Free Legal Help

Made E-Z

Matthew Lesko

Made E-Z Products, Inc.
Deerfield Beach, Florida / www.MadeE-Z.com

NOTICE:

THIS PRODUCT IS NOT INTENDED TO PROVIDE LEGAL ADVICE. IT CONTAINS GENERAL INFORMATION FOR EDUCATIONAL PURPOSES ONLY. PLEASE CONSULT AN ATTORNEY ON ALL LEGAL MATTERS. THIS PRODUCT WAS NOT PREPARED BY A PERSON LICENSED TO PRACTICE LAW IN THIS STATE.

Free Legal Help Made E-Z™
Copyright 2000 Made E-Z Products, Inc.
Printed in the United States of America
384 South Military Trail
Deerfield Beach, FL 33442
Tel. 954-480-8933
Fax 954-480-8906
http://www.MadeE-Z.com
All rights reserved.

3 3113 01972 9823

1 2 3 4 5 6 7 8 9 10 CPC R 10 9 8 7 6 5 4 3 2 1

This publication is designed to provide accurate and authoritative information in regard to subject matter covered. It is sold with the understanding that neither the publisher nor author is engaged in rendering legal, accounting, or other professional services. If legal advice or other expert assistance is required, the services of a competent professional should be sought. From: A Declaration of Principles jointly adopted by a Committee of the American Bar Association and a Committee of Publishers.

Free Legal Help Made E-Z™
Matthew Lesko

Acknowledgements

We would like to thank the hundreds of bureaucrats who contributed their time and expertise in explaining what makes a good gripe.

A Word of Caution to the Reader

We have done our best to make sure the telephone numbers and addresses in *Free Legal Help Made E-Z* are as accurate as possible, but, like everything else, they often change without notice. If a number or address has changed, don't give up. You can always get the new one by calling your local information operator and asking for the phone number of the U.S. government's Federal Information Center, or by calling the operator in your state capital.

The purpose of this book is to give the reader a quick reference to hundreds of the federal and state governments' complaint handling offices and some of the laws they enforce, but it does not claim to be the last word on the laws mentioned throughout—every complaint poses its own unique problems. Nor do we claim that these offices will resolve all your complaints to your satisfaction. We offer this material merely as an empowering tool that can expand your options and possibilities.

Table of Contents

Table of Contents

Table of Contents

Table of Contents

Table of Contents

v

Table of Contents

Table of Contents

Table of Contents

Table of Contents

Introduction

Everybody's got a complaint about something, whether it's something they bought, something about their jobs, or something about their landlords. The problem is, though, that people spend all their energy complaining to their friends about their problems rather than to those who can really do something about it, or they think their only option to get satisfaction is to hire some high-priced lawyer.

The U.S. government thought the way you complain was important enough that they authorized the U.S. Office of Consumer Affairs to research more about it. After spending a million dollars in a study called "Consumer Complaint Handling in America," here is some of what they found:

Everybody's Got a Complaint, But Nobody Complains

✔ 25 percent of all purchases result in some kind of consumer problem.

✔ Nearly 70 percent of consumers with problems don't complain.

✔ Of those who took action, about 40 percent got satisfaction by complaining only to the organization who caused the problem.

Why Aren't People Complaining?

The study found three major reasons why people with gripes don't complain:

 They didn't think it was worth their time and effort.

 They didn't know how or where to complain.

✔ They believed that complaining wouldn't do any good.

Introduction

The purpose of **Free Legal Help** is to show you where to complain, that complaining can be worth your time, and that it can do plenty of good, not just for yourself but for everybody.

Where People Complain

 Nearly 90 percent of consumers with problems complained where they purchased the product or service.

 Less than 10 percent of those with complaints went to third party complaint handlers: government agencies or private voluntary consumer agencies, like the Better Business Bureau.

After complaining to the place where they bought something and getting nowhere, most people give up. They're frustrated and feel powerless. We've learned to accept being dissatisfied with the things we buy, our jobs, our neighbors, and everything else.

If they knew how little effort it took to get a state or federal agency to help them out, they might take that extra step and take control of their problems. When a business gets a telephone call from the state's Attorney General's office, or the U.S. Department of Justice, or the Interstate Commerce Commission, they're much more likely to see things the way you do.

Who Complains

 Those with high incomes are more likely to complain than those with low incomes.

 The young are more likely to complain than the old.

The older we get, the more cynical we become about getting real satisfaction, so we resign ourselves to getting taken advantage of.

What To Do About It

All of these findings seem to suggest that people just don't know how to complain in a way that gets satisfying results, so they usually don't complain at all. Part of learning how to complain effectively is knowing where the best

Introduction

places to complain are and what will be done when you do. *You should almost always try to resolve a complaint directly with the party you have the problem with, whether it's a store, your boss, or your government.* But as the government study show, only 40 percent of those who went this route were satisfied with the results. It's at this point that you need to know where to go for a third party resolution.

Both the federal and state governments are very effective in getting results for you. There's nothing like a call from a state's Office of the Attorney General to get a store or gas station that ripped you off to see things more fairly. Your boss is more likely to listen to your complaints about discrimination if he/she gets a call from the U.S. Equal Employment Opportunity Commission or the U.S. Department of Justice. And your home improvement contractor will be a little more sympathetic to your complaint if the state Licensing Board investigates your case.

It's Free To Complain

And the great thing about using these government sources is that they are free: there are no attorney fees or court costs for you to pay. Before you threaten to take a business to court if they don't resolve your complaint, contact the appropriate government office, and they may do it for you, especially if many others just like you have complained. But chances are, it will never get that far. Getting dragged into arbitration hearings is costly for a business, and when faced with this, they'll often settle with you before it goes to a hearing.

Why You Should Complain

If a business or an individual breaks a federal or state law in dealing with you, the federal or state government may go to court on your behalf. More often, however, those government agencies wait until a pattern of complaints against a certain party develops before they'll investigate a business for possible civil or criminal prosecution. Even if you don't have enough evidence alone against a company to get a settlement in your favor, if enough people like you lodge complaints, government agencies may decide to investigate and get that company from stopping their unethical or illegal practices.

Introduction

How Government Regulation Helps You

For the last ten years or so, we've been hearing from certain politicians how bad government regulations are for the economy. What they don't tell you is that when regulations are removed, the first ones to suffer are the consumers, who often get shoddier merchandise, poorer service, and fewer options to get complaints resolved.

Businesses and individuals are regulated by the government to protect the public. If a business or individual is government regulated or licensed, you may have more leverage in dealing with them through the regulatory offices. Here are some questions to ask:

Is the company federally regulated? Examples include airlines, interstate bus lines, cruise ships, and interstate moving companies.

Is the company state licensed? Examples include everything from barbers and funeral homes to home improvement contractors, landscapers, and car dealerships, depending on the state.

Tips on Complaining

Keep in mind, though, that many state and federal agencies are swamped with complaints each year, so to ensure that your problem is being taken care of, you should always follow up on your complaint with a letter or telephone call to find out about its status. The loudest voices are heard the clearest.

Another thing to keep in mind is that *you shouldn't treat the government agency that's trying to help you as if they are the ones you have the complaint with.* Yelling at them will only make them want to put your complaint at the bottom of the pile. For help in how to handle a government office, see page 9, *Ten Basic Telephone Tips.*

Another thing to remember is that unless your complaint is taken to binding arbitration, you don't necessarily have to accept the results of a government agency if you aren't satisfied with their handling of your case. You can always take the company or individual to court yourself.

Introduction

Some More Facts

According to the U.S. Department of Commerce, American consumers complain the most about the following:

1. Automobiles
2. Mail orders
3. Banking/Credit
4. Insurance
5. Publications
6. Recreation and Travel

We've tried to make sure that **Free Legal Help** shows you where to go to get something done about these most popular gripes, along with hundreds of others. But if you've got a gripe about something we haven't covered, see the section *When All Else Fails* on page 207 where you'll find some helpful starting places in your quest for getting some satisfaction.

Organization Of The Book

This book is arranged alphabetically by subject matter with subject headings, such as *Airline Service*, *Cosmetics*, and *Ocean Cruises*. If you can't find quite what you're looking for under the subject headings, check the index in the back of the book, which goes into much greater detail about where to find what you're looking for. We've also included key words running along the top of each page to give you a quick reference to what's on the page below.

Each entry is organized exactly the same way, so that at a glance you can see what a government office can do for you if you've got a complaint:

Types of Complaints

Under each subject heading, we've given you at least three examples of the kinds of problems you might have a complaint about. For example, under *Banking Services* you'll find examples of problems with car loans, mortgages, and account deductions. But keep in mind that the examples we've given aren't the only kinds of problems that the government agency will handle.

Contact

Here you'll find the complete mailing address and telephone numbers of the appropriate government agency to contact with your complaint. And while they will usually listen to your complaint over the phone, for them to act on it, they'll usually ask you to submit a formal written complaint.

Help Available

Here you'll see five different possibilities of what may be available to you:

Information:
Investigation:
Mediation/Arbitration:
Legal advice:
Legal representation:

Organization of the Book

Information:
Every office in this book can give you further information on the complaint process, especially if you're not sure if they are the appropriate office to handle your type of problem. Also, many of these offices have very helpful consumer education publications they can send you for free to help you avoid problems in the future. Many of these offices also keep track of complaints against certain businesses and manufacturers and can tell you right over the phone if any other complaints have been lodged against a company, and whether the government has ever taken action against them.

Investigation:
This answers whether or not this office will investigate your complaint for you. Depending on the kind of problem, they may make a few telephone calls to the company in question to find out their side of the story, but if they think a serious violation has occurred, they may actually send out an investigator to look into the situation more thoroughly.

Mediation/Arbitration:
An agency may decide that the best way to solve your complaint is to bring you and the other party together and help the two of you work out a settlement. If this happens, and you aren't satisfied with the outcome, you usually aren't obligated to accept whatever settlement comes out of this--you can always go somewhere else, like small claims court.

Legal Advice:
Since what the offices in this book do is enforce the law, they have people there who can listen to your problem and tell you if any relevant laws may have been broken. Although some of these offices will be hesitant to discuss the specific aspects of your complaint before they see it in writing, most will discuss the general laws that apply to your case over the phone, and you can often decide for yourself if any have been violated. Remember, though, by "legal advice" we don't mean that a government office is necessarily going to assign you a personal lawyer to handle your case from beginning to end. So don't ask for a free lawyer.

Legal Representation:
Some, but not many, of these offices may decide to pursue your complaint for you through court proceedings on your behalf. This is especially true of complaints involving your job, such as discrimination, wages, working conditions, and pensions.

Organization of the Book

What Happens Next

Here you'll find a general explanation of how your complaint might be handled by a particular government agency. However, since every complaint is unique, you'll have to find out for yourself once you've submitted your complaint what to expect.

Ten Basic Telephone Tips

Here are a few pointers to keep in mind when dealing with government offices and officials. These guidelines amount to basic common sense but are often forgotten by the time you have been put on hold or passed around to several people.

Introduce Yourself Cheerfully

The way you open the conversation will set the tone for the entire interview. Your greeting and initial comment should be cordial and cheerful. Your telephone attitude should give the official the feeling that this is not going to be just another telephone call, but a pleasant interlude in someone's day.

Be Open And Candid

You should be as candid as possible with your source since you are asking the same of him. If you are evasive or deceitful in explaining your needs or motives, your source will be reluctant to provide you with information.

Be Optimistic

Throughout the entire conversation you should exude a sense of confidence. If you call and say "You probably aren't the right person" or "You don't have any information, do you?" it makes it easy for the person to say, "You're right, I can't help you." A positive attitude will encourage your source to stretch his mind to see what information he might have that could possibly help you and maybe even save you some money.

Be Humble And Courteous

You can be optimistic and still be humble. Remember the old adage that you can catch more flies with honey than you can with vinegar. People in general, and experts in particular, love to tell others what they know, as long as their position of authority is not questioned or threatened. In fact, if they are made to feel like an expert by the way you treat them, chances are that they will give you more information than they originally intended to give.

Ten Basic Telephone Tips

Be Concise

State your problem simply. Be direct. A long-winded explanation may bore your contact and reduce your chances for getting a thorough response.

Don't Be A "Gimme"

A "gimme" is someone who says "give me this" or "give me that," and has little consideration for the other person's time or feelings. Remember to "ask" for information or a particular document that you're interested in.

Be Complimentary

This goes hand in hand with being humble. A well-placed compliment about your source's expertise or insight about a particular topic will serve you well. In searching for information in large organizations, you are apt to talk to many colleagues of your source, so it wouldn't hurt to convey some respect for your source's abilities. A good example of a favorable comment might be, "Everyone I spoke to said you are the person I must talk with." It is reassuring for anyone to know that they have the respect of their peers.

Be Conversational

Avoid spending the entire time just talking about your complaint. Briefly mention a few irrelevant topics such as the weather, or the latest political campaign. The more social you are without being too chatty, the more likely that your source will open up and want to help you.

Return The Favor

You might share with your source information or even gossip you have picked up elsewhere. However, be certain not to betray the trust of another source. If you do not have any relevant information to share at the moment, it would still be a good idea to call back when you are further along in your research when you might have information of value to offer to an especially valuable source.

Send Thank You Notes

A short note, typed or handwritten, will help ensure that your source will be just as cooperative in the future, should you need their help.

Aging-Related:

You're Never Too Old To Get Help

Type of Complaints

✔ The Social Security Administration has stopped your monthly checks because they say you've died.

✔ Because of a physical disability, you can no longer walk to the bus stop to go shopping.

✔ The food in your nursing home is often cold and horrible tasting.

✔ You're having trouble paying your heating bills because your house isn't insulated.

✔ Your social security checks aren't enough to pay your monthly bills.

Contact:
State Agencies on Aging
See page 212 for the office nearest you

Help Available:
Information: yes
Investigation: yes
Mediation/Arbitration: yes
Legal advice: yes
Legal representation: no

What Happens Next?
Besides the general consumer protection services available to the elderly through the state and local consumer protection offices, each state also has Agencies on Aging that help the elderly with all kinds of special problems, such as:

- sheltered housing
- insurance counseling
- adult day care
- in-home care
- employment opportunities
- home delivered meals
- transportation
- recreation
- pharmacy problems
- tax relief on investments
- income finance assistance
- medicaid/medicare counseling
- nursing home information and complaints
- weatherization and home repair
- fuel assistance
- continuing care
- home equity conversion
- social security benefits
- unemployment insurance
- veterans benefits
- legal services
- education

The state Agencies on Aging will often act on your behalf to help you resolve problems that are special to older people. This could involve calling a nursing home, a bus company, or the Social Security Administration for you. And if the aging agencies can't solve the problems directly, they'll often refer you to the state or federal agency that can. For aging-related problems, the state Agencies on Aging are simply the best starting places.

Aircraft:

When The Live-At-Five Chopper Buzzes Your Barbecue Party

Type of Complaints

✔ A helicopter from the local television station keeps buzzing your backyard to get pictures of your daughter's wedding.

✔ Jets flying over your neighborhood keep making sonic booms.

✔ A small airplane is performing stunt maneuvers over your house.

Contact:
Federal Aviation Administration
800 Independence Ave., SW
Washington, DC 20591
(800) FAA-SURE (322-7873)

Help Available:
Information: yes
Investigation: yes
Mediation/Arbitration: n/a
Legal Advice: yes
Legal Representation: n/a

What Happens Next?

If you've got a complaint about loud or dangerous airplanes, jet airliners, or helicopters flying in your area, call the Federal Aviation Administration's (FAA) hotline. If the problem isn't urgent, the FAA will ask you to submit your complaint in writing, and based on that letter, they will investigate the problem, and usually let you know the outcome of their findings.

Low Flying Aircraft * Sonic Booms

If it's a continuing problem, they may be able to get it stopped for you, depending on if there are violations of the law. But there really isn't much they can do about a one-time occurrence, unless they have others who witnessed the problem and can identify the aircraft, or if it posed serious harm to people.

Airline Safety:

Watching Soap Operas On The Airport Metal Detecting X-Ray Video Screens

Type of Complaints

✔ Your seatbelt won't come undone, and while they work to get you free, you miss your connecting flight.

✔ The guards at the airport metal detector chat while people pass through unnoticed.

✔ A flight attendant neglects to demonstrate safety features on your airplane before it takes off.

✔ There are no safety instructions in your seat pocket.

Contact:
Federal Aviation Administration
800 Independence Ave., SW
Washington, DC 20591
(800) FAA-SURE (322-7873)

Help Available:
Information: yes
Investigation: yes
Mediation/Arbitration: yes
Legal advice: yes
Legal representation: no

15

What Happens Next?

For complaints involving safety violations on airlines--such as seat belts that don't work, overhead compartments that won't close, or anything else that you think might be unsafe--contact the Federal Aviation Administration's (FAA) Air Safety Hotline. They'll investigate your complaint and let you know what they find and what, if anything, was done to correct the problem.

Airline Service:

Rude Stewardesses, Delayed Flights, And Lost Luggage

Type of Complaints

✔ You have a prepaid ticket, but miss a flight because the airline has overbooked it.

✔ The airline loses or damages your baggage.

✔ Your flight attendant is rude.

✔ A flight delay causes you to miss a connecting flight.

Contact:
U.S. Department of Transportation
Office of Consumer Affairs
C-75, Room 4107
Washington, DC 20590
(202) 366-2220

Help Available:
Information: yes
Investigation: yes
Mediation/Arbitration: yes
Legal advice: yes
Legal representation: no

What Happens Next?

You should first try to resolve any complaints about airline service directly with the airlines themselves. But if you can't get the results you are looking for, contact the office above. They will register your complaint on computer, and depending on the case, contact the airlines for you to resolve the problem.

Overbooking * Canceled Flights

Under the U.S. Department of Transportation's rules, an airline must compensate you if you've bought a ticket for a flight but miss it because they've overbooked it.

- The airline must book you on one of their own flights or on another airline that arrives at your destination or first stop over within one hour of the arrival time of your original flight.

- If the flight they reschedule you on is scheduled to arrive between one and two hours after your original arrival time, you are immediately entitled to the price of your ticket in cash or up to $200.

- If the flight they reschedule you on is scheduled to arrive at your destination over two hours after your original scheduled flight, they owe you twice the ticket amount in cash or up to $400 due immediately.

Although not often, airlines will sometimes compensate you for inconveniences that you may experience, such as having to sit in a seat that won't recline all the way to Paris, by awarding you travel credit, and sometimes hotel accommodations, depending on the situation. This office can help you negotiate inconvenience compensation along with lost, delayed, and damaged baggage claims and settlements.

Alcohol Advertising:

Naked Women And Fake Beer

Type of Complaints

✔ Looking closely at a whiskey ad in a magazine, you notice a picture of a naked woman in the glass.

✔ You buy a "medicine" advertised in a magazine that guarantees to cure arthritis pain, but it turns out to be a bottle of 90% alcohol.

✔ A beer ad on television uses scenes and language that you think are obscene.

✔ There's a picture of a naked woman on the label of a can of beer you bought.

✔ The label on a bottle of wine says the alcohol content is 11%, but after tasting it, you think it is much less.

Contact:

Chief, Market Compliance Branch
Bureau of Alcohol, Tobacco, and Firearms
U.S. Department of the Treasury
650 Massachusetts Ave., NW, Room 5400
Washington, DC 20226
(202) 927-7777

Help Available:

Information: yes
Investigation: yes
Mediation/Arbitration: yes
Legal advice: yes
Legal representation: no

What Happens Next?

If you think an alcohol advertisement on TV, in a magazine or newspaper, on a billboard, or anywhere else, is obscene, misleading, or inaccurate, you can file a complaint with the Bureau of Alcohol, Tobacco, and Firearms (ATF). If you see an offensive and misleading ad in a publication, cut it out and send it to ATF, along with the name and date of the publication you found it in. If it's a television ad, send in the channel, time, and date you saw it. With any complaint, be sure to explain why you think what you saw is objectionable.

Keep in mind, though, that ATF does not have power to go after the publications and television and radio stations that run the advertisements. ATF holds only the company whose product is represented in the ads responsible for the contents of the advertisements and labels.

After receiving your complaint, ATF will look into the ad and/or label for you and find out if it violates any of the federal regulations for alcohol advertising. If they find something that violates the law, depending on the specifics of the violation, they may demand that the company whose product is involved withdraw the ad or change the label in question. And depending on how severe the offense is, and whether it has harmed or misled a great number of people, AFT may decide to fine the company or suspend its operating license.

Animal Welfare:
Mistreating Man's Best Friends

Type of Complaints

✔ You suspect that a pet wholesaler is selling stolen animals to pet stores in your area.

✔ A dog breeder and wholesaler keeps his dogs in filthy, unsanitary cages.

✔ An elephant trainer in a circus whips his elephants mercilessly during "training" sessions.

✔ Your neighbor runs a dogfighting betting ring in his garage.

✔ A circus keeps its bears in cages that are too small for them to move around in.

Contact:
Animal and Plant Health Inspection Service
Information Office
6505 Belcrest Rd., Room 531
Hyattsville, MD 20782
(301) 734-7833

Help Available:
Information: yes
Investigation: yes
Mediation/Arbitration: n/a
Legal advice: yes
Legal representation: n/a

Puppy Farms * Animal Trainers * Circuses

What Happens Next?

The U.S. Department of Agriculture's (USDA) Animal and Plant Health Inspection Service (APHIS) will investigate your complaints about the mistreatment of animals that fall under their authority. They are:

Pet wholesalers	Wild animal dealers
Pet breeders	Suppliers of specimens
Laboratory animal dealers	Animal transporters
Laboratory animal breeders	Zoos
Animal brokers	Marine mammal shows
Auction operators	Roadside zoos
Promoters giving animal prizes	Carnivals
Exotic animal wholesalers	

APHIS does *not* regulate:

Retail pet stores	Boarding kennels
Retail chain stores	Farm exhibits
Direct sales	Pet shows
Hobby breeders	Rodeos
Public pounds	Animal preserves
Private animal shelters	Hunts
Trade-day sales sponsors	

What this means is that APHIS does not have the authority to investigate conditions in your local pet store, but it can investigate the wholesale distributor who sells the dogs, cats, fish, or whatever other animals, to your local pet store.

After receiving your complaint through one of its regional offices (listed on page 217), APHIS may decide to send out an investigator to look into the alleged mistreatment. When they've completed their investigation, APHIS will send the owner an inspection report, and if violations have been discovered, the owner will be given a chance to correct the situation. To make sure that they have, APHIS will conduct a follow up inspection, and if they find that the owner has not corrected the violation, APHIS may decide to take the case before an administrative law judge to have the owner's violations formally stopped. If the owner is found guilty in administrative court, he or she could be fined and have his/her license revoked.

Puppy Farms * Animal Trainers * Circuses

Keep in mind that APHIS will investigate only certain kinds of animal mistreatment--they will not investigate your neighbor for kicking his dog or having 200 cats in his living room. Your local Animal Welfare Office or Animal Welfare Society would most likely handle those types of abuse. But if you're not sure if APHIS has authority over certain animals, feel free to call them; they'll be more than happy to tell you about the law or refer you to the proper organization that can best handle your complaint.

Appliance Energy Labeling:

Energy Savings That Cost Big Bucks

Type of Complaints

✔ You buy a new refrigerator that doesn't have a label on it telling you how much electricity it will use.

✔ Your new dishwasher is using much more electricity than its energy consumption label says it should.

✔ Your new "energy saving" air conditioner actually causes your summer electric bills to increase.

Contact:
Federal Trade Commission
Appliance Labeling Enforcement Division
6th and Pennsylvania Ave., NW
Washington, DC 20580
(202) 326-3035
Fax (202) 326-3259

Help Available:
Information: yes
Investigation: yes
Mediation/Arbitration: no
Legal advice: yes
Legal representation: no

What Happens Next?

Not only do some refrigerators cost twice as much as others, some refrigerators consume twice as much electricity as others. And over the time you own a refrigerator, the amount you spend on electricity to run it can end up costing you much more than the bargain you thought you were getting.

Air Conditioners * Refrigerators

To better protect you about the hidden costs of appliances, there is a federal law that requires that the manufacturers of home appliances let consumers know by labeling how much energy the appliances use.

If you buy an appliance, such as a refrigerator, an air conditioner, or space heater, and find that it doesn't come with any energy consumption information, or if you suspect that the energy information is incorrect, contact the Federal Trade Commission (FTC) (see page 249 for the office nearest you). Depending on your complaint and others like yours, the FTC will look into the mislabeling and contact the manufacturer to have the inaccurate labels changed. In the unlikely event that the company doesn't make the necessary changes, the FTC can impose fines and bring legal action against them.

Automobile Safety:

Calling Before You Face A Recall

Type of Complaints

✔ The brakes on your new car don't work properly.

✔ The seatbelts in your new car lock closed, making you a prisoner in your own car.

✔ The airbag in your new car opens when you merely apply the brakes.

Contact:
Office of Defects Investigation (NEF-10)
National Highway Traffic Safety Administration
U.S. Department of Transportation
400 7th St., SW, Room 5319
Washington, DC 20590
(202) 366-0123 (DC metro area)
(800) 424-9393 (elsewhere)
Internet: www.nhtfa.dot.gov

Help Available:
Information: yes
Investigation: yes
Mediation/Arbitration: no
Legal advice: yes
Legal representation: no

What Happens Next?
If you've bought a new car, but it's got problems with a safety feature, you should first try to resolve the problems with the dealer you bought the car from. If this doesn't satisfy you, or if you think that your problem is not unique to just your car, contact the National Highway Traffic Safety Administration's (NHTSA) hotline.

26

Recalls * Brake Problems * Airbags

After NHTSA receives your complaint in writing, they will compare it with other complaints to see if a pattern is developing. They'll also send a copy to the manufacturer, who, in many cases, will take action on their own to resolve your complaint.

When NHTSA thinks there's a possibility of a safety-related defect in a car's design, they'll ask the manufacturer for information related to the problem. After analyzing the data, the NHTSA may ask the manufacturer to conduct a voluntary recall. If the manufacturer refuses, the NHTSA may further investigate the problem, and if they determine that a recall is in fact required, they may order the manufacturer to conduct a recall to fix the defect.

Banking Services:

Where To Go When Your Banker Gives You The Run-Around

Type of Complaints

✔ Even though you have a good credit and a good job, your bank won't give you a car loan because you are divorced.

✔ You notice that your bank is making unusual deductions from your bank accounts each month for maintenance charges you don't understand.

✔ Your monthly credit card bill shows purchases that you never made.

✔ The annual percentage rate on your mortgage unexpectedly rises even though your mortgage contract says that it should remain the same.

Contacts:

State Banking Authorities
See page 218 for the office in your state

Federal Deposit Insurance Corporation
Office of Consumer Affairs
550 17th St., NW, Room F-130
Washington, DC 20429
(202) 898-3535
(800) 934-3342
Internet: www.fdic.gov

Comptroller of the Currency
Compliance Management
U.S. Department of the Treasury
250 E. St., SW
Washington, DC 20219
(202) 622-2000

Loan Discrimination * Credit Rights

Office of Thrift Supervision
U.S. Department of the Treasury
1700 G St., NW
Washington, DC 20552
(202) 906-6000
Fax: (202) 906-7755
Internet: www.ots.treas.gov

Help Available:
Information: yes
Investigation: yes
Mediation/Arbitration: yes
Legal advice: yes
Legal representation: no

What Happens Next?

If you have any complaints about your bank, you should always insist on speaking with a high-level manager, not a teller, and in most cases they will solve the problem. But, if you still feel that they are giving you the run-around, the following agencies can help you out.

National Banks

If your bank has "national" in its name, such as The First National Bank of America, the U.S. Treasury's Comptroller of the Currency handles complaints about it (see page 229 for the office nearest you). After receiving your written complaint, an investigator will send a copy of it to the bank in question and ask for a response within two weeks. If after receiving their response the investigator decides that you still have a basis for a complaint, they will recommend to the bank that it promptly corrects the problem for you. And since the Comptroller gives them their license to do business, these National banks tend to follow the Comptroller's recommendations promptly.

Savings & Loans

The U.S. Department of the Treasury's Office of Thrift Supervision (OTS) handles consumer complaints about S&Ls insured by the Federal Deposit Insurance Corporation (FDIC). As with National Banks, OTS regional offices will investigate your complaint, contact the Savings & Loan for you, and if necessary, request that they resolve your complaint (see page 334 for the office nearest you).

Loan Discrimination * Credit Rights

State Regulated Banks
The state Banking Commissioners handle complaints about state-chartered banks doing business in their states. Although their function varies from state to state, these agencies, for the most part, will take your complaint and contact the bank on your behalf to get the bank's side of the dispute. If after hearing the bank's response the investigator decides that you still have a legitimate complaint, they will ask the bank to promptly correct the problem. (See page 218 for your state banking commissioner.)

FDIC-Insured Institutions
The Federal Deposit Insurance Corporation (FDIC) handles complaints about all institutions that it insures, including banks and savings and loans. Upon receiving your complaint, the FDIC will refer it to the appropriate federal or state banking agencies, such as the ones listed above, that can best handle it.

Barbers, Hairdressers, And Manicurists:

A Permanent Wave That Won't Go Away

Type of Complaints

 You ask your barber for just a trim, and you end up looking like Telly Savalas.

 Your new perm curls your hair just the way you like it. Unfortunately, it also turns your hair green.

The nail polish remover that your manicurist uses causes the skin on your fingers to peel off.

Contact:
State Licensing Boards
See page 289 for the office nearest you

Help Available:
Information: yes
Investigation: yes
Mediation/Arbitration: yes
Legal advice: yes
Legal representation: no

What Happens Next?

Have you ever been sitting in a barber shop and noticed the barber's license hanging on the wall? Because your barber is licensed by the state where he or she cuts hair, you have some consumer protection that you may not be aware of. Not only do those licenses look impressive in a frame, they can also just as easily be taken away if your barber or cosmetologist does something shady while undertaking his or her trade. And because they can't cut hair without a license, you'd be surprised how much more cooperative they will be in resolving your complaint if they get a call from the state licensing board.

If you've got a complaint against any of these beauty specialists, contact your state's licensing board. They'll look into your complaint for you by contacting the business for their side of the story. And if the board decides that a violation has taken place, they may ask them to correct the problem for you, or they may decide to bring the barber in for a formal hearing that could result in fines and/or suspension of their license to cut hair, do nails, or give facials.

Bids On Government Contracts:

Getting A Fix On The Fixers

Type of Complaints

✔ Fewer bids than normal are submitted for a contract.

✔ The same company repeatedly has been the low bidder who has been awarded contracts for a certain service or in a particular geographical area.

✔ Bidders seem to win contract bids on a fixed rotation: A then B then C then A then B then C.

✔ There is an unusually large dollar difference between the winning bid and all the others.

Contact:
U.S. Department of Justice
Antitrust Division, Room 3109
950 Pennsylvania Ave., NW
Washington, DC 20530
(202) 514-2401
Fax: (202) 616-2645
Internet: antitrust@justice.usdoj.gov

Help Available:
Information: yes
Investigations: yes
Mediation/Arbitration: n/a
Legal advice: yes
Legal representation: n/a

What Happens Next?

There's big money in landing government contracts for all types of businesses--construction, manufacturing, services, data processing. Many of these contracts are awarded to companies on a bid basis, with the contract going to the lowest bidder. Because the money at stake is so large, the temptation to fix the bidding process is equally large.

If the contract being bid upon is from the government, you have the right to see the other bids after the contract has been awarded. If you have noticed or even suspect anything unusual with the bidding process for a contract, contact the U.S. Department of Justice regional office nearest you listed on page 273. Many of their investigations begin with information from private citizens like yourself. If found guilty, bid riggers may face heavy fines and/or imprisonment.

Billboards And Junkyards:

When A Burma Shave Sign
Isn't Nostalgic

Type of Complaints

✔ A billboard that was just put up along an interstate highway is so big that it blocks out the view of an entire mountain.

✔ An automobile junkyard along an interstate doesn't have a fence around it that hides it from the view of the road.

✔ An old billboard sign has been left in disrepair, with the sign peeling off and the legs falling down.

Contact:
Office of Right-of-Way
Federal Highway Administration
U.S. Department of Transportation
400 7th St., SW
Washington, DC 20590
(202) 366-3713

Help Available:
Information: yes
Investigation: yes
Mediation/Arbitration: yes
Legal advice: yes
Legal representation: n/a

What Happens Next?

There are all kinds of laws about the appearance, placement, and condition of signs and junkyards along interstate highways and state highways. And the Federal Highway Administration (FHWA), along with your state Highway Department, will look into any complaints you have about the appearance of signs and junkyards along the highways. If you file a complaint with the

FSWA, they will send it on to the appropriate state Highway Department, which will look into the matter to see if a violation has taken place. If so, they can force the owner of a billboard to remove it or change it, and they can force the owner of a junkyard to build a fence around the yard so that the junk can't be seen from the road.

Boating Safety:

Call Before You Sink Or Swim

Type of Complaints

✔ The gear shift lever on your new boat is too close to the steering wheel, making it impossible to turn the wheel without taking the boat out of gear.

✔ When you open the windows on your new boat, they extend into the walkway, and the sharp edges cut people's legs when they walk by.

✔ The life preserver you bought soaks up water like a sponge.

✔ The fiberglass hull on the boat you just bought begins cracking after only a week.

Contact:
Consumer and Regulatory Affairs Branch (G-NAB-5)
Boating, and Consumer Affairs Division
Office of Navigation Safety and Waterways Services
U.S. Coast Guard
2100 2nd St., SW, Room 1109
Washington, DC 20593-0001
(202) 267-0780
(800) 368-5647
(202) 267-0780
Fax: (703) 313-5920
Internet: www.naucen.uscg.mil/gnab/gnab.htm

Help Available:
Information: yes
Investigation: yes
Mediation/Arbitration: yes
Legal advice: yes
Legal representation: no

Boat Recalls * Life Preservers

What Happens Next?

The U.S. Coast Guard receives all kinds of complaints about safety-related defects in new boats and boating equipment. If you think that you've got a safety problem on your new boat because of a design flaw or manufacturing defect, contact the Coast Guard through their toll-free hotline above.

Depending on how many complaints come in on a certain product, the Coast Guard will decide how quickly they need to respond and what action to take. If they're getting a lot of calls about, say, a faulty life preserver, they may contact the manufacturer immediately to investigate the problem. If they find out that there's been a defect in the product, the Coast Guard may require that the manufacture recall the product and either fix or replace it for those who purchased it. By law, the manufacturer must pay all costs and expenses necessary for correcting any defect, even if it means giving you a completely new life preserver or boat.

Chance are, if there's a design flaw in your new boat, you won't be the only one to have it. It's always a good idea to contact the Coast Guard so that if a recall is necessary, anyone who didn't notice the problem will find out about it. And by law, if the Coast Guard does require a recall, you won't have to pay for any of the repairs.

Bus Service:

Making Fusses About Bad Buses

Type of Complaints

✔ A bus company charges you more for a ticket than the price it was advertised for.

✔ A bus driver drives recklessly.

✔ You are denied a place on a bus because of a physical handicap.

✔ A bus company loses you luggage.

Contact:
Interstate Commerce Commission
Office of Compliance
and Consumer Assistance
12th St. & Constitution Ave., NW, Room 4412
Washington, DC 20423
(202) 927-5500
Fax: (202) 565-1576

Help Available:
Information: yes
Investigation: yes
Mediation/Arbitration: yes
Legal advice: yes
Legal representation: no

What Happens Next?

Since all interstate bus service is regulated by the Interstate Commerce Commission (ICC), they can handle your complaints about lost baggage, rate disputes, discriminatory practices, and other service-related problems. After receiving your complaint, they will try to determine if the bus company has violated any laws that they enforce. If they think a violation has occurred, they will contact the bus company on your behalf and ask that they resolve the matter. As a result, the bus company may send you a letter of apology, along with their resolution. To file a complaint, contact the ICC regional office that serves your state (listed on page 264).

Campaign Finance:

Making Too Much Political Hay

Type of Complaints

✔ After receiving a $500 campaign contribution in cash, a Senator goes out for a $500 dinner with his secretary.

✔ Your boss gives you $2,500 in cash and tells you to contribute it to a certain presidential candidate.

✔ A Political Action Committee makes all its contributions in cash so it can give more money than is allowed by law.

Contact:
Federal Election Commission
999 E St., NW
Washington, DC 20463
(202) 219-3440
(800) 424-9530
Internet: www.fec.gov

Help Available:
Information: yes
Investigation: yes
Mediation/Arbitration: no
Legal advice: no
Legal representation: n/a

What Happens Next?

If you've noticed any shady or questionable dealings involving the making, receiving, or reporting of campaign financial contributions of a candidate running for Congress, the U.S. Senate, or the Presidency, you should report them to the Federal Election Commission (FEC). The FEC will investigate your complaint, and if they find any violations of federal law, they--along with the U.S. Justice Department--can impose civil or criminal penalties, which include fines and, in cases of fraud, possible imprisonment.

41

Car Dealers:

When Honest John Is Stealing You Blind

Type of Complaints

✔ A new car dealer tries to sell you rustproofing even though the manufacturer says it's unnecessary.

✔ A car dealer won't honor a warranty on your new car.

✔ A car dealer insists on charging you for repairs on your new car that you think are covered by your warranty.

Contacts:
State Consumer Protection Offices
See page 230 for the office nearest you

State Licensing Boards
See page 289 for the office nearest you

Help Available:
Information: yes
Investigation: yes
Mediation/Arbitration: yes
Legal advice: yes
Legal representation: no

What Happens Next?

You'd never guess by watching all those slick ads on TV that one of the most frequent things people complain about is the sale and repair of new cars. If you feel that the dealership that you bought your new car from is giving you the runaround about honoring your warranty, you can start by contacting your state Consumer Protection Office. They'll contact the dealer for you and find out why they're not listening to your complaint. If they find that the dealer hasn't treated you fairly, they'll ask them to resolve the problem promptly.

Rustproofing * Warranties * Auto Repairs

To better protect consumers, many states also require that new car dealerships be licensed--usually through the state Licensing Board or Motor Vehicle Administration. The licensing office can contact the dealership on your behalf to make sure that they honor your warranty. Because dealerships can't sell cars without a business license, don't be surprised to find that after being contacted by the licensing board your problem is quickly taken care of.

Chain Mail:

How Not To Make A Million
In Your Spare Time

Type of Complaints

✔ A letter you get tries to recruit you as part of a multi-level marketing plan that will reward you with big money for recruiting others like you.

✔ You receive a chain letter that includes a prayer, telling you to send it out to others or else you'll die a fiery death.

✔ You get a letter promising that if you send a dollar to everyone on a list, you'll get back ten times your investment.

Contact:
U.S. Postal Inspection Service
475 L'Enfant Plaza, SW
Washington, DC 20260-2100
(202) 268-4267 or your local postmaster
Fraud Hotline: (800) 654-8896

Help Available:
Information: yes
Investigation: yes
Mediation/Arbitration: yes
Legal advice: yes
Legal representation: no

What Happens Next?

Chain mail that promises you financial rewards for participating is a form of lottery and may violate federal mail fraud laws. Besides that, any contest promising that every participant will be a winner is mathematically impossible.

Pyramid Schemes * $ Stuffing Envelopes

 And while chain letters that threaten anyone who doesn't continue the chain aren't illegal, they are a nuisance that people often complain about.

To complain about chain mail that you've received, contact your local Post Office or the U.S. Postal Inspector nearest you. In the case of nuisance letters, the Postal Service will contact other names on the chain mail list for you and ask them to stop the mailings. For letters involving lottery-like schemes, the Postal Service will investigate it for possible violations of mail fraud. If the Postal Service takes a shady company to court for ripping off customers and wins, the company may be ordered to repay its customers.

Child Support:

Tracking Down Dead Beat Dads

Type of Complaints

✔ The father of your child denies that he's the father and refuses to pay child support.

✔ You need help in getting a child support order.

✔ Your spouse has moved to another state and refuses to pay child support.

Contact:
Child Support Enforcement Offices
See page 224 for the offices nearest you

Help Available:
Information: yes
Investigation: yes
Mediation/Arbitration: yes
Legal advice: yes
Legal representation: yes

What Happens Next?

You don't necessarily need to hire a high-priced lawyer to get the child support payments you have coming to you. Each state has a child support enforcement program that can help you find an absent parent, establish legal paternity of your children, get a legal support order, and collect child support payments from a non-custodial parent even if he or she lives in another state.

To make sure that child support payments are made regularly and in the correct amount, these agencies can take the following steps on your behalf:

46

Child Support * Paternity * Absent Parents

A percentage of the non-custodial parent's income can be withheld and forwarded to you.

Overdue child support payments exceeding 1,000 dollars are reported to credit bureaus, which make it difficult for those owing child support to get loans, credit cards, and other financial services.

Under some state laws, an order can be issued to any person, company, or institution that is holding property belonging to the non-custodial parent, including bank accounts, investments, and personal property. This property can be seized and sold to pay the child support debts owed to you.

A percentage of the wages and retirement pensions of active, reserve, and retired members of the military and federal government civilian employees can be withheld to cover child support debts owed to you.

All states with state income tax will withhold income tax refunds for past-due support.

Federal income tax refunds can be withheld for past-due child support.

Unemployment compensation, and other state and federal benefits can be garnished to cover past-due child support.

Under federal law, the non-custodial parent can be required to post security, bond, or other financial guarantees to cover support obligations.

Those receiving assistance under the Aid to Families with Dependent Children (AFDC), Medicaid, or Foster Care programs do not have to pay for these services. For all others an application fee of up to $25 is charged, although some states may waive all or part of this fee or collect it from the parent who owes the past-due child support to you.

Civil Rights:

No Reason Not To Vote

Type of Complaints

✔ Someone threatens to harm you if you vote in a local election.

✔ The mayor of your town won't allow your group to peacefully demonstrate because he doesn't agree with your point of view.

✔ A bank requires Black loan applicants to obtain cosigners and then charges borrowers with cosigners higher interest rates.

✔ An individual isn't allowed to vote because he can't read or write.

Contact:
U.S. Commission on Civil Rights
624 9th St., NW
Washington, DC 20425
(202) 376-8513
(800) 552-6843
Fax: (202) 376-8315

Help Available:
Information: yes
Referrals: yes
Investigation: no
Mediation/Arbitration: no
Legal advice: yes
Legal representation: no

Voting Rights * Discrimination

What Happens Next?

Any violation of your civil rights is a serious matter, and if you feel that you have been the victim of a civil rights violation, contact the Commission on Civil Rights. Although the Commission does not have any enforcement power of its own to investigate your case, they will examine your complaint and refer it to the proper federal or state agency for further investigation, and, if necessary, take legal action on your behalf.

Commodity Brokers:

When Your Pork Bellies
Turn Into Bull S___

Type of Complaints

✔ Your broker was submitting reports to you that your account was losing money when in fact he was simply taking your money for himself and writing it off as market losses.

✔ To buy a new house in the Bahamas, your commodity broker skims off larger commissions than you agreed to.

✔ Your broker makes several trades on your account just so he can make more commissions on the sales.

✔ Your brokerage firm makes trades on your account that you didn't authorize.

Contact:
Commodity Futures Trading Commission
3 Lafayette Center
1155 21st St., NW
Washington, DC 20581
(202) 418-5080
Fax: (202) 418-5525
Internet: www.cftc.gov

Help Available:
Information: yes
Investigation: yes
Mediation/Arbitration: yes
Legal advice: yes
Legal representation: no

Broker Commissions * Embezzlements

What Happens Next?

If you feel that a commodity broker or firm may have violated the law in dealing with you, contact the Commodity Futures Trading Commission (CFTC), the federal agency that regulates these brokers. The CFTC has a formal reparations program that can help you recover money you've lost if your case involves both the loss of money and a broker who was registered with the CFTC at the time of your complaint. However, if you were ripped off by a broker who wasn't registered with the CFTC, you can't participate in the CFTC's reparations program.

For claims involving $10,000 or less, the CFTC has two arbitration programs that you can chose from. Under the voluntary programs, both you and the commodity broker submit written evidence to a CFTC judgment officer who will reach a decision based only on that evidence--no oral testimony is allowed. Under the Summary Procedure, both written and oral evidence can be brought before the judgment officer. In either case, the judgment officer decides the cash award that you'll receive if the case is found in your favor.

If your claim involves more than $10,000, a CFTC investigator will notify the broker or firm in question on your behalf and arrange for a formal hearing before an administrative law judge. If the broker is found guilty of a violation at the hearing, he/she may be fined and you may be awarded a cash settlement determined by the court. If the broker does not pay the fine or your cash settlement, his/her license will be revoked, making it impossible for him/her to legally practice as a commodity broker.

Cosmetics:

Hot Lipsticks & Irritable Eyeliners Or The Tammy Faye Bakker Syndrome

Type of Complaints

 Your lipstick burns your lips.

 A skin cream gives you a rash.

 An eyeliner causes eye irritation.

Contact:
Food and Drug Administration
5600 Fishers Lane
Rockville, MD 20857
(301) 443-1240
Fax: (301) 443-3757
Internet: www.fda.gov

Help Available:
Information: yes
Investigation: yes
Mediation/Arbitration: no
Legal advice: yes
Legal representation: no

What Happens Next?

If you have any complaints about the performance of any cosmetic product, contact the Food and Drug Administration (FDA) regional office nearest you (listed on page 250). When reporting cosmetics complaints involving injury or illness, make sure that you have all of the relevant information available, including where and when you bought it, who manufactured it, the product code on the packaging, and so on.

52

Lipstick * Skin Creams * Makeup

Although the FDA can't take action against a company based on a product opened by an individual consumer, they may investigate other unopened products from the same manufacturing lot and use those findings to take action against the company if they find further contamination. This may include ordering the product off the store shelves, product recalls, or even fines, depending on the severity of the violation.

Depending on the situation, the FDA may ask you to send the product in question to them, or in urgent cases, they may even arrange to pick up the product from your home. After a laboratory test, the FDA will then send you the results of their chemical analysis of the product. Although the FDA will not sue or seek compensation for you from a company, you can use the FDA analysis report for any action you decide to take on your own.

Counterfeit Products And Import Fraud:

Kalvin Klein Jeans Can Get You $250,000

Type of Complaints

✔ You buy Gucci ice skates only to later discover that Gucci doesn't make ice skates, especially ones made in Peru.

✔ Instead of admiring your new designer jeans, your friend points out that your "Calvin Klein" label reads "Kalvin Klein."

✔ You discover that your expensive Seiko watch is actually a "Sieko."

✔ You suspect a business in your community is putting designer labels on low quality goods so that they can sell them at premium prices.

✔ A business competitor is intentionally undervaluing a product he is importing to avoid paying duty charges.

Contact:
U.S. Customs Service
Fraud Division
Washington, DC 20229
(800) BE-ALERT, or
(800) USA-FAKE

Help Available:
Information: yes
Investigation: yes
Mediation/Arbitration: yes
Legal advice: yes
Legal representation: no

Bogus Products * Counterfeit Labels

What Happens Next?

If you find yourself the victim of product counterfeiting, call the U.S. Department of the Treasury's Counterfeit Goods toll-free hotline above. U.S. Customs agents will investigate your complaint, and if it leads to the seizure of other counterfeit goods or the arrest of a product counterfeiter, you may get a reward of up to $250,000, depending on the size of the case. Your complaint will be kept completely anonymous.

Crime On Public Lands:

A Party In The Woods
That's Too Wild

Type of Complaints

✔ While out hiking you come across a crop of marijuana being grown on land owned by the federal government.

✔ Your neighbor brags to you that he gets enough free firewood for the entire winter by cutting down trees on public land.

✔ You go to a party where the host shows you his valuable collection of Indian artifacts that he "found" on public lands.

✔ To give his cattle more land to graze on, a rancher you know has moved his fences so that they include public lands.

Contact:
Bureau of Land Management
U.S. Department of the Interior
1849 C St., NW, Room 504-LS
Washington, DC 20240-1849
(202) 653-8815
Fax: (202) 452-5124
Internet: www.blm.gov

Help Available:
Information: yes
Investigation: yes
Mediation/Arbitration: n/a
Legal advice: yes
Legal representation: n/a

Marijuana Crops * Archeological Digs

What Happens Next?

If you've witnessed people growing marijuana, stealing firewood, killing or capturing wild horses, looting Indian archeological sites, or hunting illegally on public lands, contact the Bureau of Land Management (BLM) regional office nearest you (listed on page 223). BLM officers and investigators will look into your complaint, and if necessary, make arrests, impose fines, and prosecute offenders of the federal laws which govern the public lands.

Crime Victims:

Muggers Money

Type of Complaints

✔ When you were mugged, your front teeth were knocked out and you don't have the money to get them fixed.

✔ A member of your family was killed while your house was being burglarized, and you need help paying for the funeral.

✔ A family member was raped, but you don't have money for the therapy she needs to help her recover.

Contact:
Crime Victims Programs
See page 236 for the office nearest you

Help Available:
Information: yes
Investigation: no
Mediation/Arbitration: n/a
Legal Advice: yes
Legal representation: no

What Happens Next?

Millions of people and their families are victimized by crime every year in the U.S. And to better address the growing belief that the law was better at protecting the rights of criminals than those of the victims, Congress enacted a law to establish a Crime Victims Fund to compensate innocent victims of violent crime. Part of the money is given to help compensate victims or their families for costs relating to such crimes as muggings, sexual crimes, and even murder.

And one of the nice things about this money is that it does not come out of the pockets of taxpayers; rather it is collected from the criminals themselves through criminal fines, forfeited bail bonds, penalty fees, and forfeited literary profits. Each state gets a portion of this fund each year.

Most states have grant programs for victims of violent crimes, so if you or a family member find yourselves the innocent victims of violent crime, you can contact the office in your state to get free money to help pay for medical costs, lost wages and support, mental health counseling, funeral expenses, and other kinds of related costs, such as cleaning up the scene of a crime or paying for personal property held for evidence or analysis by the police.

Keep in mind, though, that these grants aren't very large--they average about $2,000, and about 60% of these awards are used to pay for victims' medical expenses. One of the nice things about these awards, though, is that you don't have to be a state resident to get an award. So if you live in California and are mugged in Texas on vacation, you can collect money from the Victims Fund in Texas.

Although Georgia, Maine, New Hampshire, South Dakota, and Vermont do not currently give direct cash payments to victims of violent crime, they may in the future, so it might be a good idea to check with your state's Office of the Attorney General (see page 230) to find out if or when they might be starting such a program.

Delicatessens:

Heavy Thumbs On Your Meat Man's Scale

Type of Complaints

✔ Your local deli sells you a pound of ham that you later discover is only three quarters of a pound.

✔ The two pounds of sausage you bought at the supermarket turns out to be only a pound and a half.

✔ The scales in the produce department at your local market are falling apart but used anyway.

Contact:
State Offices of Weights and Measures
See page 340 for the office nearest you

Help Available:
Information: yes
Investigation: yes
Mediation/Arbitration: yes
Legal advice: yes
Legal representation: no

What Happens Next?

If you suspect that the pound of salami you bought at the deli or supermarket is less than a pound, and the deli insists that it is, contact your state's Office of Weights and Measures. This office can investigate your complaint, and if it finds that the scale in question is indeed inaccurate, they can make sure that the deli fixes their scales, and sometimes they may even ask them to refund your money.

Doctors:

When Your Hemorrhoid Operation Becomes More Than A Pain In The A--

Type of Complaints

✔ Your new nose job makes you look like Porky Pig

✔ Your doctor charges you for procedures that weren't performed.

✔ You thought you were going to have your broken arm set in a cast but ended up having it amputated.

✔ You doctor makes repeated sexual advances toward you, even with his assistants in the room.

✔ The surgeon who operated on your hernia left a sponge in your stomach.

Contact:
State Medical Examining Boards
See page 307 for the office nearest you

Help Available:
Information: yes
Investigation: yes
Mediation/Arbitration: yes
Legal advice: yes
Legal representation: no

Medical Malpractice * Ethical Conduct

What Happens Next?

Each state licenses the doctors who practice in it, and each Medical Examining Board will take your complaint and bring it before a panel of doctors and lawyers for review. If they find evidence that a violation of the law or ethical code has taken place, the panel may decide to bring the case up in front of the state Medical Board.

Depending on the complaint, if the doctor is found guilty, he or she could face formal reprimands, suspensions, and license revocations. You can also call these offices and find out if a doctor has been brought up on any public formal hearings involving his/her conduct.

The Medical Boards will also look into billing complaints that you have with your doctor. They'll contact the doctor for his or her side of the dispute and then decide what action should be taken to resolve the problem.

Door To Door Sales:

You're Covered From The Aluminum Siding Con

Type of Complaints

✔ A vacuum salesman pressures you into buying a top of the line model, but when you try to cancel the order the next day, he won't let you and threatens to take you to court if you try.

✔ You buy 5,000 dollars worth of aluminum from a door-to-door salesman, and when three weeks pass without hearing from him, you call the number on his calling card only to discover that it's a pay phone in the bus station.

Contact:
State Consumer Protection Offices
See page 230 for the office nearest you

Help Available:
Information: yes
Investigation: yes
Mediation/Arbitration: yes
Legal advice: yes
Legal representation: no

What Happens Next?

Keep in mind that under a federal Door-To-Door Sales Law, you have three business days to cancel any sales contract that you sign in your home. Be sure to use those three days to examine the contract and perhaps call a consumer protection office to find out if there are any unresolved complaints against the company. And if you feel that you've been the victim of unfair sales practices by these salesmen, contact your state Consumer Protection Office (see page 230 for a listing). This office can advise you on your rights, and if necessary, investigate your case on your behalf.

```
┌─────────────────────────────────────────┐
│              Contact:                    │
│        Federal Trade Commission          │
│          Enforcement Division            │
│   6th & Pennsylvania Ave., NW, Room 4631 │
│          Washington, DC 20580            │
│            (202) 326-2996                │
│        Internet: www.ftc.gov             │
│                                          │
│           Help Available:                │
│          Information: yes                │
│          Investigation: no               │
│       Mediation/Arbitration: no          │
│          Legal advice: yes               │
│       Legal representation: no           │
└─────────────────────────────────────────┘
```

What Happens Next?

Your complaint about a door-to-door salesperson may not be the only one against a company, so it is also a good idea to let the Federal Trade Commission (FTC) know about it (see page 249 for the office nearest you). Although they won't investigate individual complaints, if they get enough of them against a certain company or industry, they may decide to undertake a formal investigation that could result in forcing the company to change its illegal practices or reimburse consumers that it has cheated.

Dial-A-Porn:

Big Phone Bills From Your Hyperactive Teenager

Type of Complaints

✔ You call a Dial-A-Porn number, but when you get your telephone bill, you discover that you've been charged twice as much as the price that was advertised in small print on the TV commercial.

✔ Your 12-year-old keeps calling a 900 Dial-A-Porn number advertised on TV during the afternoon.

✔ Even after writing and calling your telephone company to block 900 numbers from being called from your house, your 12-year-old is still able to call them.

Contact:
Federal Communications Commission
Complaints Division
Enforcement Division
Common Carrier Bureau
2025 M St., NW
Washington, DC 20554
(202) 632-7553

Help Available:
Information: yes
Investigation: yes
Mediation/Arbitration: yes
Legal advice: yes
Legal representation: no

---

900 Numbers * Late Night TV Commercials

What Happens Next?

The Federal Communications Commission (FCC) handles all types of complaints involving "900" and "976" numbers, including obscenity, accessibility to minors, and overcharges. Upon receiving your complaint, the FCC will contact the company in question and ask for their side of the story. And after looking over their response, the FCC will decide if the company has violated any federal laws regarding dial-a-porn phone services. If they have, the FCC has the authority to revoke licenses, levy fines, and pursue other enforcement procedures against these telephone services to help you resolve your complaint.

Drug Smugglers:

$250,000 For Squealing On A Drug Runner

Type of Complaints

✔ Your neighbor in Miami receives late-night shipments on his dock from a boat with Panamanian markings.

✔ A neighbor farmer uses his fields as an airdrop for low-flying planes coming from the direction of Mexico.

✔ Your neighbor works as a garbage collector but seems to take a lot of trips out of the country and buy expensive cars and boats.

Contact:
U.S. Customs Service
Fraud Division
Washington, DC 20229
(800) 542-USCS, or
(800) BE-ALERT

Help Available:
Information: yes
Investigation: yes
Mediation/Arbitration: n/a
Legal advice: yes
Legal representation: n/a

What Happens Next?

To report drug smuggling activity that you may have witnessed, call the U.S. Customs Service's Narcotics hotline. U.S. Customs agents will investigate your report, and if it leads to the arrest of smugglers or seizure of narcotics, you may get a reward of up to $250,000, depending on the size of the case. All calls are kept strictly confidential and anonymous.

Dry Cleaning:

Stop Your Wallet From Being Taken To The Cleaners

Type of Complaints

✔ The sweater you dropped off to be dry cleaned comes back the size of a potholder.

✔ You take your jacket in for cleaning, thinking it's going to cost the price advertised, but when you get it back, they charge you more.

✔ You drop off a wool jacket to be dry cleaned, but when you go to pick it up, the dry cleaner gives you a pair of wool pants instead.

Contact:
State Licensing Boards
See page 289 for the office nearest you.

State Consumer Protection Offices
See page 230 for the office nearest you

Help Available:
Information: yes
Investigation: yes
Mediation/Arbitration: yes
Legal advice: yes
Legal representation: no

What Happens Next?

Besides contacting your state Consumer Protection Office with a complaint against a dry cleaner, you might also try your state's Licensing Board. If your state requires dry cleaners to be licensed, the Licensing Board will look into your complaint for you to find out if the dry cleaner has acted unfairly or negligently. They'll contact the dry cleaner and ask for their side of the story, and if the Licensing Board finds that the cleaners has taken you to the

Missing Buttons * Damaged Clothing

cleaners, they will usually ask the cleaners to voluntarily correct the problem. If the cleaners refuses, the Licensing Board can suspend the cleaner's operating license or refuse to renew it. And without a license, a dry cleaner can't do business.

Environmental Hazards And Pollution:

Give A Hoot When You See A Polluter

Type of Complaints

✔ A factory is disgorging a white ash into the air that has fallen all over your neighborhood.

✔ You see a large number of dead fish floating in a local stream next to a garbage dump.

✔ Walking past a factory, you're overcome by a strong odor that burns your eyes and nose.

✔ Someone has abandoned a load of fifty-gallon metal drums in an empty lot near your home.

Contact:
Office of Ombudsman
Room 2111, Mail Code OS-130
U.S. Environmental Protection Agency
401 M St., SW
Washington, DC 20460
(202) 260-9361

Help Available:
Information: yes
Investigation: yes
Mediation/Arbitration: n/a
Legal advice: yes
Legal representation: n/a

Oil Spills * Smelly Factories

What Happens Next?

The Environmental Protection Agency's (EPA) Hazardous Waste Ombudsman handles all kinds of complaints and reports of pollution. Although it's okay to report pollution through the headquarters above, it's better to do it through one of the EPA's ten regional offices that serves your state (see listing on page 243), not only because headquarters will send your report on to the regional office anyway, many of the regional offices have toll-free telephone numbers for you to use, so it won't cost you anything to call.

Although they handle each kind of complaint differently, basically what happens is that when the regional office gets the complaint, they notify the headquarters of it in Washington, D.C., and then they investigate it and report their findings back to headquarters. The Ombudsman in Washington then will decide the best way to respond to the problem, and this may include, for example, notifying the factory that is spewing the ash into the air or the owner of the land dump of the poisonous run-off.

On the other hand, they might decide to refer the problem to another agency that is in a better position to address the problem, such as the U.S. Coast Guard if it is a case of an oil spill or a local health department if your neighbor is dumping his used motor oil directly into the sewer. However the EPA decides to respond to your report, they will usually notify you in writing of their decision.

When State Agencies Aren't Doing Their Jobs:
The EPA also accepts complaints about state environmental offices that haven't done anything about pollution you may have reported. If you've complained to your state environmental office about an incident of pollution, but they've done nothing about it, call the U.S. EPA's Inspector General's toll-free hotline at (800) 424-4000. The hotline staff will pass your complaint on to the appropriate EPA regional office for investigation. And if they find that your state environmental office hasn't been doing what it should to remedy the problem, the EPA has the ability to force them to do something about it.

Sue The EPA For Not Doing Its Job And Companies That Pollute:
Under the Clean Air and Clean Water Acts, private citizens and interest groups are allowed to sue the U.S. EPA for not doing its job or sue companies for violating federal laws and polluting the environment. For more information on these citizen lawsuits, contact the following EPA offices:

71

Oil Spills * Smelly Factories

Clean Air:
Office of Enforcement, Air Division, LE-134A, U.S. Environmental Protection Agency, 401 M St., SW, Washington, DC 20212; (202) 260-2817

Clean Water:
Office of Enforcement, Water Division, LE-134W, U.S. Environmental Protection Agency, 401 M St., SW, Washington, DC 20460; (202) 260-8180

Since these types of lawsuits are often very expensive, they are most often undertaken by private environmental organizations that have the collective resources to follow them through. But the experts at the above EPA offices will explain the law to you just in case you're feeling ambitious.

Ethnic Tensions:

A Neighborhood Problem That's Not Black And White

Type of Complaints

✔ A Korean grocery store is being boycotted by Blacks because of an alleged racial remark.

✔ A Jewish temple in a Catholic neighborhood is defaced with anti-Semitic graffiti.

✔ The White police in your neighborhood seem to act with extreme force toward the minorities who live there.

Contact:
Community Relations Service
U.S. Department of Justice
5550 Friendship Blvd., Suite 330
Chevy Chase, MD 20815
(800) 347-4283

Help Available:
Information: yes
Investigation: yes
Mediation/Arbitration: yes
Legal advice: yes
Legal representation: no

What Happens Next?

Did the movie, "Do The Right Thing," remind you of ethnic or racial tensions in your own neighborhood? If your community is being torn apart by ethnic disputes, and the local police just don't seem to be able to anything about it, you should contact the U.S. Department of Justice's Community Relations Service.

Police Brutality * Race Wars

This Service will help your community set up information conferences and training workshops, and distribute publications designed to avoid and resolve ethnic disputes. However, if tensions do break out, this Service will take whatever steps are necessary to bring about a resolution, starting with extensive informal discussion with public or police officials and local community leaders. If the informal discussions aren't effective, the Service will set up and mediate formal negotiations to bring about a settlement.

Experimental Testing At School:

When Passing (Out) A Test Is Illegal

Type of Complaints

✔ Your kid's school won't allow you to review the films that they plan to use in an upcoming educational testing program.

✔ Your daughter's elementary school is requiring her class to take part in testing their antisocial behavior.

✔ Your son's third grade teacher conducted a test to reveal his feelings about your family without your consent.

Contact:
Family Policy Compliance Office
U.S. Department of Education
600 Independence Ave., SW
Washington, DC 20202-4605
(202) 260-3887
Internet: www.ed.gov/offices/fpcd.html

Help Available:
Information: yes
Investigation: yes
Mediation/Arbitration: yes
Legal advice: yes
Legal representation: no

What Happens Next?

There's a federal law that requires elementary and secondary schools to get parental permission before they have your kids take part in any kind of psychological research tests primarily designed to find out information about your kids' personal attitudes, habits, traits, opinions, and beliefs or feelings that aren't directly related to academic instruction. This law, though, covers only tests that are conducted with federal funding. So if the tests are funded locally, the federal government can't do anything about it, and you'll have to solve the problem locally. The law also requires schools to make sure that parents are allowed to inspect any instructional materials such as films, tapes, and books that are used in any of these federally funded education research tests.

If you have a complaint about your child's participation in these exams, you should first contact your local board of education. But if nothing gets done through local agencies, you should then contact the U.S. Department of Education (see page 241 for listing of regional offices). After receiving your complaint, an investigator will contact the school for their side of the story. If after receiving their response the investigator decides that a violation has taken place, they will notify the school to insist that they stop the illegal testing. If the school still doesn't comply with the law, its federal funding could be cut off.

Explosions:

The Big Bang Theory May Be Real

Type of Complaints

✔ You suspect that your neighbor is making bombs in his basement.

✔ The shock from a loud explosion breaks the front windows of your house.

✔ A box of dynamite was stolen from your warehouse.

✔ Your neighbor is setting off sticks of dynamite in his backyard.

Contact:
Explosives Enforcement Branch
Bureau of Alcohol, Tobacco, and Firearms
U.S. Department of the Treasury
650 Massachusetts Ave., NW
Washington, DC 20226
(800) 800-3855
(202) 927-7777

Help Available:
Information: yes
Investigation: yes
Mediation/Arbitration: n/a
Legal advice: yes
Legal representation: n/a

What Happens Next?

If you've witnessed a large explosion or bombing, or suspect that someone is illegally manufacturing or transporting explosives, contact the Bureau of Alcohol, Tobacco, and Firearms (ATF) Explosives Hotline above. Your report will be taken down and referred to the AFT response team that serves your area for investigation.

False Advertising:

Bait And Switch Or Forever Going Out Of Business

Type of Complaints

✔ You buy an oven at a going-out-of-business sale only to discover that six months later the store is still in business.

✔ You go to a store advertising great savings on stereo equipment only to find that store has never sold the items at the non-sale price.

✔ An ad for low-priced lawn mowers lures you into a store where the salesman tells you they are temporarily out of stock of the lawn mower you want and then tries to sell you a higher priced one that can be delivered immediately.

✔ A fast food restaurant advertises that their food is wholesome and healthy for you and your kids.

Contact:
State Consumer Protection Offices
See page 230 for the office nearest you

Help Available:
Information: yes
Investigation: yes
Mediation/Arbitration: yes
Legal advice: yes
Legal representation: no

What Happens Next?

Your state and local Consumer Protection Offices can usually advise you over the phone whether or not you've been the victim of fraudulent or deceptive advertising practices, and they can also tell you what legal options you have.

Depending on the circumstances, the office may contact the offending company and try to resolve the complaint on your behalf, which may involve getting the company to change the advertisement, refund your money, or sell you exactly what the advertisement promised. They often ask for you to write a formal complaint letter if you wish them to take action against the company on your behalf.

Contact:
Federal Trade Commission
Bureau of Consumer Protection
6th and Pennsylvania Ave., NW, Room 466
Washington, DC 20580
(202) 326-3131

Help Available:
Information: yes
Investigation: yes
Mediation/Arbitration: no
Legal advice: yes
Legal representation: no

What Happens Next?

Like your state Consumer Protection Office, the Federal Trade Commission (see page 249 for the office nearest you) also accepts written complaints from individuals about deceptive advertising, and although they cannot directly solve your individual case, they can advise you on the legality of an ad and investigate a company if they receive enough letters like yours complaining against a certain company's or industry's advertising practices.

FBI Files On You:

Find Out If Big Brother
Is Watching You

Type of Complaints

 Guys in cheap suits and dark sunglasses have been hanging out in your neighborhood ever since you sent the President a letter telling him that his cat, Socks, is ugly.

 You think the FBI may be developing a file on you because of your environmental activism.

 When you get a copy of your FBI file, you read that it says you are a communist when in fact you are an anarchist.

Contact:
FBI Headquarters
Freedom of Information Request
9th St. & Pennsylvania Ave., NW
Washington, DC 20535
(202) 324-5520

Help Available:
Information: yes
Investigation: yes
Mediation/Arbitration: no
Legal Advice: yes
Legal Representation: no

What Happens Next?

You can request to see a copy of the contents of any file that the Federal Bureau of Investigation (FBI) has compiled on you, provided that releasing the information poses no threat to any on-going investigations. To request your file, write to the FBI Headquarters at the above address. In your request, you must include your complete name, place and date of birth, your social security number, a daytime phone number, your current mailing address, and your notarized signature.

If you want to dispute the accuracy of any of the contents of your file, you can do so by submitting a complaint form that will come with a copy of your file to the U.S. Department of Justice (Office of Public Affairs, U.S. Department of Justice, 10th and Constitution, Room 1216, Washington, DC 20530, 202-514-2007). The Justice Department will review your complaint, and depending on the evidence that you can provide them to support your claim, they might act to have the disputed contents changed.

Federal Contractors:

Your Boss Can Lose The Business

Type of Complaints

✔ The missile manufacturer you work for won't let you install the firing pins because you're a woman.

✔ While working on an interstate highway, the construction company you work for keeps the women workers directing traffic with flags while the men get promoted to jackhammer duties.

✔ None of the managers in your company that does contract work for the federal government are minorities or women.

Contact:
Office of Federal Contract Compliance Programs
See page 245 for the office nearest you

Help Available:
Information: yes
Investigation: yes
Mediation/Arbitration: yes
Legal advice: yes
Legal representation: yes

What Happens Next?

If you work for a federal contractor and are discriminated against based on your sex, race, color, religion, or national origin, there's a special law protecting you. All federal contractors must take affirmative action in such areas as recruitment, hiring, upgrading, demotions, layoffs or firings, pay rates and compensation, and more.

Although you can't privately sue a company for a violation of the law governing federal contractors, you can file a complaint at the U.S. Department of Labor's Office of Federal Contract Compliance Programs.

Overtime Pay * Job Discrimination

Investigators will look into your complaint on your behalf and try to reach an agreement with the contractor. This agreement might include back pay, seniority credit, or promotions, depending on the nature of your complaint.

If this avenue doesn't bring about a settlement, the contractor may be brought in front of an administrative law judge for a decision. Contractors who don't comply with the findings may lose their government contracts, have payments withheld, or even be prohibited from federal contract work in the future. Contact the U.S. Department of Labor's regional office nearest you (listed on page 274) to file a complaint.

Firewood:

When A Cord Isn't A Cord

Type of Complaints

✔ The cords of firewood you buy from your local wood seller seem to noticeably change in size from one purchase to another.

✔ The wood seller you buy your wood from won't show you how he measures the wood into cords, so you can't tell if he's cheating you out of money.

Contact:
State Offices Weights and Measures
See page 340 for the office nearest you

Help Available:
Information: yes
Investigation: yes
Mediation/Arbitration: yes
Legal advice: yes
Legal representation: no

What Happens Next?

Since firewood is usually sold in standard units of cords, the sales are often regulated by your state's Office of Weights and Measures. If you feel that you paid for a certain amount of firewood but got less than that, and you can't get anywhere with the firewood dealer, contact your state's Office of Weights and Measures. Depending on the evidence of your complaint, this office may send an investigator out to look into it, and if they do in fact find that your cord isn't a cord, or that the dealer is selling less wood to other customers than they paid for, they can make sure that the dealer corrects his "mistake" and, depending on your case, they can make sure that the wood dealer reimburses you for the wood he cheated you out of.

Fish And Seafood:

When Charlie The Tuna Is Mean To You

Type of Complaints

✔ A can of tuna you opened has bones in it.

✔ The processed lobster substitute you bought smells like beef.

✔ The clam chowder you bought has half an inch of sand on the bottom of the can.

Contact:
National Marine Fisheries Service
National Oceanic and Atmospheric Administration
U.S. Department of Commerce
1335 East-West Hwy., Room 6142
Silver Spring, MD 20910
(301) 443-8910
Internet: www.kingfish.ssp.nmfs.gov/

Help Available:
Information: yes
Investigation: yes
Mediation/Arbitration: yes
Legal advice: n/a
Legal representation: no

What Happens Next?

Unlike meat and poultry, the processing of seafood is not regulated by the federal government. The National Marine Fisheries Service (NMFS), however, has a voluntary inspection program for seafood processors that want their products and facilities inspected and graded. Currently only about 12 percent of the seafood processors in the U.S. participate in this program, but the ones that do have to obey any findings of NMFS inspections.

85

Seafood Packaging * Lobster Substitutes

If you've got a complaint about a seafood product, and you want to report it to the NMFS, you'll have to keep a couple of things in mind: 1) The NMFS has authority only over the processing of the seafood, which means that if your complaint has to do with, say, spoilage, the problem could have been caused by the store you bought it from or by the company that shipped the product from the processor. That is not to say that spoilage can't be caused by the processing, but the chances of pinpointing the cause will be more difficult. Whereas finding a rock in your can of tuna is more clearly a processing problem. 2) For the NMFS to act on your complaint, the product must have been processed by a company that is participating in their inspection program.

Once you submit a complaint to the NMFS (see page 312 for the office nearest you), they'll first look to see if the company that processed the seafood is participating in their inspection program. If the company is participating, the NMFS will contact the company about the complaint and ask them to look into it, or, depending on the seriousness of the problem, the NMFS may inspect the processing company first hand. Either way, if the investigation shows that the processor has a problem with the way they're making the seafood, the NMFS can force them to correct the problem, and if they don't, they can be dropped from participating in the inspection program.

Free Medical Care:

It's The Law

Type of Complaints

✔ When you ask for information about free medical care at your hospital, they say they don't have any, even though they do.

✔ A hospital won't give you free medical care because they say your income is too high, even though it isn't.

✔ You end up paying for medical care at a hospital that you wouldn't have had to if they had let you know about how you could get it for free.

Contact:
U.S. Department of Health and Human Resources
Health Resource and Services Administration
Rockville, MD 20857
(800) 492-0359 (in MD)
(800) 638-0742 (outside MD)

Help Available:
Information: yes
Investigation: yes
Mediation/Arbitration: yes
Legal advice: yes
Legal representation: no

What Happens Next?

Under the federal Hill-Burton law, hospitals and other health facilities that receive money for construction and modernization from the federal government must provide certain services free to those who are unable to pay. If you think a facility that is participating in the Hill-Burton program has unfairly denied you free medical care, write the regional office of the U.S. Department of Health and Human Services serving your state listed on page 262.

Hospital Bills * No Medical Insurance

Be sure to include copies of all relevant documents, along with the names of people and facilities involved. Your complaint will be looked into, and if the investigator finds that a facility has unfairly denied you health care that you are entitled to under the Hill-Burton law, they can demand that the facility provide you with the health care coming to you. In the unlikely event that the hospital refuses to comply, it could have its federal funding cut off.

Funeral Homes:

Going Out In Style

Type of Complaints

✔ A funeral home won't give you the price of their caskets and services over the telephone.

✔ A mortician tells you that by law your deceased grandmother must be embalmed.

✔ An undertaker tells you that you must purchase a regular casket for you dearly departed aunt, even though she will be cremated.

Contacts:

State Funeral Service Examining Boards
See page 252 for the Board in your state

Federal Trade Commission
Bureau of Consumer Protection
Division of Marketing Practices, Room 238
Washington, DC 20580
(202) 326-3128

Help Available:

Information: yes
Investigation: yes
Mediation/Arbitration: yes
Legal advice: yes
Legal representation: no

What Happens Next?

In 1984 Congress passed a law that protects you against unscrupulous funeral service businesses. The law gives you certain rights concerning telephone price disclosures, general price lists, embalming, cremation, and required purchases.

Your state's Consumer Protection Office (see page 230 for the office nearest you) will look into your complaint by contacting the funeral home in question and getting their side of the problem. Depending on the situation, they may then ask the funeral home to resolve the dispute directly with you or they may set up a meeting between you and the funeral home where the three of you can work out a settlement that satisfies both sides. Like the Consumer Protection Offices, your state Funeral Service Licensing Board will also investigate complaints against funeral service providers. But unlike the Consumer Offices, the Licensing Boards have the power to suspend or revoke a funeral home's operating license if they find that the funeral home has cheated many consumers and is not acting to responsibly remedy their complaints.

Although it doesn't act on individual complaints, the Federal Trade Commission (FTC) may decide to investigate a funeral home if they receive enough complaints against one. It is a good idea to submit your complaint to the FTC (see page 249 for the office nearest you) because if they do decide to investigate your funeral home and if they do find that they've cheated customers out of money, you may be able to receive compensation from the funeral home if they are forced to make refunds to consumers.

Garnishment Of Wages:

When A Collector Collects Too Much From Your Paycheck

Type of Complaints

✔ You can't pay your rent because too much money is being garnished from your paychecks to pay off a bill you owe.

✔ Your boss discovers that you are having your wages garnished and decides to fire you because you are bad for the company's image.

Contact:
Wage and Hour Division
Fair Labor Standards
U.S. Department of Labor
200 Constitution Ave., NW, Room S3516
Washington, DC 20210
(202) 219-8305
Internet: www.dol.gov

U.S. Department of Labor local offices
See page 274 for the office nearest you

Help Available:
Information: yes
Investigation: yes
Mediation/Arbitration: yes
Legal advice: yes
Legal representation: yes

What Happens Next?

If you owe money to a bank, a department store, or anyone else, and you don't pay them, they can go to court and get an order to have a portion of your wages from each paycheck paid directly to them. However, there are both state and federal laws that protect you from having your wages garnished too much, or from being fired because your wages are being garnished. If you feel that your wages have been unfairly garnished or have lost your job because of it, contact the U.S. Department of Labor's Wage and Hour Division office.

Your case will be investigated, and if they find that a violation of the garnishment law has taken place, you may be able to have the amount garnished reduced, or if you've been fired, you may get your job back with back pay. See page 274 for the U.S. Department of Labor office nearest you, or your state's own Department of Labor, which has wage garnishment laws of its own that it enforces.

Government Benefits:

When You're Not Getting Your Fair Share

Type of Complaints

✔ The monthly Social Security checks that you're supposed to receive aren't being sent to you.

✔ You are denied your Black Lung benefits even though you worked as a coal miner for forty years.

✔ You are having trouble getting reimbursed from the VA for your husband's funeral, even though he was a World War II veteran.

✔ While in a nursing home, the government threatens to cut off your Medicare funding for no apparent reason.

Contact:
Your U.S. Senator or House Representative:

U.S. Senator (*name*)
Washington, DC 20510
(202) 224-3121

U.S. House Representative (*name*)
Washington, DC 20515
(202) 224-3121

Help Available:
Information: yes
Investigation: yes
Mediation/Arbitration: yes
Legal advice: yes
Legal representation: no

Social Security * Disability

What Happens Next?

If you're getting the runaround in trying to solve a problem with your government benefits, such as Social Security, Medicare and Medicaid, Veterans' benefits, and Black Lung benefits, contact your U.S. Senator or House Representative. They have staffs just to answer inquiries from the public and help solve your problems. You'd be surprised how quickly the Social Security Administration or VA will solve your problem when they get a call from a U.S. Senator or Representative. Where government benefits are concerned, never take a "No" from a bureaucrat as the final word, especially when your representatives in Congress specialize in getting a "Yes" for people like you who can vote them into, or out of, office. If you don't know who your Senators and House members are, your local library should be able to tell you along with the addresses of their local offices in your home state.

Government Benefits Fraud:

Picking Uncle Sam's Pocket

Type of Complaints

✔ Your loudmouthed neighbor brags that he's getting veteran's benefits for a mental condition that he's been faking for ten years.

✔ A guy you know has been cashing his wife's Social Security checks for the past five years even though she died three years ago.

✔ Your co-worker is bragging about how she is able to use food stamps at a local liquor store to buy beer and cigarettes.

Contact:

General Accounting Office
Fraud Hotline
600 E St., NW, Room 1000
Washington, DC 20548
(202) 272-5557, or
(800) 424-5454 (toll-free)

Help Available:

Information: yes
Investigation: yes
Mediation/Arbitration: n/a
Legal advice: yes
Legal representation: n/a

What Happens Next?

Acting as the federal government's personal accountant, the General Accounting Office (GAO) receives all kinds of complaints about people who abuse and rip off government benefit programs. The GAO will either investigate the report itself or refer it to the federal agency that administers the benefits program directly. If you wish, your call will be kept anonymous.

95

Food Stamps * VA Benefits

Here's a list of the benefit programs along with the direct federal toll-free hotlines that handle complaints:

Black Lung benefits: .... (800) 347-3756
Food Stamps: .... (800) 424-9121
Housing Subsidies: .... (800) 347-3735
Medicare & Medicaid: .... (800) 368-5779
Railroad Retirement benefits: .... (800) 772-4258
Social Security benefits: .... (800) 368-5779
Student Loans: .... (800) 647-8733
Unemployment Compensation: .... (800) 347-3756
Veterans benefits: .... (800) 488-8244

All reports will be investigated, and if criminal violations are discovered, the case may be referred to the U.S. Department of Justice (Office of Public Affairs, U.S. Department of Justice, 10th and Constitution, Room 1216, Washington, DC 20530, 202-514-2007) for review and possible prosecution, which could lead to fines and imprisonment for the violators.

Government Waste And Mismanagement:

Cheating On Uncle Sam

Type of Complaints

✔ A federal employee uses government telephones to make personal long distance telephone calls.

✔ While on official business, a government employee earns airline bonus mileage that he uses to get free tickets for personal travel.

✔ You suspect that a government contractor is bribing a federal employee to get a better chance at landing a large military contract.

Contact:

General Accounting Office
Fraud Hotline
600 E St., NW, Room 1000
Washington, DC 20548
(202) 272-5557, or
(800) 424-5454 (toll-free)

Federal Inspector General's Whistleblower Hotlines
See page 345 for listing of agencies.

Help Available:

Information: yes
Investigation: yes
Mediation/Arbitration: n/a
Legal advice: yes
Legal representation: n/a

Lazy Bureaucrats * Whistleblowers

What Happens Next?

Each of the major departments and agencies in the federal government has a special hotline in their Inspector General's office that takes reports about waste, fraud, and mismanagement involving employees working for them. If you witness any kind of questionable conduct by a federal employee or contractor, contact the appropriate whistleblower hotline listed on page 345. If you wish, your call will be kept anonymous.

Every complaint is investigated to determine whether it can be substantiated. If it can, the Inspector General will take whatever steps are necessary to remedy the situation, including undertaking financial audits, criminal investigations, and even firing a dishonest employee. If a criminal investigation is necessary, the case may be referred to the U.S. Department of Justice for review and prosecution. If you are a federal employee yourself and your complaint leads to recovery of money or to saving the government money, you may be eligible for a reward up to $10,000, or as much as $20,000 if it is granted by the President of the United States, depending on how good your tip is.

Handicap Access:

Getting Over The Hurdles
For Wheelchairs

Type of Complaints

✔ The restroom stalls in the building where you take adult education classes are too narrow to fit your wheelchair.

✔ There are no special handicap parking spaces at your local Small Business Administration Office.

✔ The building where you have to apply for Food Stamps doesn't have a wheelchair ramp.

Contact:
Architectural and Transportation Barriers
Compliance Board
1331 F Street, NW, Room 1000
Washington, DC 20004-1111
(202) 653-7834
(800) USA-ABLE

Help Available:
Information: yes
Investigation: yes
Mediation/Arbitration: yes
Legal advice: yes
Legal representation: n/a

What Happens Next?

By law, buildings that have received certain federal funding since 1969 to make architectural changes are required to comply with federal accessibility standards for the handicapped. These standards make sure that entrances have wheelchair access, rest room facilities have the appropriate fixtures, light switches and door handles are low enough for those in wheelchairs, and so on.

Bathrooms * Stairways * Curbs

Upon receiving your complaint, the Board will determine if the building in question falls under their jurisdiction. If so, they will contact the building's occupying agency, along with the agency from which the building gets its funding, and ask that the access problem be corrected. In most cases, this action will solve the problem. If not, the Board may take legal action to make sure that the changes are made.

Since state and local governments have their own standards for handicap access, if the building in question does not fall under the Board's jurisdiction, they will refer your complaint to the appropriate federal, state, or local agency that can do something about it.

Health And Safety Hazards At Work:

A Messy Desk Can Get The Boss In Trouble

Type of Complaints

✔ The repetitious work on the assembly line at work is causing chronic pain in your arms and hands.

✔ You were fired because you pointed out health hazards on the job to your boss.

✔ There is asbestos insulation falling from the ceiling above your desk at work.

✔ Your boss continues to make you use power tools with faulty wiring even after you've pointed it out to him.

Contact:
Office of Field Programs
Occupational Safety and Health Administration
U.S. Department of Labor
200 Constitution Ave., NW, Room N3603
Washington, DC 20210
(202) 523-8111

Help Available:
Information: yes
Investigation: yes
Mediation/Arbitration: yes
Legal advice: yes
Legal representation: yes

Repetitious Work * Dirty Offices

What Happens Next?

Without knowing it, you might be exposed to situations on the job that violate federal health and safety standards. But if you suspect that conditions on your job threaten your health or safety, contact the nearest Occupational Safety and Health Administration (OSHA) regional office nearest you (listed on page 274).

OSHA will review your complaint and decide if a federal OSHA safety standard is possibly being violated. To do this, they will send out an investigator to inspect your work place. If the inspection proves that OSHA laws have been violated, they may give your company a citation, impose financial penalties, and force the company to correct the violation. If the company refuses, OSHA may take them to court to enforce the law.

If you think you've been fired, demoted, transferred, or have experienced other forms of discipline for bringing health and safety violations to the attention to your boss, OSHA will investigate your complaint, and if they find that you've been mistreated for reporting an OSHA violation, they can force your company to reinstate you with back pay to your former position. Keep in mind, though, that if you feel that you might lose your job by reporting a health violation, contact OSHA directly. To protect your job, OSHA will not tell your company who filed the complaint against them.

Health Clubs:

When Pumping Iron Flattens Your Wallet

Type of Complaints

✔ You pay $500 for a membership to a health club but they close down the very next day.

✔ You buy a membership to a health club because they claimed they'd have an olympic size swimming pool built within two months. Six months later, there's still no pool.

✔ That personal fitness trainer the health club promised you turns out to be the personal trainer for the other 500 members too and has no time for you.

Contact:
Your State Consumer Protection Office
See page 230 for the office nearest you

Help Available:
Information: yes
Investigation: yes
Mediation/Arbitration: yes
Legal advice: yes
Legal representation: no

What Happens Next?

Because of the increasing complaints about health clubs, many states have enacted special laws specifically to protect consumers against unfair practices. In fact, some states now require that new health clubs post a bond or put money into a special account before they open just in case any problems arise.

Health Club Memberships * Health Spas

If you have been lied to or cheated out of money by a health club, contact your state's Consumer Protection Office. They'll investigate your complaint and find out if the club has acted dishonestly. They may decide to set up a meeting between you and the health club to mediate a settlement, or if the case is clear cut, they may simply ask the club to refund your money.

When a Consumer Protection Office gets several complaints against the same health club, they will often conduct an investigation that could result in legal action against the club. Penalties might include revoking the club's operating license, imposing civil fines, and forcing the club to refund their clients' money.

Health Fraud:

Taking The Cure From A Snake Oil Salesman

Type of Complaints

✔ A medical supply company sells you a miracle cure for cancer that turns out to be aspirin.

✔ A man, posing as a doctor, promises to cure your arthritis by giving you injections of a new drug that turns out to be sugar water.

✔ The $1,000 cure for AIDS you bought is actually a bottle of multi-vitamins along with advice to drink a lot of water.

Contact:
Your State Consumer Protection Office
See page 230 for the office nearest you

Help Available:
Information: yes
Investigation: yes
Mediation/Arbitration: yes
Legal advice: yes
Legal representation: no

What Happens Next?

Con artists have been selling miracle cures for diabetes, cancer, arthritis, old age, and hair loss for centuries, and unsuspecting people have been making them rich for just as long. And if you find yourself the victim of one of these scams, contact your state's Consumer Protection Office.

After receiving your complaint, they will investigate it by contacting the company in question and getting their side of the story. They may then decide to mediate a settlement between you and the company, which could result in you getting your money back and getting the company stopped from continuing their illegal practices.

If a state's Consumer Protection Office gets enough complaints about a particular company, they may decide to start a formal investigation that could result in legal action against the company. If the company is found guilty of fraud, it may be forced to pay back money to the people they cheated and stop selling their product, and they may even have their business license revoked and have to pay civil fines.

Health Maintenance Organizations:

Getting To Know Your HMO

Type of Complaints

 An HMO won't provide you with care because you're too old.

 The physician at your HMO treats you for the same condition three times in the last month with no improvement, and then he says the pain is all in your head.

 Medicare paid for your gallstone treatment, but the HMO still billed you for it.

Contact:
Office of Prepaid Health Care
Operation and Oversite Office of Operation
Health Care Financing Administration
7500 Security Blvd.
Baltimore, MD 21244
(410) 786-3000
Internet: www.hcfa.gov

Help Available:
Information: yes
Investigation: yes
Mediation/Arbitration: yes
Legal advice: yes
Legal representation: no

What Happens Next?

If a Health Maintenance Organization (HMO) receives Medicare or Medicaid payments, and most do, they've got to follow certain federal guidelines regarding the quality of care they provide. If you feel that the care you received from a federally-qualified HMO was less than what you expected, contact the Health Care Financing Administration (HCFA).

The HCFA will look into your complaint by first finding out if what you're complaining about is something that they have jurisdiction over, and if it is, they'll contact the HMO on your behalf and ask for their side of the story. If the HMO's response shows that they have violated a federal guideline, the Health Care Financing Administration will ask the HMO to promptly correct the problem. If the HMO still doesn't do anything about your complaint, the HCFA has the ability to deny the HMO's participation in the Medicare and Medicaid programs, which could severely hurt them financially.

Home Improvements:

Repairing A Contractor's Contract

Type of Complaints

✔ You have your house painted, but it begins to peel again after only two months.

✔ A contractor makes you put down a 50 percent deposit before he remodels your kitchen but never returns to do the work.

✔ The new addition you have put on your house has only half the square footage that the contractor said it would.

✔ Ever since the plumber installed your new water heater, all the water in your house has been the color of rust.

Contact:
State Licensing Boards
See page 289 for the office nearest you

Help Available:
Information: yes
Investigation: yes
Mediation/Arbitration: yes
Legal advice: yes
Legal representation: no

What Happens Next?

If trying to work out your complaint directly with the contractor doesn't satisfy you, contact your state's Home Improvement Commission, which is often located within your state's Licensing Board. The Commission will send a copy of your written complaint to the contractor who did the work for you and ask them to resolve your problem.

If the contractor still disputes the complaint, the Commission may send out an investigator to look at the work done. If after doing so the investigator decides that your complaint is justified, they may arrange a meeting between you and the contractor to work out a solution. But if this still doesn't work, the Commission may bring the contractor before a formal hearing.

Some states require that their licensed contractors be bonded, meaning that they have to put a certain amount of money into an escrow account just in case they have a dispute with a customer. If you show the state Licensing Board that the contractor has cheated you out of money, the Board may request that funds be released from the escrow account to cover your damages. It's always a good idea to find out if your contractor is bonded before work is started.

Contact:
State Consumer Protection Offices
See page 230 for the office nearest you

Help Available:
Information: yes
Investigation: yes
Mediation/Arbitration: yes
Legal advice: yes
Legal representation: no

What Happens Next?
Like your state Licensing Board, your state Consumer Protection Office will contact the contractor on your behalf and try to arrange a settlement. This will often do the trick, but if it doesn't, you may have to pursue the complaint further in court on your own.

Hospital Care And Service:
Dealing With Unhealthy Health Care

Type of Complaints

✔ You had to wait three hours in the emergency room with a compound fracture in your leg before you were taken care of.

✔ The hospital insisted on discharging you after surgery even though you were still in extreme pain.

✔ Dirty towels and bed sheets were piled in the hallways in the hospital where you stayed.

✔ The linens on your hospital bed were dirty and the food was cold.

✔ The nurse who took care of you was rude and impatient when she was explaining how you were supposed to take your medication.

Contact:
Health Care Financing Administration
U.S. Department of Health
and Human Services
7500 Security Blvd.
Baltimore, MD 21244
(410) 786-3000
Internet: www.hcfa.gov

Help Available:
Information: yes
Investigation: yes
Mediation/Arbitration: yes
Legal advice: yes
Legal representation: no

111

What Happens Next?

Visits to the hospital are stressful enough without having to also deal with rude nurses, unsanitary conditions, long waits, and any other annoying problems that sometimes come up. If you have a complaint about your treatment while at the hospital, contact the U.S. Department of Health and Human Services regional office serving your area listed on page 262.

The Health Care Financing Administration (HCFA) is the federal agency that handles complaints involving any hospital that participates in the Medicare funding program, and that covers about 95 percent of all hospitals in the U.S. Once they receive your written complaint, HCFA will review it to determine if there's enough evidence to warrant them taking any action. If they decide that there is, they'll refer the complaint to one of their regional offices or to the Medicare state agencies who will investigate the complaint and relay the results back to the HCFA.

If the investigation of your complaint finds that a violation of federal guidelines has taken place, they will contact the hospital in question and request that it correct the problem, whether this means making sure the nurses are more courteous, the linens are cleaned properly, or the food is heated and served more efficiently. If the hospital doesn't do anything about remedying the complaints, the HCFA, depending of the seriousness of the violation, may choose to cut the hospital off from participating in the Medicare funding program.

Hospital Discrimination:

Discrimination In Health Facilities

Type of Complaints

✔ You are denied dialysis because you are HIV positive.

✔ A hospital refuses to allow your Seeing Eye dog to accompany you during your stay.

✔ You were denied medical services at a hospital because your physician doesn't have staff privileges.

Contact:
Office for Civil Rights
U.S. Department of Health and Human Services
330 Independence Ave., SW, Room 5250
Washington, DC 20201
(202) 619-0403

Help Available:
Information: yes
Investigation: yes
Mediation/Arbitration: yes
Legal advice: yes
Legal representation: no

What Happens Next?

These and other discriminatory acts occur more often that you might think. If you feel that a hospital, nursing home, or mental health facility that receives funding from the U.S. Department of Health and Human Services (HHS) has denied you services or discriminated against you in other ways based on your race, color, age, religion, national origin, or medical condition, contact the HHS regional office nearest you (listed on page 262).

If the HHS investigator determines that your complaint has cause for action, HHS will arrange a meeting with the health care facility representatives, hear the evidence, and make a decision. If they decide in your favor, the health care facility can be forced to treat you and others like you or risk losing their federal funding. And if your case is life-threatening and requires that the investigation process be speeded up, HHS will do that so that you can get the services you need as soon as possible.

Housing Discrimination:

When You're Too Old, Too Young, Or Too Something To Buy Or Rent

Type of Complaints

✔ A landlord won't rent an apartment to you because he's had bad experiences with other people who are Jewish.

✔ A landlord refuses to rent to you because he thinks divorced women are too much of a financial risk.

✔ You call about a house for sale, and the owner says it's still available. When you get there ten minutes later, and she sees that you are Black, she tells you that the house is already sold.

Contact:
Office of Investigation
U.S. Department and Housing and Urban Development
451 7th Street, SW, Room 5208
Washington, DC 20410-2000
(800) 669-9777
(202) 708-0836

Help Available:
Information: yes
Investigation: yes
Mediation/Arbitration: yes
Legal advice: yes
Legal representation: yes

What Happens Next?
If you feel that you've been discriminated against in housing on the basis of your race, color, religion, sex, national origin, family status, or because of a handicap, be sure to document everything you can about the incident and

contact the U.S. Department of Housing and Urban Development's (HUD) hotline.

Upon receiving your complaint, HUD will send out an investigator to look into the problem, and then arrange a meeting between you and the person you've complained about to resolve the problem. If this meeting doesn't bring about a satisfying resolution to your complaint, and if the HUD investigator decides that there is justifiable cause for legal action, HUD may recommend to the U.S. Department of Justice that your case be tried in court. If it is tried and the defendant is found guilty of discrimination, that person may be jailed, fined, or be forced to compensate you financially for any damages resulting from his/her actions.

Insurance:

Canceled Policies & Unpaid Claims

Type of Complaints

✔ Your insurance company cancels your car insurance without properly notifying you.

✔ Your health insurance premium goes up after one year even though your broker said it would go down.

✔ An insurance company won't honor your claim for reasons you can't understand.

Contact:
State Insurance Commissioners
See page 265 for the office nearest you

Help Available:
Information: yes
Investigation: yes
Mediation/Arbitration: yes
Legal advice: yes
Legal representation: no

What Happens Next?

Contact your state's Insurance Commissioner if you have any complaints involving insurance policies, including premiums, deductibles, claims, or anything else related to your insurance coverage. They will review your complaint, and if they find that your insurance company has acted in an unlawful or unethical way, they have the power to force the insurance dealer to compensate you or correct whatever mistake they've made.

If you have a policy claim, but your state-licensed insurance company goes out of business before you can collect, you may not be completely out of luck. Some states, like Maryland, have organizations funded by the industry that pay

Deductibles * Premiums * Claims * Agents

policy claims if your state-licensed insurance company goes out of business. These funds, though, do not pay all types of claims, and because they are not insured by the state, there is no guarantee that your claim against them will be paid. Contact your state's Insurance Commission to find out if your state has such an organization.

Interstate Land Sales:

How To Get Out Of Swamp Land

Type of Complaints

✔ You're interested in buying some undeveloped land by mail, but the real estate developer won't give you a property report before you make the purchase.

✔ Within a week after signing a contract to buy some land in another state, you change your mind, but the company that sold you the property won't let you out of the contract.

✔ You buy some undeveloped land in another state with the understanding that within a year a golf course and marina would be built next to it. A year later you still have a swamp as a neighbor.

Contact:
Interstate Land Sales Registration Division
U.S. Department of Housing and Urban Development
451 7th St., SW
Washington, DC 20410-8000
(202) 708-0502

Help Available:
Information: yes
Investigation: yes
Mediation/Arbitration: yes
Legal advice: yes
Legal representation: yes

Deeds * Land Developers * Real Estate

What Happens Next?

If you feel you are the victim of a shady interstate land developer, you may be able to get help in resolving your complaint through the U.S. Department of Housing and Urban Development (HUD). HUD will assign an investigator to your case, and depending on the circumstances of your complaint, the investigator will present the evidence to the land developer and ask them for a voluntary settlement. If the developer refuses to settle, HUD may decide to prosecute the developer on your behalf in civil or federal court depending on the nature of the case.

HUD has jurisdiction only over land sales between individual consumers and developers with at least 25 or more lots to sell. They do not get involved with single land sales that occur between individuals. If the sale that you were involved in does not fall under HUD authority, you should contact your own state's Consumer Protection Agency, which enforces state laws that protect consumers in land sales.

Keep in mind that HUD encourages people who even suspect but aren't sure that they've been cheated in a land sales deal to contact them. Chances are that if you feel you've been cheated, there are a number of other people just like you, and all your complaints can add up to a strong legal suit against a dishonest land developer.

Whenever you decide to invest money in a land development project, be sure to keep complete records of the transaction--contracts, receipts, advertisements, and especially conversations. HUD will need all of this evidence to investigate your case.

Job Discrimination:

Hiring, Firing, And Promoting

Type of Complaints

✔ A factory refuses to hire you because you have pre-school-age children, even though there is no such restriction for the male employees.

✔ The company you work for pays male packers 21 cents an hour more than the female workers because they say that the men can do things that the women can't, such as lifting and stacking cartons and using hand trucks.

✔ You take a leave of absence from your job because of pregnancy, but when you return, you are given a temporary position and denied the seniority you've accumulated.

Contact:
Equal Employment Opportunity Commission
1400 L St., NW
Washington, DC 20005
(800) 669-4000
(202) 663-4264

Help Available:
Information: yes
Investigation: yes
Mediation/Arbitration: yes
Legal advice: yes
Legal representation: yes

What Happens Next?
If you believe you have been discriminated against by an employer, labor union, or employment agency when applying for a job or on the job because of your race, color, sex, religion, national origin, age, or handicap, you can file a charge of discrimination with the Equal Employment Opportunity Commission

Promotions * Jobs * Bosses * Pay Raises

(EEOC). Between 1986 and 1988, the EEOC recovered $394 million for victims of job discrimination, so they obviously work hard in getting victims of discrimination what's coming to them.

You can file discrimination charges with EEOC in person, by mail, or by telephone. Before lodging your complaint, make sure that you document everything that happened, including dates, conversations, and so forth. If after looking at the evidence, the EEOC investigator decides that there are grounds for making a charge against the company in question, they will notify the company of the charges on your behalf.

If the company denies the charges, EEOC will set up a hearing to seek a resolution. If the company still denies the charges and EEOC believes there are grounds for further action, EEOC will file charges against the company in federal court on your behalf. If they win your case, the company may be fined and you may be awarded monetary compensation in the form of cash payments, back pay, or benefits.

Labor Union Corruption:

Using Your Muscle On Labor Bosses

Type of Complaints

✔ For the last three years, the same leaders win the union elections even though no one you've talked to voted for them.

✔ Your union president bought a Rolls Royce two days after he gave the union's support to a candidate in the upcoming election for mayor.

✔ Your union dues were doubled last year, and the only improvement you can see is the new swimming pool in your boss's backyard.

Contact:
U.S. Department of Labor
Office of Labor-Management Standards
Office of Policy and Program Support
200 Constitution Ave., NW, Room N5605
Washington, DC 20210
(202) 523-7337

Help Available:
Information: yes
Investigation: yes
Mediation/Arbitration: n/a
Legal advice: yes
Legal representation: n/a

What Happens Next?

To report any complaints about unfair elections, financial reporting violations, or embezzlement in labor unions, contact the U.S. Department of Labor regional office nearest you (listed on page 274). When this office investigates your complaint, your name and the specific details of the complaint will not be disclosed, and the union will not be allowed to review the complaint or obtain a copy of it. If investigators find out that criminal violations have taken place, the case will be referred to the U.S. Justice Department for further investigation and possible prosecution.

Landlords And Tenants:

Tightening Up On Leaky Landlords

Type of Complaints

✔ Your landlord won't return your security deposit and wouldn't give you a good reason why.

✔ You sign a lease stating that you can move in on the first of the month, but when you arrive, the previous tenants haven't moved out yet, and the landlord says you'll just have to wait a week.

✔ When you ask your landlord to fix a plumbing leak, he gives you thirty days to move out.

Contact:
State Consumer Protection Office
See page 230 for the office nearest you

Help Available:
Information: yes
Investigation: yes
Mediation/Arbitration: yes
Legal advice: yes
Legal representation: no

What Happens Next?

Not surprisingly, people commonly complain about their landlords. If you have an unresolved dispute with your landlord about your lease, security deposit, evictions, application fees, repairs, or anything else that deals with your rental housing, don't give up. Each state, and each county within each state, often has its own laws to protect your rights as a renter against dishonest or irresponsible landlords. And probably the best place to start with lodging a complaint is your state or local Consumer Protection Agency.

Leases * Rental Agreements * Deposits

If, for example, your landlord has broken any laws by withholding your security deposit or refusing to make necessary repairs, this office will contact your landlord for you, and ask that the situation be resolved. This action usually brings results, but if it doesn't you can always take your landlord to small claims court.

If your complaint involves a safety or health hazard, such as a leaky gas pipe, lead paint peelings, or rodent infestation, you can also try reporting your landlord to your state or local housing office for possible violations of local building codes. They may send out an investigator to look at the problem, and if they find a violation, they will force your landlord to make needed repairs. Keep in mind, though, that cosmetic repairs, such as a torn shower curtain or dirty rugs do not qualify as safety or health hazards, and in these cases your housing office won't investigate them. Also remember that it is illegal for a landlord to evict you because you complain about any health or safety hazards, but if this happens, your Consumer Protection Office can help you get a fair settlement with your landlord.

Lawyers:

Where To Go When You Get The Legal Runaround

Type of Complaints

✔ Your lawyer bills you for preparing a will that he won't let you see.

✔ Because of a slip-up by your lawyer, you went to jail for a parking ticket.

✔ After you pay an expensive retainer to your lawyer, she skips town.

Contact:
Attorney Grievance Offices
See page 279 for the Board in your state

Help Available:
Information: yes
Investigation: yes
Mediation/Arbitration: yes
Legal advice: yes
Legal representation: no

What Happens Next?

Each state has an agency that investigates complaints against lawyers and law firms. These offices will investigate complaints about lawyers practicing in their state, and if necessary, take disciplinary actions on your behalf, that can include reprimands, dismissals, suspensions, and even disbarments. Many of these offices will help arbitrate disputes about fees between you and your lawyer, and some also have set up funds to reimburse clients who have had money stolen by their lawyer.

Licensed Professionals:

From Acupuncturists
To Veterinarians

Type of Complaints

✔ While treating you for back pain, your acupuncturist punctures your eardrum.

✔ All of the trees that your landscaper planted for you last month have died.

✔ The private detective you hired to follow your wife ended up having an affair with her and emptying your bank account.

✔ The mortician who handled your Aunt Zelda's funeral accidentally cremated her and then lost the ashes.

✔ After a taxidermist stuffed and mounted your dog, all of its hair fell out.

Contact:
State Licensing Boards
See page 289 for the office nearest you

Help Available:
Information: yes
Investigation: yes
Mediation/Arbitration: yes
Legal advice: yes
Legal representation: no

What Happens Next?

Depending on the state, you may be surprised to find out what professionals require business licenses, like manicurists, taxidermists, or even morticians.

Barbers * Taxidermists * TV Repairmen

If you've got a complaint against someone who has to have a license to do business, you've got an advantage when you go to complain: they can't cut hair, stuff your dog, or bury your favorite aunt without that license. And if they've got a lot of unresolved complaints lodged against them at your state Licensing Board, they are going to have a tough time getting that license renewed.

Your state's Licensing Board can tell you which professions it licenses, along with whatever disciplinary actions resulting from consumer complaints that it can carry out. Although most require that you submit a written complaint, they can often listen to the facts over the phone and advise you whether or not you have a legitimate grievance. Depending upon the situation, the state Licensing Boards have the power to investigate and take disciplinary action, including probation, license suspension, or license revocation, against the professional in question.

Although each state differs in the professions it regulates, here is a sampling of those licensed across the 50 states. Remember, though, not every state licenses the professions listed here. You'll have to contact your state's licensing board to find out if the professional you are having a problem with is licensed.

Accountants
Acupuncturists
Architects
Auctioneers
Audiologists
Bailbondsmen
Barbers
Beauticians
Beer Distributors
Blood Alcohol Analysts
Boxing Trainers
Burglar Alarm Installers
Carnivals
Chiropractors
Clergy
Collection Agencies
Concert Promoters

Cosmetologists
Cut Flower Dealers
Dental Hygienists
Dentists
Dieticians
Doctors
Dry Cleaners
Electricians
Electrologists
Embalmers
Emergency Medical Technicians
Engineers
Family Support Counselors
Fumigators
Funeral Directors
Gas Fitters
General Contractors

Barbers * Taxidermists * TV Repairmen

Geologists
Hairdressers
Hearing Aid Specialists
Heating and Air Conditioning
  Contractors
Insurance Agents
Interior Designers
Investment Advisors
Land Dealers
Landscapers
Land Surveyors
Lawyers
Livestock Dealers
Manicurists
Marriage Counselors
Midwives
Morticians
Nurses
Occupational Therapists
Optometrists
Osteopaths
Pawnbrokers
Pharmacists
Physical Therapists

Pilots
Plant Breeders
Plumbers
Podiatrists
Polygraph Examiners
Private Detectives
Private Security Guards
Psychologists
Radio Repair Technicians
Real Estate Brokers
River Boat Pilots
School Bus Drivers
Sewer Installers
Shorthand Reporters
Social Workers
Speech Pathologists
Taxidermists
Tax Preparers
Television Repair Technicians
Tow Truck Operators
Tree Surgeons
Used Car Dealers
Veterinarians
Well Drillers

Mail Schemes:

Did Ed McMahon Lie To You?

Type of Complaints

✔ You send away $25 for a solar powered clothes dryer advertised in a magazine, but all you receive is 10 feet of rope and two nails.

✔ You send away $100 for a new cure for arthritis and get a bottle of rubbing alcohol in return.

✔ The "fine metallic etching" of a U.S. president that you sent $50 away for turns out to be a penny.

✔ You receive a sweepstakes notice in the mail that says if you send $100 for shipping costs, you'll get a brand new car that you've won. You send the money, but no car arrives.

Contact:
Postal Inspection Service
U.S. Postal Service
475 L'Enfant Plaza, SW
Washington, DC 20260-2175
(202) 268-4293
(800) 654-8896 or
Your local Postmaster

Help Available:
Information: yes
Investigation: no
Mediation/Arbitration: yes
Legal advice: yes
Legal representation: no

What Happens Next?

If you feel that anything you sent away for isn't what you bargained for, submit a consumer complaint through your local Post Office or the U.S. Postal Inspector. Based upon your complaint, the U.S. Postal Inspector will send a letter on your behalf to the company in question, asking that they resolve the problem. This is as far as the U.S. Postal Service can take a single consumer complaint against a company that does business through the mail.

If, on the other hand, the Postal Service receives many complaints just like yours against the same company, they may choose to investigate for the possibility of mail fraud. If they decide it's necessary, the Postal Service may temporarily hold the mail of the company being investigated, or they may intercept their mail orders and return them to consumers before the company gets them.

Marine Mammal Protection:

$2,500 Reward For Turning In A Dolphin Poacher

Type of Complaints

✔ You witness a weekend fisherman shooting at dolphins with a shotgun to scare them away from his fishing lines.

✔ A business imports fur seal skin wallets and is trying to get other businesses to buy them for resale.

✔ A fishing boat allows much more than the legal limit of dolphins to get caught in their nets.

Contact:

National Marine Fisheries Service
Office of Protected Resources
National Oceanic and Atmospheric Administration
U.S. Department of Commerce
1335 East-West Highway, 6th Floor
Silver Spring, MD 20910-3226
(301) 443-8910

Help Available:

Information: yes
Investigation: yes
Mediation/Arbitration: n/a
Legal advice: yes
Legal representation: n/a

What Happens Next?

If you witness the illegal capture, killing, or harassment of any marine mammal, such as bottlenose dolphins, whales, and seals, you may be able to receive a reward of up to $2,500 from the federal government. To get a reward, the information you provide has to lead to a conviction for a violation of the Marine Mammal Protection Act. You can receive up to one-half of the fine that the government collects based on your complaint. (See page 312 for the National Marine Fisheries Service office nearest you.)

Marine Worker Safety:

When The Rats Move Their Nests To The Lifeboats

Type of Complaints

✔ The boat you work on doesn't have proper life saving equipment.

✔ The oil tanker you work on loads and unloads its fuel in an unsafe way.

✔ The fishing boat you work on is leaking gasoline, but your boss won't do anything about it.

Contact:
U.S. Coast Guard (G-TGC-1)
2100 2nd St., SW
Washington, DC 20593-0001
(202) 267-1933 or
(800) 323-7233
Internet: www.defenselinu.mil/
factfile/chapter1/uscg.html

Help Available:
Information: yes
Investigation: yes
Mediation/Arbitration: no
Legal advice: yes
Legal representation: no

What Happens Next?
The U.S. Coast Guard's Marine Safety Alert Hotline is set up to take complaints from workers stationed on board commercial vessels who observe hazardous conditions, such as malfunctioning equipment and unsafe operating procedures. If you wish, the Coast Guard will keep your complaint anonymous. The Hotline will pass your complaint on to the Coast Guard's Marine Inspection Office

Life Jackets * Oil Tankers * Fishing Boats

serving your area where it will be investigated if necessary. If the investigation finds that violations have taken place, the Coast Guard has the authority to make sure the company who owns the vessel you work on promptly corrects the problems.

Medical Bills:

When You're Sick Of Doctor's Fees

Type of Complaints

✔ You pay your doctor for a lab test, and he also receives payment for the tests from Medicare, but he won't give you a refund.

✔ Even after repeated calls to your insurance company, they give you the runaround about sending you a refund for doctor's fees that you paid for out-of-pocket.

✔ You overpaid your doctor for a visit, but you haven't received the refund she promised you months ago.

Contacts:
State Consumer Protection Office
See page 230 for the office nearest you

State Medical Boards
See page 307 for the office nearest you

Help Available:
Information: yes
Investigation: yes
Mediation/Arbitration: yes
Legal advice: yes
Legal representation: no

What Happens Next?

Errors in your medical bills and insurance claims are more common than you might think. If you find problems with your medical bill and your physician or Health Maintenance Organization (HMO) isn't responding to your complaint, contact your state's Consumer Protection Office or Medical Board.

If necessary, they will contact your doctor or hospital on your behalf to help solve your problems with your medical records, billing errors, insurance claim delays, denied or delayed refunds, and much more.

Keep in mind, though, that your state's Consumer Protection Office does not handle complaints about the quality or accuracy of your doctor's treatment and diagnosis. For information on this subject contact your state Medical Board.

Medical Devices:

Listening To The Radio With Your Hearing Aid

Type of Complaints

✔ A piece of your new hearing aid falls off and gets lodged in your ear canal.

✔ The baby monitor you bought shuts off whenever you use the television remote control.

✔ Your in-home respirator has the annoying habit of switching off after you've fallen asleep.

Contact:
MedWatch
Office of Consumer Affairs
Food and Drug Administration
(HFE-88)
U.S. Department of Health
and Human Services
5600 Fishers Lane
Rockville, MD 20857
(301) 443-1240
(800) 532-4440
Internet: www.fda.gov

Help Available:
Information: yes
Investigation: yes
Mediation/Arbitration: no
Legal advice: yes
Legal representation: no

What Happens Next?

The Food and Drug Administration (FDA) is the federal agency that regulates the manufacture of medical devices, and they take all kinds of complaints about the performance of these devices. And if you think the one you have may have some kind of defect, you should contact the FDA (see page 250 for the office nearest you) along with the place where you bought it.

Although the FDA won't act on your behalf to recover damages from the manufacturer of a defective medical device, they will look into your complaint to see if they should take some kind of action against the manufacturer to make sure that the problem isn't widespread or life threatening. If the FDA determines that there is a serious threat to the public from a defective medical device, they can insist that the manufacturer stop making the product and issue a recall on those they've already sold.

As far as your own case against the manufacturer, the FDA will make the results of their investigation available to you and anyone else so that if you wish to take the company to court on your own, you can use the FDA results to help you prove your case.

Medicare Fraud And Abuse:

When Your Doctor Is Dead Wrong

Type of Complaints

✔ You think your doctor is billing Medicare for procedures that you may not have needed.

✔ A pharmacist dispenses generic drugs to fill prescriptions and then bills Medicare for more expensive, non-generic drugs.

✔ The ambulance company you work for is billing Medicare for transporting patients who never existed.

Contact:
U.S. Department of Health and Human Services
OIG Hotline
P.O. Box 17303
Baltimore, MD 21203-7303
(800) 368-5779 (toll-free)

Help Available:
Information: yes
Investigation: yes
Mediation/Arbitration: n/a
Legal advice: yes
Legal representation: n/a

What Happens Next?

The U.S. Department of Health and Human Services, the federal agency that administers the Medicare program, has set up a toll-free hotline so that you can report Medicare fraud or abuse. Your report will be investigated, and if it is found to be true, the case may be referred to the U.S. Department of Justice for criminal prosecution, which could lead to imprisonment and fines. If you wish, your call will be kept anonymous.

Migrant And Farm Workers:

Getting Picked Clean When Working On The Farm

Type of Complaints

✔ The farm labor contractor you work for has been making deductions from your pay check but won't give you a written explanation why he's making them.

✔ A farmer who hires you as a migrant worker didn't tell you when he hired you that you were replacing other farm workers who were on strike.

✔ Your employer tells you that while working for him, you must buy your groceries from a particular store.

✔ The housing provided for you while working as a migrant has health hazards such as peeling lead paint, broken plumbing fixtures, or a leaking roof.

Contact:
Employment Standards Administration
U.S. Department of Labor
200 Constitution Ave., NW, Room S3325
Washington, DC 20210
(202) 219-8743

Help Available:
Information: yes
Investigation: yes
Mediation/Arbitration: yes
Legal advice: yes
Legal representation: yes

What Happens Next?

If you feel that your rights as a migrant or seasonal agricultural worker might being violated by your employer, the U.S. Department of Labor wants to know about it (see page 274 for the office nearest you). By law your employer is required to display a poster in a conspicuous place at the job site outlining your rights.

After receiving your complaint, the Department of Labor will send out an investigator to look into it if they think any federal labor laws may have been violated. If investigators find out that a violation has taken place, the employer will be advised to make the necessary changes, such as making needed housing repairs or providing itemized written statements of your earnings. Depending on how serious the violations are, the U.S. Department of Labor may also decide to take the employer into an administrative court of law to have fines imposed or his registration certificates revoked. Without this certificate, an employer cannot legally employ migrant and seasonal agricultural workers.

If the employer refuses to comply with the court's findings, the Department of Labor may decide to hand the case over to the U.S. Department of Justice for criminal prosecution, which may lead to heavy fines and prison sentences. Also keep in mind that it is illegal for an employer to fire, harass, or intimidate you for bringing violations to the attention of the Department of Labor, and they will also investigate these incidents and, if they feel they have a case, may go to court on your behalf to protect your rights to complain.

Moving Companies:

When Your Furniture Is Taken For A Ride

Type of Complaints

✔ A moving company loses half your household items, but they still charge you for moving them.

✔ Your moving company won't allow you to be present when your shipment is being weighed.

✔ The moving company shows up at your new house with your furniture three weeks after the agreed delivery date.

Contact:
Interstate Commerce Commission
Office of Compliance
and Consumer Assistance
12th St. & Constitution Ave., NW, Room 5500
Washington, DC 20423
(202) 927-5500

Help Available:
Information: yes
Investigation: yes
Mediation/Arbitration: yes
Legal advice: yes
Legal representation: no

What Happens Next?

To protect your rights when you hire interstate moving companies, the Interstate Commerce Commission (ICC) handles service complaints, such as billing errors, delivery delays, and damaged property.

Damaged Goods * Late Arrivals

After receiving your complaint, the ICC will contact the moving company in question and ask for their side of the story. If the ICC then finds that the moving company has violated your rights, they will ask the company to resolve the problem for you. Because the ICC has the ability to revoke a company's operating license, a letter or call from the ICC will often resolve the problem.

Keep in mind, though, that the ICC cannot force a moving company to resolve loss and damage claims with you. If you can't settle such claims directly with the mover, you may have to take them to court on your own. Many moving companies, however, participate in dispute resolution programs that can arbitrate your claim if you'd rather not go to court on your own. See page 264 for the ICC office nearest you.

Contacts:

State Utility Commissions
See page 335 for the office nearest you

State Consumer Protection Offices
See page 230 for the office nearest you.

Help Available:

Information: yes
Investigation: yes
Mediation/Arbitration: yes
Legal advice: yes
Legal representation: no

What Happens Next?

The ICC does not regulate moves within one state. For complaints in these cases, you should contact your state's Consumer Protection Office or Utility Commission. Your state Utility Commission regulates the rates for these in-state moving services, and they will contact the moving company on your behalf to help resolve your problem. If your complaint doesn't involve a rate dispute, you may have to contact your state's Consumer Protection Office, who will help arbitrate a solution between you and the moving company.

Nuclear Power Plants:

Vegetable Gardens That Glow In The Dark

Type of Complaints

✔ The nuclear plant in your neighborhood emits a strange, glowing green gas at night.

✔ The nuclear plant you work for is cutting corners on safety regulations so they won't have to pay for costly needed repairs.

✔ A nuclear power plant is scheduled to be built in an area that would be next to impossible to evacuate in case of an accident.

Contact:
Nuclear Regulatory Commission
Office of Governmental and Public Affairs
11555 Rockville Pike
Rockville, MD 20852
(301) 492-7000

Help Available:
Information: yes
Investigation: yes
Mediation/Arbitration: no
Legal advice: yes
Legal representation: no

What Happens Next?

The Nuclear Regulatory Commission (NRC) will look into all reported violations or irregularities involving nuclear energy. Because they license all nuclear facilities, the NRC has the power to force them to correct any violations of the law that investigators may find based on your complaint. If they refuse to comply, the NRC can shut them down.

Nursing Homes:

Careless Caring

Type of Complaints

✔ The food at your nursing home is often served cold.

✔ The fees seem to rise every month without notice.

✔ The staff has treated you abusively.

✔ You've been unfairly denied admission to a nursing home for reasons that don't make sense to you.

Contact:
Nursing Home Ombudsmen
See page 313 for the office nearest you

Help Available:
Information: yes
Investigation: yes
Mediation/Arbitration: yes
Legal advice: yes
Legal representation: no

What Happens Next?

There are many complaints common to nursing homes and other health care facilities across the country. To help resolve these special complaints, most states have established Ombudsman offices that act to ensure that these facilities provide their services appropriately and fairly.

Ombudsman offices act as mediators or go-betweens in disputes involving consumer complaints. The Ombudsman, however, are not enforcement agencies: they don't "police" nursing homes and other health agencies in their areas to make sure these facilities are conforming to regulations. And they cannot force a nursing home to change or correct their practices--this can be done through the state office which licenses the nursing home.

What they can do is contact the nursing home on your behalf and try to work out a voluntary solution to your complaint. Often a phone call or a letter is enough to correct the situation, but in more serious cases, a formal meeting between the nursing home, you, and an Ombudsman staff member may be necessary. Since it's to the nursing home's advantage to take care of problems before they are referred to enforcement agencies, such as the state Office of the Attorney General or the state Department of Health and Social Services, you may find that the help of the Ombudsman is all you'll need to correct the problem. If it isn't, the Ombudsman may in fact send your complaint on to an enforcement agency for you.

Of course if you aren't satisfied with the Ombudsman's help, you don't have to accept their findings, and you can always contact the state's Consumer Protection Office (see page 230 for the office nearest you) or the Licensing Board (see page 289 for the office nearest you), who will also investigate your complaint.

Ocean Cruises:

High Seas High Jinks

Type of Complaints

✔ Your cruise was canceled, but you weren't compensated.

✔ A cruise line won't sell you a ticket because of your handicap.

✔ Your cabin was next to the boiler room.

✔ When you were introduced to the captain, he smelled of gin.

Contact:
Federal Maritime Commission
800 N. Capitol
Washington, DC 20573
(202) 523-5807
Fax: (202) 523-0014
E-mail: joseph@fmc.gov
Internet: www.fmc.gov/

Help Available:
Information: yes
Investigation: yes
Mediation/Arbitration: yes
Legal advice: yes
Legal representation: no

What Happens Next?

If you have any problems about a cruise you took, and the cruise line just can't remedy the problem to your satisfaction, you might try contacting the Federal Maritime Commission (FMC). The FMC regulates all shipping commerce, including cruise lines. If you were physically injured on the cruise, didn't get compensation for a cancellation, were discriminated against because of a

149

handicap, or even if you were just generally unsatisfied with the service, the FMC will try to work out a settlement with the cruise line on your behalf.

Through FMC district offices across the country, investigators will look into your complaint, even if it doesn't involve the violation of a law that they enforce, and try to get you satisfaction, either financially or perhaps through having the cruise line offer you another trip, depending on your case.

Odometer Tampering:

Turn In A Tamperer And Get $1,500

Type of Complaints

✔ When you take that used car you bought with only 30,000 miles on it into a mechanic, he tells you there's no way the car has less than 90,000 miles on it.

✔ A car company disconnects the odometers on new cars and allows corporate executives to drive them. The company then reconnects the odometers and sells the cars as new.

✔ You buy a used car only to find that when you register it at the department of motor vehicles, it has less mileage on it now than it did when the previous owner registered it two years ago.

Contact:
Odometer Fraud Staff
Office of Chief Counsel
National Highway Traffic Safety Administration
U.S. Department of Transportation
400 7th St., SW, Room 5219
Washington, DC 20590
(800) 424-9393
(202) 366-0123 (DC metro area)
Internet: www.nhtsa.dot.gov/

Help Available:
Information: yes
Investigation: no
Mediation/Arbitration: no
Legal advice: yes
Legal representation: no

What Happens Next?

To report odometer tampering on a car you bought or are considering buying, call the Auto Safety hotline. Although they will not personally investigate your complaint, the National Highway Traffic Safety Administration (NHTSA) will help you gather the material you'll need to build a case against the dealership, auction house, or individual whom you think has violated the odometer tampering laws. It is then up to you to take the car seller in question to court. Under the law, if the dealership or individual is found guilty, you are entitled to $1,500 or three times the damages that you incurred because of the tampering.

If the NHTSA receives a series of odometer complaints against the same seller, they will undertake an investigation for possible acts of fraud, and if found guilty, that seller may face criminal charges from the U.S. Department of Justice.

Contact:
Your State Consumer Protection Offices
See page 230 for the office nearest you

Help Available:
Information: yes
Investigation: yes
Mediation/Arbitration: yes
Legal advice: yes
Legal representation: no

What Happens Next?

It's also a good idea to contact your state's Consumer Protection Office if you think the odometer has been rolled back on a car you've bought. Unlike the National Traffic Safety Administration, they will investigate your complaint directly, and if they find that the car seller has tampered with the odometer on your car, they can get you financial compensation and perhaps fine the seller. To better protect you against odometer fraud, some states have created special task forces that include the Attorney General, state motor vehicle department, and the FBI.

Oil And Chemical Spills:

When Spilling Crude Is More Than Rude

Type of Complaints

✔ While sailing on the bay one day, you notice a purple sludge being discharged from a oil tanker.

✔ The chemical transport tanker you work on is leaking toxins into the water, but the captain doesn't want to fix it because of the cost involved.

✔ While walking on the beach, you discover a dead bird covered in crude oil.

Contact:
Commandant (G-TGC)
U.S. Coast Guard
National Response Center
2100 2nd St., SW
Washington, DC 20593
(800) 424-8802
(202) 267-2188 (DC metro area)

Help Available:
Information: yes
Investigation: yes
Mediation/Arbitration: n/a
Legal advice: yes
Legal representation: n/a

What Happens Next?

The Coast Guard will look into any reports from the public of oil and chemical spills on the water. If they investigate a complaint and find that there has been a violation of federal environmental regulations, the Coast Guard may decide to take the offending parties to court so that civil penalties can be enforced. The Coast Guard will also monitor the clean up of a spill, making sure that the environmental impact is minimized, and if possible, make sure that the violators pay for the clean up.

Pensions:

Is Your Boss Messing With Your Pension Money?

Type of Complaints

✔ You think you've just been fired so that your boss won't have to pay your pension benefits.

✔ Your boss says you can't join the company pension plan because you're too old.

✔ You leave your job before retirement age, but your former company won't give you the vested benefits you've accumulated.

✔ Your spouse owes you thousands of dollars in unpaid child support, but his company refuses allow money from his pension plan to be paid to you to cover what he owes you.

Contact:
Pension and Welfare Benefits Administration
U.S. Department of Labor
200 Constitution Ave., NW, Room N5658
Washington, DC 20210
(202) 219-8776

Help Available:
Information: yes
Investigation: yes
Mediation/Arbitration: yes
Legal advice: yes
Legal representation: yes

What Happens Next?

The U.S. Department of Labor investigates all kinds of complaints regarding the federal laws that protect your pension rights. If you think that a company has violated your legal rights regarding your or your spouse's pension, contact the U.S. Department of Labor's Pension and Welfare Benefits Administration. They will look into your complaint to see if there has been a violation of the law, and if there has been, they will ask the company in question to comply. If they refuse to comply or say they will but don't, the Department of Labor may decide to file a lawsuit in federal court on your behalf against the company to get you the pension benefits that you're entitled to.

Pharmacists And Pharmacies:

When Your Drugstore Makes You Sick

Type of Complaints

✔ Your pharmacist neglects to warn you about taking a certain drug while operating heavy machinery.

✔ You were charged for 100 pills, but the pharmacist gave you only 75.

✔ Your pharmacist is rude and impatient with you when you ask questions about your prescription.

✔ Your pharmacist dispenses the wrong prescription for you and you have a serious allergic reaction to the drug.

Contact:
State Pharmacy Boards
See page 318 for the Board in your state

Help Available:
Information: yes
Investigation: yes
Mediation/Arbitration: yes
Legal advice: yes
Legal representation: no

What Happens Next?

Like many licensed professionals, pharmacists are required to be licensed by the state they practice their trade in. Although that license doesn't guarantee that the pharmacist will always do his or her job correctly, it does give you some recourse if you feel that the pharmacist has acted unprofessionally or negligently. If you have a complaint about a pharmacist, contact your state's

Pharmacy Board (listed on page 318), either by calling or writing, and they will look into the matter for you.

If the Board's investigation shows that you do have a legitimate complaint, they will decide what action to take against the pharmacist. Depending on the seriousness of the complaint, the Board may just tell the pharmacist to cease his or her offensive behavior, or they may conduct a formal hearing that could result in a suspension or revoking of their license to practice.

Political Broadcasting:

Getting Back At An Unfair Talk Show Host

Type of Complaints

✔ A TV station airs an editorial against a political candidate but doesn't offer the candidate an opportunity to respond.

✔ A radio station invites only pro-life advocates as guests on their talk shows.

✔ A TV station overcharges candidates for political commercials.

✔ A newspaper will print letters that support only one point of view concerning a pending piece of legislation on a gun law.

Contact:
Federal Communications Commission
Political Programming
2025 M St., NW, Room 8202
Washington, DC 20554
(202) 632-7586

Help Available:
Information: yes
Investigation: yes
Mediation/Arbitration: yes
Legal advice: yes
Legal representation: no

What Happens Next?

If you think a political candidate hasn't been given equal access to media opportunities--on television, radio, editorial advertising, and so forth--contact the Federal Communication Commission's (FCC) Political Broadcasting Division. They will investigate equal time issues, billing disputes, and will also look into how evenly a political issue such as abortion, hand guns, or even strip mining, is handled by news stations on TV and radio.

After receiving your complaint, an FCC staff member will investigate it, usually by sending a letter to the broadcast station involved and asking for their side of the issue. If after hearing the station's side the FCC decides that a violation has occurred, they may ask the station to voluntarily remedy the situation. Depending on how serious the violation is, the FCC may also decide to impose sanctions against the station, which may include fines, revocation of licenses, or denial to renew their license.

Politicians In Washington:

Trouble With Your Congressman

Type of Complaints

✔ You discover that the house of ill-repute that you frequent is run out of one of your U.S. Congressman's homes.

✔ A U.S. Senator makes huge cash deposits in a corporate account at the bank you work at.

✔ You discover that a U.S. Senator is paying his wife as a full-time member of his staff, even though she shows up for work only once a month.

Contacts:
U.S. Senators:
Senate Select Committee on Ethics
Hart Senate Office Bldg., Room SH-220
Washington, DC 20510
(202) 224-2981

U.S. Representatives:
House Committee on Standards
of Official Conduct
HT2, U.S. Capitol
Washington, DC 20515
(202) 225-7103

Help Available:
Information: yes
Investigation: yes
Mediation/Arbitration: n/a
Legal advice: yes
Legal representation: n/a

Senators * Kickbacks * Scandal

What Happens Next?

Senate:

If you've witnessed unethical conduct by a U.S. Senator, submit your evidence to the Senate Select Committee on Ethics. They'll look into the allegations to decide if a formal investigation and hearing is warranted, which could lead to reprimands, disciplining actions, or removal from office.

House of Representatives:

If you've witnessed a member of the U.S. House of Representatives acting in an unprofessional or unethical manner, the law allows you to report your complaint to the Committee on Standards and Official Conduct that investigates such allegations. To report allegations to this Committee, however, you must first have submitted your allegations to three members of Congress who have in turn rejected them and refused to do anything about the matter. Once it has been rejected three times, you can then make a report directly to this committee accompanied by copies of the three letters of rejection. The committee will then investigate your allegations, and if they find them to be true, recommend disciplinary actions, or in the case of criminal violations, refer the case to the proper federal authorities for possible prosecution.

Price Fixing:

One Price Fits All & Stores That Won't Sell To You

Type of Complaints

✔ A store tells you they won't sell you an item because they have an agreement with another store that only they can sell it in your area.

✔ You notice that the only two stores that sell an item have fixed the price to keep it artificially high.

✔ You're a furniture store owner, and the wholesale distributor that you buy your chairs from tells you to sell the chairs at a certain price and no lower or else they won't supply you with the chairs anymore.

Contact:
Antitrust Division
U.S. Department of Justice
10th St. & Constitution Ave., NW, Room 3103
Washington, DC 20530
(202) 514-2401

Help Available:
Information: yes
Investigation: yes
Mediation/Arbitration: yes
Legal advice: yes
Legal representation: no

What Happens Next?

When competing businesses get together to fix prices on certain products and services, to limit their output, or to divide business between them without any benefits to consumers, chances are that federal antitrust laws are being violated.

If you know, or even suspect, that a business is engaging in this kind of sleazy activity, even if it's the company you work for, the U.S. Department of Justice wants to hear about it. A large part of their investigations start off as complaints or tips from consumers and businesses. To lodge a complaint, contact the Antitrust Division of the U.S. Department of Justice above or one of their regional offices listed on page 273.

After receiving your complaint, an investigator will try to determine from the evidence you provide whether an antitrust law has been broken. If they find that there's reason to believe that one has been, depending on the seriousness of the situation, they may start a formal investigation into the company or companies involved. And if an investigation uncovers antitrust violations, those guilty could be heavily fined and sentenced to prison.

Prescription Fraud:

Bad Medicine

Type of Complaints

✔ Your friend brags to you that his doctor sells her prescriptions for valium under the table.

✔ Your doctor offers to sell you a prescription for codeine.

✔ Even though you've recovered from your depression, your doctor offers to sell you anti-depressants directly whenever you want them at half the normal price.

Contact:
Office of Diversion Control
Drug Enforcement Agency
Washington, DC 20537
(202) 307-8010

Help Available:
Information: yes
Investigation: yes
Mediation/Arbitration: n/a
Legal advice: no
Legal representation: no

What Happens Next?

If you know of a doctor who's got his or her own drug dealership going on the side, selling drugs or prescriptions for drugs that are controlled substances, the Drug Enforcement Agency (DEA) wants to know about it. Not only does the DEA investigate drug dealers on the street, they also respond to complaints involving physicians who are abusing their privileged access to drugs that under any other circumstances would be illegal.

Pharmacists * Controlled Substances

Upon receiving your complaint about a doctor, DEA investigators will look into it and try to determine if there's evidence to support your report. If they believe there is evidence that the doctor is dealing illegally in prescription drugs, they can bring criminal charges against the doctor, and if he's found guilty, have his license revoked or send him to prison.

Product Safety Defects:

Your Lawnmower Blade Kills
The Neighbor's Dog

Type of Complaints

✔ The paint on a toy doll is peeling off, and your kid eats it.

✔ You buy a new high chair that has sharp metal screws exposed that scratch your baby's legs.

✔ Your new electric blender falls apart when you puree.

✔ A Halloween mask interferes with your child's breathing.

✔ The smoke detector you just bought won't go off even when you set fire to it.

✔ Your son is injured when his all terrain vehicle flips over at a low speed.

Contact:
Consumer Product Safety Commission
5401 Westbard Ave.
Washington, DC 20207
(800) 638-2772
TDD: (800) 638-8270
Internet: www.cpsc.gov/

Help Available:
Information: yes
Investigation: yes
Mediation/Arbitration: no
Legal advice: yes
Legal representation: no

What Happens Next?

There are a few steps you should take to complain about the safety of a product that you've bought. First report the defective product to the store from which you bought it, and then report it to the U.S. Consumer Product Safety Commission's (CPSC) toll-free hotline. The CPSC will review your complaint, and depending on the circumstances and the number of similar complaints they are getting, they might decide to begin an investigation of the product and the manufacturer.

The CPSC, however, will not sue a company for you or help you get compensation from it for any injuries you may have suffered from one of their defective products. What they can do is investigate a company on the behalf of the general public, and order a recall of the products, or if necessary, seek legal action against it to stop them from manufacturing and distributing their unsafe products.

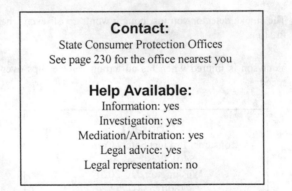

Contact:
State Consumer Protection Offices
See page 230 for the office nearest you

Help Available:
Information: yes
Investigation: yes
Mediation/Arbitration: yes
Legal advice: yes
Legal representation: no

What Happens Next?

As far as your own particular complaint against the company, you should contact your state's Consumer Protection Office. They will help by investigating your complaint and trying to work out a solution with the manufacturer or seller of the defective product. Also keep in mind that when negotiating a settlement with a company concerning a defective product, you can get plenty of useful statistics on product-related injuries from the Consumer Product Safety Commission to support your case.

Product Tampering:

Someone Messing With Your Cereal

Type of Complaints

 Your box of cereal has more broken glass and sharp pins in it than you had expected.

 Your aspirin tastes like turpentine.

 A can of orange soda smells like gasoline.

Contacts:
Federal Bureau of Investigation

Food and Drug Administration
See page 250 for the office nearest you
Internet: www.fda.gov

State Consumer Protection Offices
See page 230 for the office nearest you

Help Available:
Information: yes
Investigation: yes
Mediation/Arbitration: no
Legal advice: yes
Legal representation: no

What Happens Next?

Most stores will replace any package of food or drugs you buy that shows evidence of tampering, but you may want to take further action to make sure that others aren't hurt. The Federal Bureau of Investigation (FBI), the Food and Drug Administration, and your state's Consumer Protection Office will all investigate tampering incidents and decide if an official recall or public warning is necessary.

Property Damage By Diplomats:

An Unfriendly Foreign Affair

Type of Complaints

✔ An employee from a foreign embassy throws a baseball through a window in your house and refuses to pay for the damage.

✔ After a foreign diplomat runs a red light and hits your car, you find out that he has no insurance.

✔ A diplomat signs a year-long lease for your apartment but breaks the agreement and refuses to pay the money he owes you.

Contact:
Office of Foreign Missions
Department of State
2201 C St., NW, Room 2238
Washington, DC 20520
(202) 647-3417

Help Available:
Information: yes
Investigation: yes
Mediation/Arbitration: yes
Legal advice: yes
Legal representation: no

What Happens Next?

If you've got a dispute with a foreign diplomat living in the U.S. who has broken leases, windows, rental agreements, your car, or anything else, contact the State Department. Although they cannot force a foreign diplomat to pay you whatever money he or she owes you, they can contact the diplomat on your behalf and ask that the problem be resolved voluntarily.

Diplomatic Immunity

To better protect U.S. citizens against uninsured drivers with diplomatic immunity, the State Department now requires that members of foreign missions stationed in the U.S. carry high levels of automobile insurance coverage--at least $100,000--before they can register their cars with the State Department.

Like most state's auto insurance laws, the State Department will revoke a diplomat's car registration if the insurance isn't kept up to date. And just like if you get into an accident with an uninsured private citizen, if the same happens with an uninsured diplomat, there's little you or the State Department can do aside from contacting the diplomat and requesting that the matter be settled quickly and fairly.

Property Seized By Foreign Governments:

Start The Revolution Without You

Type of Complaints

✔ During a recent political coup, your vacation home in the Pacific was seized by the new government as their new headquarters because they liked the view.

✔ Your business in Central America was seized by the newest military junta in exchange for your life and a plane ticket out of the country.

✔ Your family lost millions in property during the Iranian revolution.

Contact:
Department of State
Office of Legal Advisor
2100 K St., NW, Suite 402
Washington, DC 20037-7180
(202) 632-5040

Help Available:
Information: yes
Investigation: yes
Mediation/Arbitration: yes
Legal advice: yes
Legal representation: no

What Happens Next?

If you've had property--such as businesses, real estate, and personal property-- unfairly seized by a foreign government, you should first exhaust all of the local remedies in that country. If this doesn't provide a solution, contact the State Department. Depending on the circumstances of your case, the State Department will contact the country for you to seek a voluntary resolution to the problem, but if this doesn't work, they may decide to take your case to international arbitration, involving such programs as the World Bank's

172

Foreign Ownership * Military Juntas

International Centre for the Settlement of Investment Disputes or the International Chamber of Commerce.

If local remedies have been exhausted and the dispute still isn't resolved, the U.S. government has the choice of "espousing" the claim as its own and trying to settle it in the International Court of Justice, with the proceeds received turned over to you at the conclusion of the case.

Radio And Television Broadcasts:

Stopping Dirty DJs

Type of Complaints

✔ The DJ on the morning radio show uses language that you've seen only on the walls in public bathrooms.

✔ A TV show depicts graphic nudity on a late night broadcast.

✔ A local television station "forgets" to bleep out all the obscene language in a movie that they broadcast.

✔ A TV station airs a program with adult subject matter and language during a time when children are likely to be watching.

Contact:
Federal Communications Commission
Mass Media Bureau, Enforcement Division
Complaints and Investigations Branch
2025 M St., NW, Room 8210
Washington, DC 20554
(202) 632-7048

Help Available:
Information: yes
Investigation: yes
Mediation/Arbitration: n/a
Legal advice: yes
Legal representation: n/a

What Happens Next?

If you think that a morning DJ on the radio is using language that may violate federal obscenity laws, be sure to submit your complaint soon after the incident takes place. In your complaint, be sure to include your name and address, the call letters and location of the station; the name of the program involved

Obscene TV * Censorship * Talk Shows

with the date and time of broadcast; the reason you think the subject is offensive; and what you want the station and/or the Federal Communications Commission (FCC) to do to remedy the situation.

The FCC will review your complaint letter, and if they think that you've given sufficient evidence that a violation has occurred, they will investigate. They will send a letter to the station in question and ask them to explain their side of the story. After receiving the station's response, the FCC will decide whether a violation has occurred, and if so, what sanctions to impose. Sanctions may include a formal warning, fines, or revocation of their broadcasting license.

Keep in mind, though, that the FCC cannot censor the content of a television show or commercial unless it violates certain federal obscenity laws, which follow a 1978 Supreme Court ruling that defines obscenity using such guidelines as context, subject matter, and contemporary community standards. This means that the FCC cannot do anything for you if you don't like the quality of the broadcasts or the merits of the actors or performers in them. That's something you'll just have to take up with the networks themselves.

Radon:

When You Can't Trust Your Nose

Type of Complaints

✔ Your neighbor says he has radon gas in his basement and thinks you should get your house tested.

✔ You can't find a contractor whom you trust to fix the radon problem in your home.

✔ You don't know where to find a reliable radon detection kit.

Contact:
Radon Division (6604-J)
Office of Radon Programs
U.S. Environmental Protection Agency
401 M St., SW
Washington, DC 20460
(202) 233-9370
(800) SOS RADON

Help Available:
Information: yes
Investigation: no
Mediation/Arbitration: no
Legal advice: yes
Legal representation: no

What Happens Next?

Since 1985 when dangerous levels of radon gas were found in homes all across the U.S., homeowners have been asking a lot of questions about their safety. To better address this large demand for information and assistance, the U.S. Environmental Protection Agency and each state have set up special Radon Offices (see page 322 for the Radon office in your state).

Although these offices won't come out and test your home for radon for you, they can answer any questions you might have, including how to test your home, where to find a licensed contractor to do any needed repairs, and information on whether or not high levels of radon have been discovered in the homes in your area.

Railroads:

Have They Been Working On Them?

Type of Complaints

✔ You see kids laying logs across railroad tracks.

✔ A train crossing signal in your area doesn't work properly.

✔ The railroad company that you work for is shipping hazardous materials in an illegal way.

Contact:
Office of Safety
Federal Railroad Administration (RRS-20)
U.S. Department of Transportation
400 7th St., SW, Room 8301
Washington, DC 20590
(202) 366-0521

Help Available:
Information: yes
Investigation: yes
Mediation/Arbitration: no
Legal advice: yes
Legal representation: no

What Happens Next?
The Federal Railway Administration (FRA) will investigate any complaints about safety on the railroads in the U.S. Be sure to include the specific details of the incident so that they can remedy the problem as quickly as possible.

Real Estate Agents & Brokers:

When Your Dream Home Is A Nightmare

Type of Complaints

✔ After buying a house, you discover that your real estate broker neglected to tell you that the house was going to be torn down to make way for the new interstate highway.

✔ Your real estate agent charges you twice what you expected for his commission fee.

✔ You can't get the money from your escrow account released after the sale of a house falls through.

Contact:
State Real Estate Commissions
See page 328 for the office nearest you

Help Available:
Information: yes
Investigation: yes
Mediation/Arbitration: yes
Legal advice: yes
Legal representation: no

What Happens Next?

Each state requires that real estate agents and brokers be licensed before they can sell property and houses. And although a license can't guarantee you that your broker is going to treat you fairly, it does give you some added protection if you find yourself the victim of a shady deal. If you have a complaint about a real estate broker, contact your state's Real Estate Commission. They will look into your complaint and contact the broker for you to help resolve the issue. If the broker refuses to act on your complaint, the Commission may decide to conduct a formal hearing that could result in fines or suspension of the broker's license to practice, especially when the broker is found to have violated the state's real estate regulations.

Keep in mind that a real estate broker has to periodically renew his or her license, so it's in their interest to resolve your complaints as quickly as possible. It's not uncommon for a Commission to hold up a broker's renewal application until complaints against him or her are resolved in a satisfactory way.

Restaurants:

What's That Fly Doing In My Soup?

Type of Complaints

✔ There's a fly in your soup. Really.

✔ You notice that the cook at a restaurant leaves the restroom without washing his hands.

✔ The cashier who takes your money at a fast food restaurant also handles the food without first washing her hands.

Contact:
State or Local Health Department
See page 257 for a listing of your state

Help Available:
Information: yes
Investigation: yes
Mediation/Arbitration: n/a
Legal advice: yes
Legal representation: n/a

What Happens Next?

If you notice unsanitary or unhealthful conditions or practices in a restaurant, contact your local health department or your state Health Department (listed on page 257) and they will investigate the problem. Since every restaurant needs a license to operate, if they violate any health codes, they risk the possibility of being shut down by the Health Department until the violations are corrected, or if they have repeatedly violated the health codes, they could be shut down permanently. The state Health Departments will either investigate your complaint themselves or they will refer you to the proper local agency nearest you that has jurisdiction.

School Records:

When Making The Grade Fails

Type of Complaints

✔ Your son's high school won't allow you to inspect the results of the psychological tests he recently took.

✔ You recently to moved to California and you want to inspect your kid's school records from New York, but the school in New York says you'll have to inspect them in person.

✔ Your college released personal information about your school record that you didn't authorize.

✔ Your daughter's school records indicate she has a drug problem and they refuse to change the records even though you've given them ample evidence to the contrary.

Contact:

Family Policy Compliance Office
U.S. Department of Education
400 Maryland Ave., SW
Washington, DC 20202-4605
(202) 732-1807

Help Available:

Information: yes
Investigation: yes
Mediation/Arbitration: yes
Legal advice: yes
Legal representation: no

Transcripts * Behavior Reports * Grades

What Happens Next?

A federal law requires that schools receiving federal funding make a student's records available to his or her parents for inspection, or to the students themselves if they are over 18 years old. The law also prohibits these school from releasing any personal records to anyone, except for official school business. Students and parents also have the right to request a school to correct any records that they believe are inaccurate or misleading.

If you feel that a school has violated your rights involving your personal school records, try to solve the problem with the school directly, but if this attempt doesn't get you the results you're looking for, contact the U.S. Department of Education (see page 241 for the office nearest you). Upon receiving your written complaint, they will assign it to an investigator who will review it. If there's reason to believe that the school has violated your rights, the investigator will contact the school and ask for their side of the story. If after hearing their side of things the investigator decides that the school has indeed violated your rights, they will require the school the comply with the law. And in the unlikely event that the school still refuses to comply, the U.S. Department of Education can decide to cut off the school's federal funding.

Sexual Harassment At School:

Perverted Professors

Type of Complaints

✔ Your anatomy professor uses centerfolds from a girly magazine as teaching guides.

✔ Your professor told you not to worry about your grade because the two of you can settle it out of class.

✔ The college financial officer told you that you could get the money you needed if you slept with him.

Contact:
U.S. Department of Education
Office for Civil Rights
Customer Service Team
Mary E. Switzer Bldg.
330 C St., SW
Washington, DC 20202
(202) 205-5413
Fax: (202) 205-9862

Help Available:
Information: yes
Investigation: yes
Mediation/Arbitration: yes
Legal advice: yes
Legal representation: no

What Happens Next?

Sexual harassment of students is a form of discrimination and a violation of federal law, and any educational institution that receives federal funds can be investigated by the U.S. Department of Education (see page 241 for the office nearest you) for complaints involving sexual harassment. If you find

184

yourself the victim of sexual harassment at school, and you think the school's been unresponsive to your complaint, contact the U.S. Department of Education's Office for Civil Rights (OCR).

Although every complaint is handled in a unique way, generally an investigator will be assigned to your case, and they will attempt to substantiate your charge. This usually involves contacting the college and the individuals involved. OCR does not, however, reveal the names or other identifying information about an individual who files a complaint unless it's necessary to complete the investigation or take action against the school that violates the law.

If they find evidence of sexual harassment, OCR attempts to get the school to voluntarily comply with the law and take immediate action to prevent further harassment, as well as initiate corrective measures against the harasser, such as formal reprimands, suspensions, denial of tenure--whatever is appropriate. If the school refuses to take any action, OCR may refer the case to the U.S. Department of Justice for possible legal action or initiate proceedings before an administrative law judge to have the school's federal funding stopped for the department where the harassment occurred.

Sexual Harassment At Work:

When Your Boss Makes A Pass At You At The Christmas Party

Type of Complaints

✔ The men in your office continue to make sexually offensive comments to you, and when you report them to your boss, he says, "Boys will be boys," and tells you to just ignore them.

✔ Your boss tells you that if you don't go along with her sexual advances, you'll lose your job, and when you don't, you do in fact get fired.

✔ Men at the factory where you work hoot and yell sexually explicit comments at the women whenever they walk past them.

Contact:
Equal Employment Opportunity Commission
1400 L St., NW
Washington, DC 20005
(800) 669-4000
(202) 663-4264

Help Available:
Information: yes
Investigation: yes
Mediation/Arbitration: yes
Legal advice: yes
Legal representation: yes

What Happens Next?

Any type of sexual harassment in the work place is against the law. You might be told that your job depends on going along with the sexual advances of your boss. Or your boss may be ignoring a situation in which sexual harassment

Discrimination * Advancement * Salary

among his/her employees is taking place. If you are being sexually harassed, you should contact the Equal Employment Opportunity Commission (EEOC) to file a sexual discrimination complaint.

Your complaint will be investigated, and if there is evidence to support your claim, EEOC may take your boss to court on your behalf to seek compensation, especially if you've lost your job, been demoted, or experienced other forms of unfair discipline. A victim of sexual harassment can also file a lawsuit on their own under state laws that protect you against assault, battery, intentional infliction of emotional distress, or intentional interference with an employment contract.

Stockbrokers:

Thinking You Bought Stocks When You Really Bought The Farm

Type of Complaints

✔ Your stock broker sells you securities at a price far above the current market value.

✔ Your broker skims off a larger commission from the sale of your stocks than what you had agreed to.

✔ Your broker advises you to buy $10,000 in stock for a company that his brother owns, although he knows it is going out of business.

Contact:
Securities and Exchange Commission
Office of Consumer Affairs
and Information Services
450 5th St., NW, MS 2-6
Washington, DC 20549
(202) 272-7440

Help Available:
Information: yes
Investigation: yes
Mediation/Arbitration: no
Legal advice: yes
Legal representation: no

What Happens Next?

You should first try to resolve complaints involving the buying and selling of securities with the brokerage firm in question. If you find that they don't return your calls or are dragging their feet, send them a certified letter that clearly outlines your complaint along with the evidence on which you base it, and be sure to ask for a response within a specified period of time.

Account Tampering * Commissions

If this avenue does not get the response you want, submit your complaint in writing to the U.S. Securities and Exchange Commission (SEC) regional office nearest you (listed on page 332). The SEC will privately investigate your charges and contact to the broker for a response. If the SEC determines that your broker has violated the law, they may get a civil injunction that prohibits him or her from continuing such illegal practices. The SEC may also decide to hold an administrative hearing that could result in revoking or suspending your broker's registration to practice.

Although the SEC cannot take sides in the matter, or represent you in a court of law, or force a broker to make restitution to you, they can open up communication between you and the broker to help bring about a resolution to your problem. Keep in mind that the SEC is not a collection agency that can recover losses for you, and if you can't resolve your complaint through the SEC's informal avenues, you may have to take legal action on your own through a private lawsuit.

On the other hand, if the broker in question sells or buys securities in your state, you should also contact your state's Securities Office, usually located within the state Attorney General's Office (see page 230 for the office nearest you). Like the SEC, the state securities office has no authority to force a broker to compensate you, but they can refer your case to an arbitrator who can then hear the evidence and offer a binding decision.

Tanning Devices And Salons:

Sex, Lies, And Tans

Type of Complaints

✔ An ad for a tanning lamp promises medical benefits such as reducing blood pressure, treating diabetes, improving your sex life, and promoting vitamin D production.

✔ The timing device on a sun lamp in a tanning salon cannot be controlled by the customer.

✔ A tanning salon does not provide you with protective eyewear because they claim it is perfectly safe without using any.

Contact:
Food and Drug Administration
Center for Devices and Radiological Health
Office of Compliance and Surveillance (HSV-312)
1390 Piccard Dr.
Rockville, MD 20850
(301) 427-1172

Help Available:
Information: yes
Investigation: yes
Mediation/Arbitration: yes
Legal advice: yes
Legal representation: no

What Happens Next?

According to Food and Drug Administration (FDA) regulations, the only labeling claim that a tanning device can make is that it browns your skin. Any other claims, such as safety, reduced blood pressure, and so on, are illegal. If you find advertising or labeling that makes illegal claims, contact the FDA

190

Tanning Booths * Sun Lights * Sunburns

or the Federal Trade Commission, and if they find that the labels and ads are in fact misleading, they can order to have them stopped.

If you've noticed or experienced a health threat involving a tanning device, whether at a tanning salon or from a product advertised in a publication or on television, contact an FDA regional office nearest you (listed on page 250).

Depending on the case, the FDA may send out an agent to investigate the complaint, and if they find a violation has occurred, they will send the manufacturer of the tanning salon involved a cease and desist letter asking for them to correct the safety violation. Usually a letter from the FDA will do the trick, but if the company in question refuses to listen to the FDA's requests, the FDA may go to court and have the equipment seized.

Keep in mind, though, that the FDA will get involved with private tanning salons only if there is a serious health risk. They aren't going to get into complaints about billing or the quality of your tan or their service, nor will they represent you in court if you are injured at a tanning salon. You can, however, use whatever findings they come up with in an investigation if you plan to pursue the matter in court on your own.

Taxi Cab Rates:

Getting Taken For A Ride

Type of Complaints

✔ The cab you take home every day all of sudden starts costing you $1 more even though the rates haven't increased.

✔ The meter in your cab blinks on and off during your trip, and when you finally arrive, your fare is twice as much as it should be.

Contacts:
State Offices of Weights and Measures
See page 340 for the office nearest you

State Consumer Protection Offices
See page 230 for the office nearest you

Help Available:
Information: yes
Investigation: yes
Mediation/Arbitration: yes
Legal advice: yes
Legal representation: no

What Happens Next?

If your cab fare seems much too high for the distance you travel, and your driver says he's charging you just what's on the meter, you can still do something about it. Contact your state's Office of Weights and Measures which regulates taxi cab fare meters and other measuring devices. Depending on the circumstances, this office may investigate your complaint and determine if the meter in the particular cab you rode in is working properly, and if it isn't, they can order the cab company to fix the faulty meter and refund the money they owe you. Your state Consumer Protection Office will also look into the problem for you and ask the taxi company to resolve your complaint.

Taxes:

When Uncle Sam Taxes Your Patience

Type of Complaints

✔ After three letters to the IRS, you still can't get your refund check.

✔ The IRS hands you a $10,000 tax bill for income you never earned.

✔ The IRS threatens to take you to court for back taxes even though you've written them numerous times with proof that you don't owe any.

Contact:
Problem Resolution Staff
Taxpayer Ombudsman
Internal Revenue Service
U.S. Department of the Treasury
1111 Constitution Ave., NW, Room 1027
Washington, DC 20224
(202) 622-4300
(800) 829-1040 (General Info)

Problem Resolution Offices
See page 270 for the office nearest you

Help Available:
Information: yes
Investigation: yes
Mediation/Arbitration: yes
Legal advice: yes
Legal representation: no

IRS * Refund Checks * Penalties

What Happens Next?

Everybody complains about taxes they have to pay, but even the IRS can make mistakes. After repeated attempts to resolve a problem you're having with the IRS, you should contact the IRS's Taxpayer Ombudsman nearest you (listed on page 270). The Ombudsman heads an independent problem resolution program that can cut through the aggravating red tape at the IRS an look at both sides of the complaint and make a decision. In 1989, they received over 400,000 complaints and resolved 90% of them to the satisfaction of those who complained.

Your problem has to meet the following guidelines to be eligible for help by the Ombudsman program:

Refund Problems
You have not received your refund 90 days after you filed your original tax return, and have made two or more inquiries about it.

Inquiries:
You have a question that requires help or information on the same issue and have not gotten a response by the date promised, or at least 45 days have passed since your first request for assistance.

Notices:
You have received a notice from the IRS telling you that they will or won't act on your case in a certain way, and you've inquired at least three times about the mistake.

When the Ombudsman receives your complaint, it is given a special number and entered into a computer. Your case is then sent to the appropriate IRS division that handles your type of problem. Your case is monitored until it is resolved, and you will be kept informed about its status. If your problem cannot be resolved within five working days, you will be notified, told about the status of your case, and provided with the name and telephone number of the IRS employee who's responsible for resolving your complaint.

Telemarketing Scams:

When The Call Is Something For Nothing

Type of Complaints

✔ You receive a telephone call congratulating you on winning a yacht. All you have to do is send $200 for shipping and handling charges. But all you receive is an inflatable raft with a leak in it.

✔ When you received your combination potato peeler/dog leash that you ordered over the phone, you didn't receive your free bonus gift they promised.

✔ You give the salesman who calls you on the phone your credit card number to reserve the free car you'd just won in a national survey. You never receive the car, and you've been billed for $1,000 on your card.

Contact:
State Consumer Protection Offices
See page 230 for the office nearest you

Help Available:
Information: yes
Investigation: yes
Mediation/Arbitration: yes
Legal advice: yes
Legal representation: no

What Happens Next?

According to the National Association of Attorneys General, people complain about telemarketing and direct mail scams more than any other consumer problem. It's become such a big business that the Federal Trade Commission, along with the state Attorneys General and the U.S. Postal Service, has developed a computer database to track the companies that engage in telemarketing scams across the country.

If you've been taken by one of these scams, contact your state Consumer Protection Office, and they'll investigate your complaint. Even if you live in Iowa and the company that cheated you operates out of Florida, they can still investigate your case. They'll contact the company on your behalf to get their side of the story. If they find that you have been conned, they may ask the company to refund your money and stop their deceptive sales practices.

It's also a good idea to submit your complaint to the Federal Trade Commission (FTC) so that they can enter it on their national computer database (see page 249 for the office nearest you). Although the FTC won't begin an investigation based on just your complaint, if they get enough complaints against the same company, they'll start a formal fraud investigation that could lead to legal actions against the company, cease and desist orders, and even restitution to the individuals who submitted complaints.

Truck Driver Working Conditions:

On The Road To Ruin

Type of Complaints

✔ You've told your boss that the brakes on your truck aren't working properly, but he tells you not to worry about it if you want to keep your job.

✔ To save money, the trucking company you work for hires drivers who have licenses revoked in ten states and pays them less.

✔ To meet your company quotas, you have to drive twice as many miles per day as the federal government allows.

Contact:
Federal Highway Administration
Federal Programs Division, HFO-10
400 7th St., SW, Room 3408
Washington, DC 20590
(202) 366-1795

Help Available:
Information: yes
Investigation: yes
Mediation/Arbitration: yes
Legal advice: yes
Legal representation: no

What Happens Next?

After receiving and registering your written complaint about trucking safety, the Federal Highway Administration (FHWA) will investigate it within 60 days. The FHWA does a quick safety review of the company you work for, and if they find any problems, they may then do an in-depth safety compliance review. Depending on what they find, the FHWA may force your company to fix

197

any equipment safety violations and change their driving hours practices. The FHWA may also levy fines against the company, depending on the number and severity of the violations. You can submit your complaints in writing to a Federal Highway Administration field office serving your area or to the headquarters in Washington, D.C.

Truck Drivers:

When They Drive You Wild

Type of Complaints

✔ A semi tailgates you for ten miles.

✔ A tractor trailer weaves in and out of traffic at high speeds.

✔ A truck following you flashes its lights at you to make you get out of its way.

Contact:
Federal Highway Administration
U.S. Department of Transportation
Attn: Motor Carrier Safety
Field Operations Office
400 7th St., SW, Room 3408
Washington, DC 20590
(202) 366-1724

Help Available:
Information: yes
Investigation: yes
Mediation/Arbitration: yes
Legal advice: yes
Legal representation: no

What Happens Next?

Almost every driver seems to have a horror story about an encounter with a reckless truck driver on the highway. If you try to report it to the police, they'll probably tell you that because they didn't see it they can't do anything about it. However, there are three better places to lodge formal complaints against truck drivers: 1) the company whose name appears on the side of the truck; 2) the U.S. Department of Transportation; and 3) the state Department of Transportation in which the truck company is based. Chances are you weren't

Reckless Truck Drivers * Speeding Convoys

the only one to notice the reckless truck driver, and if these offices receive just a few complaints against the same driver, they will often investigate the driver and decide if any disciplinary action should take place. If you are going to lodge a complaint, though, make sure you have the truck's license plate number, the company name on the truck (if available), the location of the incident, and the U.S. Department of Transportation number (USDOT #) appearing on the side or back of the truck.

Utility Companies:

Help When Your Phone Company Gives You Gas

Type of Complaints

✔ The electric company charged you twice for your hook up.

✔ Your telephone company bills you for twenty calls to Alaska that you didn't make.

✔ You were without water for an entire week, but the water company still charged you the same monthly flat rate.

✔ Your gas company sent you a notice that it's doubling your rate effective immediately.

Contact:
State Utilities Commissions
See page 335 for the office nearest you

Help Available:
Information: yes
Investigation: no
Mediation/Arbitration: no
Legal advice: yes
Legal representation: no

What Happens Next?

If your complaints about your electric, gas, or other utilities cannot be resolved with the utility company directly, contact your state's Utility Commission. Although these offices don't usually investigate individual complaints, if they receive a number of similar complaints about the same matter, they may conduct an investigation. But it's worth your while to report incidents of billing errors, disruptions in service, rate hikes, and other related problems, so that if the Commission does take any action, you may directly benefit because you were one of those who complained.

Wages And Overtime Pay:

Over-Worked And Underpaid

Type of Complaints

✔ Your boss pays you five cents less per hour than minimum wage because he says you don't work hard enough.

✔ As a waitress, you average more than minimum wage in tips, but your boss tells you that he'll pay you wages only when your tips fall below the minimum wage rate.

✔ Your boss requires you to work overtime, but refuses to pay you time-and-a-half for the extra hours you put in.

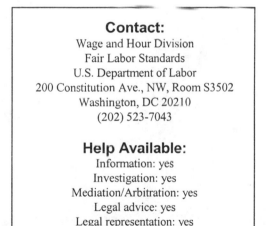

Contact:
Wage and Hour Division
Fair Labor Standards
U.S. Department of Labor
200 Constitution Ave., NW, Room S3502
Washington, DC 20210
(202) 523-7043

Help Available:
Information: yes
Investigation: yes
Mediation/Arbitration: yes
Legal advice: yes
Legal representation: yes

What Happens Next?

If you think that your boss isn't paying you the minimum wage or overtime pay that you rightfully have coming to you, you should file a complaint to the U.S. Department of Labor's Wage and Hour Division (listed on page 274). After they receive your complaint, an investigator will look into the matter to see if there has been a violation of the federal labor laws. If there has been a violation, the U.S. Labor Department will ask your employer to voluntarily comply with the law, which may include giving you the back pay he or she owes you. If nothing still happens, the Labor Department may decide to file a law suit against your boss in federal court to force your boss to pay up.

Also keep in mind that it's illegal for your employer to fire, demote, or harass you in any way for filing a complaint against him, and if he or she does, the Department of Labor will investigate your complaint and get you reinstated with back pay.

Working Conditions:

No Firing Allowed For Employee Talk

Type of Complaints

✔ You're fired for discussing your salary with another employee at the company you worked for.

✔ You and another employee talk about how unsanitary the bathrooms are where you work. When your boss finds out what you said, he demotes you.

✔ You and another employee complain to your boss that there's exposed asbestos in your office. The next day both of you are fired for insubordination.

Contact:
National Labor Relations Board
Division of Information
1717 Pennsylvania Ave., NW, Room 710
Washington, DC 20570
(202) 632-4950

Help Available:
Information: yes
Investigation: yes
Mediation/Arbitration: yes
Legal advice: yes
Legal representation: yes

What Happens Next?

Have you complained to your boss on behalf of yourself and others at work about your wages or working conditions only to find yourself fired, transferred, or demoted? By federal law, every employee has the right to participate in

205

Union Talk * Demotions * Dirty Bathrooms

union activities and to protest unfair wages and working conditions. If two or more employees get together to discuss their working conditions and then bring a complaint to their employer's attention for action, they are protected under federal law against any disciplinary action against them for bring up the complaint.

If you find yourself the victim of this kind of illegal discipline, contact the nearest regional office of the National Labor Relations Board (NLRB) listed on page 275. If upon reviewing your complaint the NLRB decides that it has merit, they will contact your employer on your behalf to get you your job back, lost pay, or whatever remedy they see as fair. Depending on the case, the NLRB may also decide to lodge an Unfair Labor Law complaint against the employer and have the case brought before an administrative law judge for possible further legal action.

When All Else Fails

This book doesn't claim to cover every conceivable complaint, so if you've got a complaint about something that just isn't addressed here, you might try one or all of the following sources.

Federal Information Centers

If you can't quite figure out what federal government agency to contact to help you out with a problem, call the Federal Information Center nearest you listed on page 247. Set up to help you through the often confusing government bureaucracy, these Centers can direct you toward the appropriate agency that can help you solve problems involving anything from Social Security and Medicare benefits to taxes, pensions, immigration laws, and veterans' benefits.

State Consumer Protection Offices

Often located within your state's Office of the Attorney General, these "all purpose" offices enforce consumer protection and fraud laws. They can help you resolve a complaint on almost any subject, everything from mechanics and dry cleaners to aluminum siding and doctors' bills. And if you aren't quite sure where to go with a complaint, these offices are great places to start. And one of the nice things about these offices is that over half of them have toll-free numbers so that the call won't cost you anything. See page 230 for the office in your state.

Governors' Offices

As an elected official, your governor is interested in keeping you happy, and one of the ways he or she accomplishes this is by helping out people. Many governors have special problem resolution centers within the Offices of Governor that are set up to resolve complaints or direct you to the agencies that can.

President of the United States

Although the President doesn't have time to personally sit down and read all of the mail he gets each day from the public, his staff does, and if your letter poses an interesting problem, they may decide to act on it themselves, or they may refer the problem to the appropriate agency that is best suited to do something about it. If you have a complaint in general or one about the President himself, write him at The White House, Washington, DC 20500.

When All Else Fails

U.S. Senators and House Representatives

Each U.S. Senator and Representative has a support staff set up to help solve the problems of the people who voted them into office and keep them happy so that they'll keep voting for them. These politicians have offices in Washington, D.C., and in your own state, and if you want to know who your representatives in the U.S. Congress are and where they are located, contact the Federal Information Center nearest you listed on page 247 or call your local library.

State Senators and Representatives

Like your representatives in the U.S. Congress, your state government representatives have support staffs to answer your complaints and direct you toward solutions. To get the telephone numbers and addresses, you can call the operators in your state capitol, or you can call your local library.

U.S. House of Representatives
Legislative Committees

How many times have you heard the expression, "There should be a law against that"? People usually say it only after they discover that what they're complaining about is legal. Well, here's your opportunity to complain about existing laws and contribute to making better ones. Since these House Committees consider and draft legislation for new federal laws, your complaints or concerns are important to them. Some of these committees may look into your complaint if there's anything they can do about it under existing laws, or they may refer it to the proper federal agency that is best equipped to solve it. What follows is a listing of some of the committees that draft laws of interest to the public, along with their areas of specialty:

House Committee on Agriculture
1301 Longworth House Office Bldg., Washington, DC 20515; (202) 225-2171; Internet: www.house.gov/agriculture. Topics covered include agriculture, rural electrification, domestic marketing, and nutrition.

House Committee on Armed Services
2120 Rayburn House Office Bldg., Washington, DC 20515; (202) 225-4151. Topics covered include defense matters such as procurement practices, weapons systems, manpower, military intelligence, naval petroleum reserves, and military applications of nuclear energy.

House Committee on Banking, Finance, and Urban Affairs
2129 Rayburn Office Bldg., Washington, DC 20515; (202) 225-7502; Internet: www.house.gov/banking/. Topics covered include banking and currency, international financial organizations, and public and private housing.

House Committee on Education and Labor
2181 Rayburn Office Bldg., Washington, DC 20515; (202) 225-4527; Internet: www.house.gov/eeo/. Topics include education, labor, vocational rehabilitation, minimum wage legislation, and school lunch programs.

House Committee on Energy and Commerce
2125 Rayburn Office Bldg., Washington, DC 20515; (202) 225-2927; Internet: www.house.gov/commerce/. Topics covered include the national energy policy, interstate commerce, communications, securities and exchanges, health care, biomedical research, railroads and railroad labor, and consumer affairs and protection.

House Committee on Interior and Insular Affairs
1324 Longworth House Office Bldg., Washington, DC 20515; (202) 225-2761. Topics covered include public lands, national parks and military cemeteries, irrigation, reclamation, Indian affairs, and regulation of nuclear energy industry.

House Committee on the Judiciary
2138 Rayburn House Office Bldg., Washington, DC 20515; (202) 225-3951; Internet: www.house.gov/judiciary. Topics covered include federal courts, constitutional amendments, immigration and naturalization, Presidential succession, antitrust and monopolies, impeachment resolutions, and patents, trademarks, and copyrights.

House Committee on the Merchant Marine and Fisheries
1334 Longworth House Office Bldg., Washington, DC 20515; (202) 225-4047. Topics include regulation and protection of fisheries and wildlife, the U.S. Coast Guard, the Merchant Marine, and the Panama Canal.

House Committee on Public Works and Transportation
2165 Rayburn House Office Bldg., Washington, DC 20515; (202) 225-4472; Internet: www.house.gov/transportation/. Topics covered include public buildings and roads, bridges and dams, flood control, rivers and harbors, watershed development, mass transit, surface transportation excluding railroads, and civil aviation.

When All Else Fails

House Committee on Small Business
2361 Rayburn House Office Bldg., Washington, DC 20515; (202) 225-5821; Internet: www.house.gov/smbiz/. Topics covered include small business development and the Small Business Administration.

House Committee on Veterans' Affairs
335 Cannon House Office Bldg., Washington, DC 20515; (202) 225-3527; Internet: www.house.gov/va/. Topics covered include veterans affairs, pensions, medical care, life insurance, education, and rehabilitation.

Contacts Close To Home

Agencies On Aging

These all-purpose offices can help the elderly and families of the elderly with all kinds of aging-related problems and complaints, from Social Security benefits to free legal assistance and home-delivered meals. See *Aging-Related* on page 11 for more detailed information.

Alabama
Commission on Aging, 770 Washington Street, ASA Plaza, Suite 470, Montgomery, AL 36130; (334) 242-5743; toll free in-state: (800) 243-5463.

Alaska
Older Alaskans Commission, P.O. Box C, Juneau, AK 99811-0209; (907) 563-5654.

American Samoa
Territorial Administration on Aging, Government of American Samoa, Pago Pago, AS 96799; 011 (684)-1251.

Arizona
Aging and Adult Administration, 1789 West Washington, 950, Phoenix, AZ 85007; (602) 542-4446.

Arkansas
Division of Aging and Adult Services, Dept. of Human Services, P.O. Box 1437, Little Rock, AR 72203-1437; (501) 682-2441.

California
Department of Aging, 1600 K Street, Sacramento, CA 95814; (916) 322-5290.

Colorado
Aging and Adult Services Division, Department of Social Services, 1575 Sherman Street, 4th Floor, Denver, CO 80203-1714; (303) 866-3851.

Connecticut
Department on Aging, 175 Main Street, Hartford, CT 06106; (203) 566-3238, or toll free in-state: (800) 443-9946.

Delaware
Department of Health and Social Services, Division of Aging, 1901 North DuPont Hwy., New Castle, DE 19720; (302) 577-4791, or toll free in-state: (800) 223-9074.

District of Columbia
Office on Aging, 1424 K Street, NW, 2nd Floor, Washington, DC 20005; (202) 724-5622.

Florida
Dept. of Elder Affairs, 4040 Esplanade Way, Tallahassee, FL 32399; (904) 414-2000, (800) 96-ELDER (FL only)

Agencies On Aging

Georgia
Office of Aging, 2 Peachtree Street, NE, Atlanta, GA 30303; (404) 657-5258.

Guam
Office of Aging, Government of Guam, P.O. Box 2816, Agana, GU 96910; 011 (671) 734-2942.

Hawaii
Executive Office on Aging, 335 Merchant St., Room 241, Honolulu, HI 96813; (808) 586-0100.

Idaho
Office on Aging, State House, Room 108, Boise, ID 83720; (208) 334-3833.

Illinois
Department on Aging, 421 East Capitol Avenue, Springfield, IL 62701; (217) 785-2870, or toll free: (800) 252-8966.

Indiana
Division of Aging and Rehabilitation Service, I.N.H.S., 402 W. Washington, Indianapolis, IN 46207-7083; (317) 232-7020, or toll free in-state: (800) 622-4972.

Iowa
Department of Elder Affairs, 914 Grand Avenue, Suite 236, Des Moines, IA 50309; (515) 281-5187, or toll free in-state: (800) 532-3213.

Kansas
Department on Aging, Docking State Office Building, 122 South, 915 Southwest Harrison St., Room R122 S, Topeka, KS 66612-1500; (913) 296-4986, or toll free in-state: (800) 432-3535.

Kentucky
Division for Aging Services, Department for Social Services, 275 East Main Street, 6th Floor West, Frankfort, KY 40621; (502) 564-6930, or toll free in-state: (800) 372-2991.

Louisiana
Governors Office of Elder Affairs, P.O. Box 80374, Baton Rouge, LA 70898; (504) 342-1700.

Maine
Bureau of the Elderly and Adult Service, Statehouse #11, Station 11, Augusta, ME 04333-0011; (207) 626-5335.

Maryland
Office on Aging, 301 West Preston Street, 10th Floor, Baltimore, MD 21201; (410) 767-1100, or toll free in-state: (800) 338-0153.

Massachusetts
Executive Office of Elder Affairs, 1 Ashburton Place, Boston, MA 02108; (617) 727-7750, or toll free in-state: (800) 872-0166.

Michigan
Office of Services to the Aging, P.O. Box 30026, Lansing, MI 48909; (517) 373-8230.

Minnesota
Board on Aging, 444 Lafayette Rd., St. Paul, MN 55155-3843; (612) 296-2544, or toll free in-state: (800) 652-9747.

Mississippi
Department of Human Services, Division of Aging and Adult Services, 421 West Pascagoula Street, Jackson, MS 39203; (601) 359-4925, or toll free in-state: (800) 345-6347.

Missouri
Division of Aging, P.O. Box 1337, Jefferson City, MO 65102; (573) 751-3082, or toll free in-state: (800) 392-0210.

Montana
Governor's Office on Aging, Aging Services Bureau, State Capital Building, P.O. Box 8005, Helena, MT 59604; (406) 444-3111, or toll free in-state: (800) 332-2272.

Nebraska
Department on Aging, State Office Building, P.O. Box 95044, Lincoln, NE 68509; (402) 471-2306, or toll free in-state: (800) 942-7830.

Nevada
Division for Aging Services, Department of Human Resources, 1665 Hot Springs Road, Suite 158, Carson City, NV 89710; (702) 687-4210.

New Hampshire
Division of Elderly and Adult Services, 6 Hazen Dr., Concord, NH 03301; (603) 271-4680, or toll free in-state: (800) 852-3345.

New Jersey
Division on Aging, Department of Community Affairs, 101 South Broad Street, CN 807, Trenton, NJ 08625; (609) 292-3766, or toll free in-state: (800) 792-8820.

New Mexico
Agency on Aging, 224 East Palace Ave., Ground Floor, Santa Fe, NM 87501; (505) 827-7640, or toll free in-state: (800) 432-2080.

New York
Office for the Aging, Agency Building 2, ESP, Albany, NY 12223; (518) 474-5731, or toll free in-state: (800) 342-9871.

North Carolina
Division of Aging, Department of Human Resources, 693 Palmer Drive, Call Box 29531, Raleigh, NC 27626-0531; (919) 733-3983.

North Dakota
Aging Services, Department of

Agencies On Aging

Human Services, 600 East Blvd., Bismarck, ND 58505; (701) 328-8910, or toll free in-state: (800) 472-2622.

Ohio
Department of Aging, 50 West Broad St., 9th Fl., Columbus, OH 43266-0501; (614) 466-5500, or toll free in-state: (800) 282-1206.

Oklahoma
Special Unit on Aging, P.O. Box 25352, Oklahoma City, OK 73125; (405) 521-2281.

Oregon
Senior Services Division, Department of Human Resources, State of Oregon, 313 Public Service Building, Salem, OR 97310; (503) 945-5811, or toll free in-state: (800) 232-3020.

Pennsylvania
Department of Aging, 231 State St., Barto Building, Harrisburg, PA 17101; (717) 783-1549.

Puerto Rico
Office of Elder Affairs, Call Box 50063, Old San Juan Station, San Juan, PR 00902; (787) 721-5710.

Rhode Island
Department of Elderly Affairs, 160 Pine St., Providence, RI 02903; (401) 277-2880, or toll free in-state: (800) 322-2880.

South Carolina
Commission on Aging, 400 Arbor Drive, Suite 500B, Columbia, SC 29223; (803) 735-0210, or toll free in-state: (800) 868-9095.

South Dakota
Office of Adult Services and Aging, 700 Governors Dr., Pierre, SD 57501; (605) 773-3656.

Tennessee
Commission on Aging, 706 Church Street, Suite 201, Nashville, TN 37243-0860; (615) 741-2056.

Texas
Department on Aging, P.O. Box 12786, Capitol Station, Austin, TX 78711; (512) 424-6840, or toll free in-state: (800) 252-9240.

Utah
Division of Aging and Adult Services, P.O. Box 45500, Salt Lake City, UT 84145-9500; (801) 538-3920.

Vermont
Department of Aging and Disability, 103 South Main Street, Waterbury, VT 05671; (802) 241-2400, or toll free in-state: (800) 642-5119.

Virgin Islands
Department of Human Services, Barbel Plaza South, Charlotte, Amalie, St. Thomas, VI 00802; (809) 692-5950.

Agencies On Aging

Virginia
Department for the Aging, 700 East Franklin St., 10th Floor, Richmond, VA 23219; (804) 225-2271, or toll free in-state: (800) 552-4464.

Washington
Aging and Adult Services Administration, P.O. Box 45600, Olympia, WA 98504-5600; (360) 586-8753, or toll free in-state: (800) 422-3263.

West Virginia
Commission on Aging, 1900 Kanawha Blvd., East, Charleston, WV 25305-0160; (304) 558-3317.

Wisconsin
Bureau on Aging, P.O. Box 7851, Madison, WI 53707; (608) 266-2536.

Wyoming
Commission on Aging, Hathaway Building, Cheyenne, WY 82002; (307) 777-7986, or toll free in-state: (800) 442-2766.

Animal And Plant Health Inspection Service

As part of the U.S. Department of Agriculture, Animal and Plant Health Inspection Service (APHIS) works to protect and improve the health of plants and animals, along with enforcing federal laws that relate to animal and plants quarantines, the humane treatment of animals, and getting rid of related pests and diseases. If you have a complaint about inhumane treatment to animals, or about any other matter under APHIS's control, contact the regional office listed below serving your state. See *Animal Welfare* on page 21 for more detailed information.

Eastern
USDA, APHIS, AC, 2568-A Riva Road, Suite 302, Annapolis, MD 21401-7400; (410) 571-8692. States served: AL, CT, DE, DC, FL, GA, KY, IL, IN, ME, MD, MA, MI, MN, MS, NC, NH, NJ, NY, OH, PA, PR, RI, SC, TN, VA, VI, VT, WV, WI

Central
USDA, APHIS, AC, 501 Felix, FWFC Bldg. #11 (packages);

P.O. Box 6258 (letters), Fort Worth, TX 76115-6258; (817) 885-6923. States served: AR, IA, KS, LA, MO, NE, ND, OK, SD, TX

Western
USDA, APHIS, AC, 9580 Micron Ave., Suite J, Sacramento, CA 95827-2623; (916) 857-6205. States served: AK, AZ, CA, CO, HI, ID, MT, NV, NM, OR, UT, WA, WY

Banking Authorities

The following State banking regulators make sure that banks chartered in their state operate fairly and follow laws that protect customers in such areas as credit cards, loans, interest rates, account errors, and discrimination. For more information, see *Banking Services* on page 28.

Alabama
Superintendent of Banks, 101 South Union Street, Montgomery, AL 36130; (334) 242-3452.

Alaska
Director of Banking, Corporations and Securities, P.O. Box 110807, Juneau, AK 99811-0807; (907) 465-2521.

Arizona
Superintendent of Banks, 3225 North Central, Suite 800, Phoenix, AZ 85012; (602) 255-4421, or (800) 544-0708 (toll free in AZ).

Arkansas
Bank Commissioner, Tower Building, 323 Center Street, Suite 500, Little Rock, AR 72201; (501) 324-9019.

California
Superintendent of Banks, 111 Pine Street, Suite 1100, San Francisco, CA 94111-5613; (415) 263-8507, or (800) 622-0620 (toll free in CA).

Colorado
State Bank Commissioner, Division of Banking, Denver Post Bldg., 1560 Broadway, Suite 1175, Denver, CO 80202; (303) 894-7575.

Connecticut
Banking Commissioner, 44 Capitol Ave., Hartford, CT 06106; (203) 244-8299, or (800) 842-2220 (toll free in CT).

Delaware
State Bank Commissioner, 555 E. Loockerman St., Suite 210, Dover, DE 19901; (302) 739-4325.

District of Columbia
Superintendent of Banking and Financial Institutions, 1250 I St., NW, Suite 1003, Washington, DC 20005; (202) 727-1563.

Florida
State Comptroller, State Capitol Building, Ste. 2102, Tallahassee, FL 32399-0350; (904) 488-0286, or (800) 848-3792 (toll free in FL).

Banking Authorities

Georgia
Commissioner of Banking and Finance, 2990 Brandywine Rd., Suite 200, Atlanta, GA 30341; (404) 986-1633.

Guam
Department of Revenue and Taxation, P.O. Box 2796, Agana, GU 96910, 01 (671) 477-5107.

Hawaii
Commissioner of Financial Institutions, P.O. Box 2054, 1010 Richards Street, Room 602A, Honolulu, HI 96813; (808) 586-2820.

Idaho
Department of Finance, 700 W. State St., State House Mall, 2nd Floor, Boise, ID 83720-2700; (208) 334-3319.

Illinois
Commissioner of Banks and Trust Companies, 117 S. 5th St., Room 100, Springfield, IL 62701; (217) 785-2837, or (800) 634-5452 (toll free in IL).

Indiana
Department of Financial Institutions, 402 West Washington, Suite W066, Indianapolis, IN 46204; (317) 232-3955, or (800) 382-4880 (toll-free in IN).

Iowa
Superintendent of Banking, 200 East Grand, Suite 300, Des Moines, IA 50309; (505) 285-4014.

Kansas
State Bank Commissioner, 700 Jackson Street, Suite 300, Topeka, KS 66603; (913) 296-2266.

Kentucky
Commissioner, Department of Financial Institutions, 911 Leawood Drive, Frankfort, KY 40601; (502) 564-3390.

Louisiana
Commissioner of Financial Institutions, P.O. Box 94095, Baton Rouge, LA 70804-9095; (504) 925-4660.

Maine
Superintendent of Banking, State House Station #36, Augusta, ME 04333; (207) 624-8570.

Maryland
Bank Commissioner, 501 St. Paul Place, 13th Floor, Baltimore, MD 21202-2272; (410) 333-6812, or (800) 492-7521 (toll free in MD).

Massachusetts
Commissioner of Banks, 100 Cambridge Street, Boston, MA 02202; (617) 727-2120.

Banking Authorities

Michigan
Commissioner of Financial Institutions Bureau, P.O. Box 30224, Lansing, MI 48909; (517) 373-3460.

Minnesota
Deputy Commissioner of Commerce, 133 E. 7th St., 3rd Floor, St. Paul, MN 55101; (612) 296-2135.

Mississippi
Commissioner of Banking and Consumer Finance, P.O. Box 23729, Jackson, MS 39225; (601) 359-1031, or (800) 826-2499.

Missouri
Commissioner of Finance, P.O. Box 716, Jefferson City, MO 65102; (314) 751-3242.

Montana
Commissioner of Financial Institutions, 1520 E. 6th Ave., Room 50, Helena, MT 59620-0542; (406) 444-2091.

Nebraska
Director of Banking and Finance, 1200 N. Street, A-311, Lincoln, NE 68508; (402) 471-2171.

Nevada
Commissioner of Financial Institutions, 406 E. 2nd St., Carson City, NV 89710; (702) 687-4259.

New Hampshire
Bank Commissioner, 169 Manchester St., Concord, NH 03301; (603) 271-3561.

New Jersey
Commissioner of Banking, 20 W. State St., CN-040, Trenton, NJ 08625; (609) 292-3420, or (800) 421-0069 (toll free in NJ).

New Mexico
Financial Institutions Division, P.O. Box 25101, Santa Fe, NM 87504; (505) 827-7100.

New York
Superintendent of Banks, Two Rector St., New York, NY 10006; (212) 618-6642, or (800) 522-3300 (toll free in NY).

North Carolina
Commissioner of Banks, P.O. Box 29512, Raleigh, NC 27626-0512; (919) 733-3016.

North Dakota
Commissioner of Banking and Financial Institutions, 600 East Blvd., 13th Floor, Bismarck, ND 58505; (701) 328-9933.

Ohio
Superintendent of Banks, 77 S. High St., 21st Floor, Columbus, OH 43266-0549; (614) 466-2932.

Oklahoma
Bank Commissioner, Malco Bldg, 4100 N. Lincoln Blvd., Oklahoma City, OK 73105; (405) 521-2783.

Banking Authorities

Oregon
Administrator, Division of Finance and Corporate Securities, Labor and Industries Bldg., Room 21, Salem, OR 97310; (503) 378-4140.

Pennsylvania
Secretary of Banking, 333 Market Street, 16th Floor, Harrisburg, PA 17101; (717) 787-6991, or (800) PA-BANKS (toll free in PA).

Puerto Rico
Commissioner of Banking, G.P.O. Box 70324, San Juan, PR 00936; (809) 723-3131.

Rhode Island
Associate Director and Superintendent of Banking, 233 Richmond Street, Suite 231, Providence, RI 02903-4231; (401) 277-2405.

South Carolina
Commissioner of Banking, 1015 Sumter Street, Room 309, Columbia, SC 29201; (803) 734-2001.

South Dakota
Division of Banking and Finance, 500 East Capital Avenue, State Capitol Building, Pierre, SD 57501-5070; (605) 773-3421

Tennessee
Commissioner of Financial Institutions, John Sevier Building, 4th Floor, Nashville, TN 37243-0705; (615) 741-2236.

Texas
Banking Commissioner, 2601 North Lamar, Austin, TX 78705; (512) 475-1300.

Utah
Commissioner of Financial Institutions, P.O. Box 89, Salt Lake City, UT 84110; (801) 538-8830.

Vermont
Commissioner of Banking and Insurance Securities, 120 State Street, Montpelier, VT 05602; (802) 828-3301.

Virgin Islands
Chairman of the Banking Board, Kongens Garde 18, St. Thomas, VI 00802; (809) 774-2991.

Virginia
Bureau of Financial Institutions, P.O. Box 2-AE, Richmond, VA 23205; (804) 371-9657, or (800) 552-7945 (toll free in VA).

Washington
Division of Banking, 1400 S. Evergreen Park Dr., Ste. 120, Olympia, WA 98504-1026; (360) 753-6520.

West Virginia
Commissioner of Banking, State Capitol Complex, 1900 Kanawha Blvd. E., Building 3, Room 311, Charleston, WV 25305; (304)

558-2294, or (800) 642-9056 (toll free in WV).

Wisconsin
Commissioner of Banking, 101 E. Wilson, 5th Floor, Madison, WI 53702; (608) 266-1621.

Wyoming
State Examiner, Herschler Bldg., 3rd Floor East, Cheyenne, WY 82002; (307) 777-7797.

Bureau Of Land Management

As caretaker of more than 300 million acres of public land, part of the Bureau of Land Management's (BLM) job is to conduct criminal investigations and make arrests of people committing crime on public lands, such as stealing wood, growing marijuana, and hunting illegally. For more detailed information, see *Crime on Public Lands* on page 56.

Alaska
222 W. 7th St. #13, Anchorage, AK 99513-7599; (907) 271-5960

Arizona
222 N. Central Ave., Phoenix, AZ 85004-2203; (602) 417-9200

California
2135 Butano Drive, Sacramento, CA 95825; (916) 978-4400

Colorado
2850 Youngfield St., Lakewood, CO 80215-7093; (303) 239-3600, Fax: (303) 239-3933, TDD: (303) 239-3635.

Eastern States
7450 Boston Blvd., Springfield, VA 22153; (703) 440-1600. Serves 31 states bordering and east of the Mississippi River.

Idaho
1387 S. Vinnell Way, Boise, ID 83709-1657; (208) 373-4000

Montana
222 N. 32nd St., P.O. Box 36800, Billings, MT 59107-6800; (406) 255-2885, Fax: (406) 255-2762

E mail· mtinfo@mt.blm.gov. Also serves North and South Dakota.

Nevada
850 Harvard Way, P.O. Box 12000, Reno, NV 89520-0006; (702) 785-6500, Fax: (702) 785-6411.

New Mexico
1474 Rodeo Rd., P.O. Box 27115, Santa Fe, NM 87502-0115; (505) 438-7400. Also serves Kansas, Oklahoma and Texas.

Oregon
P.O. Box 2965, Portland, OR 97208; (503) 952-6003, Fax: (503) 952-6308, E-mail: or912mb@or.blm.gov. Also serves Washington.

Utah
324 S. State St., P.O. Box 45155, Salt Lake City, UT 84145-0155; (801) 539-4001.

Wyoming
5353 Yellowstone, P.O. Box 1828, Cheyenne, WY 82003; (307) 775-6256. Also serves Nebraska.

Child Support Enforcement Offices

The offices listed below can help you find an absent parent who owes you unpaid child support, even if he or she is in another state. They can also help you establish paternity of your children and get a legal child support order. For more detailed information about how these offices can help you, see *Child Support* on page 46.

Alabama
Child Support Enforcement Division, Department of Human Resources, 50 Ripley St., Montgomery, Al 36130; (334) 242-9300.

Alaska
Child Support Enforcement Division, Department of Revenue, 550 West 7th Ave., 4th Floor, Anchorage, AK 99501; (907) 269-6900.

Arizona
Child Support Enforcement Administration, Department of Economic Security, 222 West Encanto, P.O. Box 6123--Site Code 776A, Phoenix, AZ 85005; (602) 252-0236.

Arkansas
Division of Child Support Enforcement, Arkansas Social Services, P.O. Box 8133, Little Rock, AR 72203; (501) 682-8398.

California
Child Support Program Management Branch, Department of Social Services, 744 P Street, Mail Stop 9-011, Sacramento, CA 95814; (916) 654-1532.

Colorado
Division of Child Support Enforcement, Department of Social Services, 1575 Sherman Street, Denver, CO 80203-1714; (303) 866-5994.

Connecticut
Bureau of Child Support Enforcement, Department of Human Resources, 1049 Asylum Ave., Hartford, CT 06105; (860) 424-5251.

Delaware
Division of Child Support Enforcement, Department of Health and Social Services, P.O. Box 904, New Castle, DE 19720; (302) 577-4863.

District of Columbia
Office of Paternity and Child Support, Department of Human Services, 3rd Floor, Suite 3013, 425 I Street, NW, Washington, DC 20001; (202) 645-7500.

Child Support Enforcement Offices

Florida
Office of Child Support Enforcement, Department of Health and Rehabilitative Services, 1317 Winewood Blvd., Building 3, Tallahassee, FL 32399-0700; (904) 922-9590.

Georgia
Office of Child Support Recovery, State Department of Human Resources, 878 Peachtree St., NE, Room 529, Atlanta, GA 30309; (404) 894-4119.

Guam
Office of the Attorney General, Child Support Enforcement Office, Union Bank Building, Suite 309, 194 Hernan Cortez Ave., Agana, Guam 96910; (671) 477-2036.

Hawaii
Child Support Enforcement Agency, Department of the Attorney General, 680 Iwilei Rd., Honolulu, HI 96805-1860; (808) 587-3700.

Idaho
Bureau of Child Support Enforcement, Department of Health and Welfare, 450 West State St., Towers Building, 5th Floor, Boise, ID 83720; (208) 334-5710.

Illinois
Division of Child Support Enforcement, Department of Public Aid, Prescott E. Bloom Bldg, 201 South Grand Ave. East, P.O. Box 19405, Springfield, Il 62794-9405; (217) 524-4602 or (800) 447-4278 (in state)

Indiana
Child Support Enforcement Division, Department of Public Welfare, 4th Floor, 141 South Meridian St., Indianapolis, IN 46225; (317) 233-5437.

Iowa
Bureau of Collections, Iowa Dept. of Human Services, Hoover Bldg, 5th Fl, Des Moines IA 50319; (515) 281-5580.

Kansas
Child Support Enforcement Program, Department of Social & Rehabilitation Services, Biddle Building, 1st Floor, 300 South West Oakley St., P.O. Box 497, Topeka, KS 66603; (913) 296-3237.

Kentucky
Division of Child Support Enforcement, Dept of Social Insurance, Cabinet for Human Resources, 275 East Main Street, 6th Floor East, Frankfort, KY 40621; (502) 564-2285.

Louisiana
Support Enforcement Services, Department of Social Services, P.O. Box 94065, Baton Rouge, LA 70804; (504) 342-4780.

Child Support Enforcement Offices

Maine
Support Enforcement Division of Social Welfare, Department of Human Services, State House, Station 11, Augusta, ME 04333; (207) 287-2886.

Maryland
Child Support Enforcement Administration, Department of Human Resources, 311 West Saratoga Street, Baltimore, MD 21201; (410) 767-7619.

Massachusetts
Child Support Enforcement Division, Department of Revenue, 141 Portland Street, Cambridge, MA 02124; (617) 577-7200.

Michigan
Office of Child Support, Department of Social Services, 235 South Grand Avenue, Suite 1406, P.O. Box 30037, Lansing, MI 48909; (517) 373-7570.

Minnesota
Office of Child Support Enforcement, Department of Human Services, 444 Lafayette Road, 4th Floor, St. Paul, MN 55155-3846; (612) 296-2499.

Mississippi
Child Support Division, State Department of Public Welfare, 507 East Capital, P.O. Box 352, Jackson, MS 39205; (601) 359-4861.

Missouri
Division of Child Support Enforcement, Department of Social Services, P.O. Box 1527, Jefferson City, MO 65102-1527; (573) 751-4301.

Montana
Child Support Enforcement Division, Department of Social and Rehabilitation Services, P.O. Box 5955, Helena, MT 59604; (406) 444-4614.

Nebraska
Child Support Enforcement Office, Dept. of Social Services, P.O. Box 95026, Lincoln, NE 68509; (402) 471-9160.

Nevada
Child Support Enforcement Program, Department of Human Resources, 2527 N. Carson St., Capital Complex, Carson City, NV 89710; (702) 687-4744.

New Hampshire
Office of Child Support Enforcement Services, Division of Welfare, Health & Welfare Building, 6 Hazen Dr., Concord, NH 03301; (603) 271-4427.

New Jersey
Division of Family Assistance, Department of Human Services, Bureau of Child Support and Paternity Programs, CN 716, Trenton, NJ 08625; (609) 588-2401.

Child Support Enforcement Offices

New Mexico
Child Support Enforcement Division, Department of Human Services, P.O. Box 25109, Santa Fe, NM 87504; (505) 827-7200.

New York
Office of Child Support Enforcement, New York State Department of Social Services, P.O. Box 14, One Commerce Plaza, Albany, NY 12260; (518) 474-9081.

North Carolina
Child Support Enforcement Section, Division of Social Services, Department of Human Resources, 437 North Harrington St., P.O. Box 351, Raleigh, NC 27602-1393; (919) 571-4114.

North Dakota
Child Support Enforcement Agency, North Dakota Department of Human Services, 1929 N. Washington St., P.O. Box 7190, Bismarck, ND 58507-7190; (701) 328-3582.

Ohio
Bureau of Child Support, Department of Human Services, State Office Tower, 27th Floor, 30 East Broad St., Columbus, OH 43266-0423. (614) 462-3275.

Oklahoma
Child Support Enforcement Division, Department of Human Services, P.O. Box 25352,

Oklahoma City, OK 73125; (405) 522-5871.

Oregon
Recovery Services Section, Adult and Family Services Division, Department of Human Resources, P.O. Box 14506, Salem, OR 97309; (503) 378-5439.

Pennsylvania
Bureau of Child Support Enforcement, Department of Public Welfare, P.O. Box 8018, Harrisburg, PA 17105; (717) 787-3672.

Puerto Rico
Child Support Enforcement Program, Department of Social Services, P.O. Box 3349, San Juan, PR 00902; (787) 767-1500.

Rhode Island
Bureau of Family Support, Department of Human Services, 77 Dorrance St., Providence, RI 02903; (401) 277-2847.

South Carolina
Child Support Enforcement Division, Department of Social Services, P.O. Box 1520, Columbia, SC 29202-9988; (803) 737-5870.

South Dakota
Office of Child Support Enforcement, Department of Social Services, 700 Governors Drive, Pierre, SD 57501-2291; (605) 773-3641.

Child Support Enforcement Offices

Tennessee
Child Support Services, Department of Human Services, Citizens Plaza Building, 12th Floor, 400 Deadrick St., Nashville, TN 37248-7400; (615) 313-4880.

Texas
Child Support Enforcement Division, Office of the Attorney General, P.O. Box 12017, Austin, TX 78711-2017; (512) 460-6000.

Utah
Office of Recovery Services, Department of Social Services, 120 North 200 West, P.O. Box 45011, Salt Lake City, UT 84145-0011; (801) 536-8500.

Vermont
Office of Child Support, 103 South Main Street, Waterbury, VT 05671-1901; (802) 244-1483.

Virgin Islands
Support and Paternity Division, Department of Law, 46 Norre Gade, St. Thomas, VI 00801; (809) 774-5666.

Virginia
Division of Support Enforcement Program, Department of Social Services, 804 Franklin Farms Dr., Richmond, VA 23229; (804) 692-1428.

Washington
Office of Child Support Enforcement, Revenue Division, Department of Social & Health Services, P.O. Box 9162, Mail Stop HJ-31, Olympia, WA 98507; (360) 586-3162.

West Virginia
Child Advocate Office, Department of Human Services, 1900 Washington, St., East, Charleston, WV 25305; (304) 558-3780.

Wisconsin
Division of Economic Support, Bureau of Child Support, One West Wilson St., Room 382, P.O. Box 7935, Madison, WI 53707-7935; (608) 266-9909.

Wyoming
Child Support Enforcement, Department of Family Services, Hathaway Bldg., 3rd Floor, Cheyenne, WY 82002-0490; (307) 777-7631.

Comptroller Of The Currency

The U.S. Department of the Treasury's Comptroller of the Currency enforces the laws and regulations relating to national banks, and they respond to and investigate consumer complaints regarding the services of these banks, including discrimination, mortgages, interest rates, credit cards, account deductions, and much more. For more detailed information, see *Banking Services* on page 28.

Northeastern District
1114 Avenue of the Americas, Suite 3900, New York, NY 10036; (212) 819-9860. States served: CT, DE, DC, ME, MD, MA, NH, NJ, NY, PA, RI, PR, VI.

Southeastern
245 Peachtree Center Ave., Marquis One Tower, Suite 600, Atlanta, GA 30303; (404) 659-8855. States served: AL, FL, GA, MS, NC, SC, TN, VA, WV.

Central
440 S. LaSalle St., One Financial Place, Suite 2700, Chicago, IL 60605; (312) 360-8800. States served: IL, IN, KY, MI, OH, WI.

Midwestern
2345 Grand Ave., Suite 700, Kansas City, MO 64108; (816) 556-1800. States served: KS, MN, MO, NE, ND, SD.

Southwestern
1600 Lincoln Plaza, 500 N. Akard, Dallas, TX 75201-3394; (214) 720-0656. States served: AR, LA, NM, OK, TX.

Western
50 Fremont St., Suite 3900, San Francisco, CA 94105; (415) 545-5900. States served: AK, AR, CA, HI, ID, MT, NV, OK, UT, WA, WY.

Consumer Protection Offices

Often located within your state's Office of the Attorney General, these "all purpose" offices enforce consumer protection and fraud laws. They can help you resolve a complaint on almost any subject, everything from car mechanics and dry cleaners to aluminum siding and doctors' bills. And if you aren't quite sure where to go with a complaint, these offices are great places to start. And one of the nice things about these offices is that over half of them have toll-free numbers so that the call won't cost you anything.

Alabama
Consumer Protection Division, Office of Attorney General, 11 S. Union Street, Montgomery, AL 36130; (205) 242-7334, or (800) 392-5658 (toll-free in AL).

Alaska
This office has been closed. Consumers with complaints are being referred to the Better Business Bureau, small claims courts, or private attorneys.

Arizona
Consumer Protection Division, Office of Attorney General, 1275 W. Washington St., Room 259, Phoenix, AZ 85007; (602) 542-3702, or (800) 352-8431 (toll-free in AZ).

Assistant Attorney General, Consumer Protection, 40 W. Congress South Bldg., Suite 315, Tucson, AZ 85701; 602-628-6504.

Arkansas
Consumer Protection Division, Office of Attorney General, 200

Tower Building, 323 Center Street, Suite 200, Little Rock, AR 72201; (501) 682-2341, or (800) 482-8982 (toll-free in AR).

California
Public Inquiry Unit, Office of Attorney General, 1515 K Street, Suite 511, or P.O. Box 944255, Sacramento, CA 94244-2550; (916) 322-3360, or (800) 952-5225 (toll-free in CA).

California Department of Consumer Affairs, 400 R Street, Sacramento, CA 95814; (916) 445-1254, (800) 344-9940.

Bureau of Automotive Repair, California Department of Consumer Affairs, 10240 Systems Parkway, Sacramento, CA 95827; (916) 366-5100, or (800) 952-5210 (toll-free in CA-auto repair only).

Colorado
Consumer Protection Unit, Office of Attorney General, 1525 Sherman Street, 5th Floor,

Consumer Protection Offices

Denver, CO 80203; (303) 866-5189, (800) 332-2071.

Connecticut
Department of Consumer Protection, State Office Building, 165 Capitol Ave., Hartford, CT 06106; (203) 566-2534, or (800) 538-CARS, (800) 842-2649 government information (toll-free in CT).

Delaware
Division of Consumer Affairs, Department of Community Affairs, 820 N. French St., 4th Floor, Wilmington, DE 19801; (302) 577-3250.

District of Columbia
Department of Consumer and Regulatory Affairs, 614 H St., N.W., Washington, DC 20001; (202) 727-7120, Fax: (203) 727-8073/7842.

Florida
Division of Consumer Services, Mayo Building, Tallahassee, FL 32399-0800; (904) 488-2226, or (800) HELP-FLA (toll-free in FL).

Georgia
Office of Consumer Affairs, 2 Martin Luther King, Jr. Drive, Plaza Level-East Tower, Atlanta, GA 30334; (404) 656-3790, or (800) 869-1123 (toll-free in GA).

Hawaii
Office of Consumer Protection, Dept of Commerce and Consumer Affairs, 828 Fort Street Mall, Suite 600B, or P.O. Box 3767, Honolulu, HI 96813-3767; (808) 586-2636, Fax: (808) 586-2640.

Idaho
Deputy Attorney General, Consumer Protection Unit, 700 W. Jefferson, ROom 119, BOise, ID 83720-0010; (208) 334-2424, Fax: (208) 334-2840.

Illinois
Governor's Office of Citizens Assistance, 100 W. Randolph, 12th Floor, Chicago, IL 60601; (312) 814-3000.

Indiana
Consumer Protection Division, Office of Attorney General, 402 W. Washington, Indianapolis, IN 46204; (317) 232-6330, or (800) 382-5516 (toll-free in IN).

Iowa
Iowa Citizens' Aide Ombudsman, 215 E. 7th St., Capitol Complex, Des Moines, IA 50319; (515) 281-3592, or (800) 358-5510 (toll-free in IA).

Kansas
Consumer Protection Division, Office of Attorney General, Kansas Judicial Center,301 West 10th St., Topeka, KS 66612-

15973) 296-3751, or (800) 432-2310 (toll-free in KS).

Kentucky
Consumer Protection Division, Office of Attorney General, 209 St. Clair St., Frankfort, KY 40601; (502) 564-2200, or (800) 432-9257 (toll-free in KY).

Louisiana
Consumer Protection Section, Office of Attorney General, 1 America Place, P.O. Box 94095; Baton Rouge, LA 70804-9095; (504) 342-9638, Fax: (504) 342-9637.

Maine
Consumer Assistance Services, Office of Attorney General, State House Station No. 6, Augusta, ME 04333; (207) 624-8527.

Maryland
Consumer Protection Division, Office of Attorney General, 200 St. Paul Pl., Baltimore, MD 21202; (410) 528-8662, or (202) 727-7000 in the Washington, DC metro area.

Massachusetts
Consumer Protection Division, Department of Attorney General, 131 Tremont St., Boston, MA 02111; (617) 727-2200.

Michigan
Consumer Protection Division, Office of Attorney General, P.O. Box 30213, Lansing, MI 48909; (517) 373-1140.

Minnesota
Office of Consumer Services, Office of Attorney General, 1440 N.C.L. Tower, 455 Minnesota Street, St. Paul, MN 55101; (612) 296-3353.

Mississippi
Consumer Protection Division, Office of Attorney General, P.O. Box 22947, Jackson, MS 39225; (601) 359-4230, Fax: (601) 359-4231.

Missouri
Public Protection Division, Office of Attorney General, P.O. Box 899, Jefferson City, MO 65102; (314) 751-3321, or (800) 392-8222 (toll-free in MO).

Montana
Office of Consumer Affairs, Department of Commerce, 1424 9th Avenue, Helena, MT 59620; (406) 444-4312.

Nebraska
Consumer Protection Division, Office of Attorney General, 2115 State Capitol, Room 2115, Lincoln, NE 68509; (402) 471-2682, Fax: (402) 471-3297.

Nevada
Consumer Affairs Division, Department of Commerce, 4600 Kietezke Lane, Bldg B, Suite 113, Reno, NV 89502; (702) 688-1800, or (800) 992-0900 (NV only).

Consumer Protection Offices

New Hampshire
Consumer Protection and Antitrust Bureau, Office of Attorney General, 25 Capitol St., Concord, NH 03301-0397; (603) 271-3641, Fax: (603) 271-2110.

New Jersey
Department of the Public Advocate, 25 Market St., CN 850, Trenton, NJ 08625; (609) 292-7087, or (800) 792-8600 (toll-free in NJ).

New Mexico
Consumer and Economic Crime Division, Office of Attorney General, P.O. Drawer 1508, Santa Fe, NM 87504; (505) 827-6060, or (800) 678-1508 (toll-free in NM).

New York
Bureau of Consumer Frauds and Protection, NY State Department of Law, The Capitol, Albany, NY 12224; (518) 474-8583

Bureau of Consumer Frauds and Protection, Office of Attorney General, 120 Broadway, Manhatten, NY 10271; (212) 416-8345.

North Carolina
Consumer Protection Division, Office of Attorney General, P.O. Box 629, Raleigh, NC 27602; (919) 733-7741.

North Dakota
Consumer Fraud Division, Office of Attorney General, 600 East Boulevard, Bismarck, ND 58505; (701) 224-3404, or (800) 472-2600 (toll-free in ND).

Ohio
Consumer Protection Division, Office of Attorney General, 30 East Broad Street, State Office Tower, 25th Floor, Columbus, OH 43266-0410; (614) 466-4986, or (800) 282-0515 (toll-free in OH).

Oklahoma
Consumer Protection Unit, Office of Attorney General, 2300 North Lincoln, Room 112, 112 State Capitol Bld, Oklahoma City, OK 73105-4894; (405) 521-4274 or (405) 512-2929.

Oregon
Financial Fraud Section, Consumer Complaints, Department of Justice, Justice Building, Salem, OR 97310; (503) 378-4732.

Pennsylvania
Bureau of Consumer Protection, Office of Attorney General, Strawberry Square, 14th Floor, Harrisburg, PA 17120; (717) 787-9707, or (800) 441-2555 (toll-free in PA).

Puerto Rico
Department of Consumer Affairs, Minillas Station, P.O. Box 41059, Santurce, PR 00940; (809) 721-2900.

Consumer Protection Offices

Rhode Island
Consumer Protection Division, Department of Attorney General, 72 Pine St., Providence, RI 02903; (401) 274-4400.

South Carolina
Department of Consumer Affairs, P.O. Box 5757, Columbia, SC 29250; (803) 734-9452, or (800) 922-1594 (toll-free in SC).

South Dakota
Division of Consumer Affairs, Office of Attorney General, 500 East Capitol, Capitol Building, Pierre, SD 57501; (605) 773-4400, (800) 300-1986.

Tennessee
Division of Consumer Affairs, 500 James Robertson Parkway, 5th Floor, Nashville, TN 37243-0600; (615) 741-3491, or (800) 342-8385 (toll-free in TN).

Texas
Consumer Protection Division, Office of Attorney General, Capitol Station, P.O. Box 12548, Austin, TX 78711; (512) 463-2070, (800) 621-0508.

Utah
Division of Consumer Protection, Department of Commerce, 160 E. 3rd South, or P.O. Box 45804, Salt Lake City, UT 84145-0804; (801) 530-6601 or (800) 721-7233.

Vermont
Public Protection Division, Office of Attorney General, 109 State St., Montpelier, VT 05609; (802) 828-3171.

Virgin Islands
Department of Licensing and Consumer Affairs, Property and Procurement Building, Subbase 8201, Ste. 2, St. Thomas, VI 00802; (809) 774-3130.

Virginia
Division of Consumer Affairs, 900 E. Main Street, Richmond, VA 23209; (804) 786-2116.

Washington
Consumer and Business Fair Practice Division, Office of Attorney General, 900 4th Ave, Ste. 2000, Seattle, WA 98164; (206) 464-6684, or (800) 551-4636 (toll-free in WA).

West Virginia
Consumer Protection Division, Office of Attorney General, 812 Quarrier St., 6th Floor, Charleston, WV 25301; (304) 558-8986, or (800) 558-0184 (toll-free in WV).

Wisconsin
Office of Consumer Protection and Citizen Advocacy, Department of Justice, P.O. Box 7856, Madison, WI 53707-7856; (608) 224-4939, or (800) 422-7128 (toll-free in WI).

Consumer Protection Offices

Wyoming
Consumer Affairs, Office of Attorney General, 123 State Capitol Building, Cheyenne, WY 82002; (307) 777-7874, Fax: (307) 777-6869.

Crime Victims Programs

Most states have a Crime Victims Fund to compensate innocent victims of violent crime. Part of the money from these funds is given out to victims as direct cash payments to help compensate for costs related to the violent crimes. Contact the office in your state if you find yourself the victim of violent crime and need money to help pay for such related costs as medical bills, lost wages, and funeral expenses. For more detailed information, see *Crime Victims* on page 58.

Alabama
Alabama Crime Victims Compensation Commission, 645 McDonugh, P.O. Box 1548, Montgomery, AL 36102; (334) 242-4007, (800) 541-9388 (Victim Only).

Alaska
Department of Public Safety, Violent Crimes Compensation Board, P.O. Box N, Juneau, AK 99811; (907) 465-3040.

Arizona
Arizona Criminal Justice Commission, 1501 West Washington, Suite 207, Phoenix, AZ 85007; (602) 542-1928.

Arkansas
Children's & Victim's Advocate, Crime Victims Reparations Board, 601 Tower Building, 323 Center St., Little Rock, AR 72201; (501) 682-1323.

California
State of California State Board of Control, Victims of Crimes, P.O. Box 3036, Sacramento, CA 95812-3036; (916) 327-2933.

Colorado
Division of Criminal Justice, Department of Public Safety, Suite 3000, 700 Kipling St., Denver, CO 80215; (303) 239-4402.

Connecticut
Commission on Victim Services, 1155 Silasdeane Highway, Wetherford, CT 06109; (860) 529-3089, (800) 822-8428.

Delaware
Delaware Violent Crimes Compensation Board, 1500 E. Newport Pike, Suite 10, Wilmington, DE 19804; (302) 995-8383.

District of Columbia
Department of Employment Services, Employment Security Building, 500 C St., NW, Suite 600, Washington, D.C. 20001; (202) 879-4216.

Crime Victims Programs

Florida
Bureau of Victims Compensation, Bureau of Grants & Planning, Office of Attorney General, The Capitol, Tallahassee, FL 32399-1050; (904) 414-3300.

Georgia
Crime Victims Emergency Funds, 503 Oak Place, Ste. 540, Atlanta, GA 30349; (404) 559-4949.

Hawaii
Dept. of the Attorney General, Resource Coordination Division, 426 Queen St., Room 201, Honolulu, HI 96813; (808) 548-3800.

Idaho
Crime Victims Programs, c/o Idaho Industrial Commission, 317 Main Street, P.O. Box 83720, Boise, ID 83720; (208) 334-6000, (800) 950-2110.

Illinois
Illinois Court of Claims, 630 S. College St., Springfield, IL 62756; (217) 782-0703.

Crime Victims Division, Office of the Attorney General, 100 W. Randolph, 13th Floor, Chicago, IL 60601; (312) 814-2581.

Indiana
Violent Crime Compensation Division, 302 W. Washington St., Room E203, Indianapolis, IN 46204; (317) 232-7103.

Iowa
Crime Victim Assistance Division, Old Historical Bldg., Des Moines, IA 50319; (515) 281-5044.

Kansas
Kansas Crime Victims Compensation Board, 700 S.W. Jackson, Suite 400, Topeka, KS 66603-3757; (913) 296-2359.

Kentucky
Crime Victims Compensation Board, 115 Myrtle Ave., Frankfort, KY 40601; (502) 564-2290.

Louisiana
Crime Victims Reparation Program, Louisiana Commission on Law Enforcement, 1885 Wooddale Blvd., Room 708, Baton Rouge, LA 70806; (504) 925-4437.

Maine
No compensation program. (207) 626-8800.

Maryland
Department of Public Safety and Correctional Services, Criminal Injuries Compensation Board, 6776 Reisterstown Rd., Suite 313, Baltimore, MD 21215-2340; (410) 764-4214.

Massachusetts
Victim Compensation Division, Office of the Attorney General, One Ashburton Place, Room 1811, Boston, MA 02108; (617) 727-2200.

Crime Victims Programs

Michigan
Crime Victims Compensation
Board, P.O. Box 30026, Lansing,
MI 48909; (517) 373-7373.

Minnesota
Crime Victims Reparations Board,
N-465 Griggs-Midway Building,
1821 University Ave., St. Paul,
MN 55104; (612) 642-0395/0396,
(800) 247-0390.

Mississippi
Mississippi Crime Victim
Compensation Program, P.O. Box
267, Jackson, MS 39205; (601)
359-6766.

Missouri
Division of Workers' Compensation, Crime Victims Compensation, P.O. Box 58, Jefferson
City, MO 65102; (573) 526-6006,
(800) 347-6881.

Montana
Board of Crime Control, Crime
Victims Unit, Scott Hart Bldg, 303
N. Roberts, 4th Flr., Helena, MT
59620; (406) 444-3653.

Nebraska
Nebraska Crime Victims
Reparation Board, Nebraska
Commission on Law Enforcement
and Criminal Justice, 301
Centennial Mall South, P.O. Box
94946, Lincoln, NE 68509; (402)
471-2194.

Nevada
Victim of Crime, State Board of
Examiners, 555 E. Washington,

Suite 3300, Las Vegas, NV
89101; (702) 486-2740.

New Hampshire
Victim Witness Assistance, Office
of Attorney General, Criminal
Justice Bldg., State House Station
Annex, Concord, NH 03301;
(603) 271-1284.

New Jersey
Violent Crimes Compensation
Board, 50 Park Place, 6th Floor,
Newark, NJ 07102; (201) 648-
2107, (800) 242-0804 (victim
only).

New Mexico
New Mexico Crime Victims
Reparation Commission, 8100
Mountain Rd., NE, Suite 106,
Albuquerque, NM 87110; (505)
841-9432.

New York
Crime Victims Board, Room 200,
270 Broadway, New York, NY
10007; (212) 417-5160.

North Carolina
North Carolina Department of
Crime Control and Public Safety,
Division of Victim and Justice
Services, P.O. Box 29588,
Raleigh, NC 27626-0588; (919)
733-7974, (800) 824-8263 (victim
only).

North Dakota
Crime Victims Reparations,
Russell Building, Highway 83
North, 4007 N. State St.,

Crime Victims Programs

Bismarck, MD 58501; (701) 328-6195.

Ohio
Victims of Crime Compensation Program, Court of Claims of Ohio, 65 E. State Street, Suite 1100, Columbus, OH 43215; (614) 466-7190, (800) 824-8263.

Oklahoma
Crime Victims Compensation Board, 2200 Classen Blvd., Suite 1800, Oklahoma City, OK 73106-5811; (405) 557-6704.

Oregon
Department of Justice, Crime Victims' Compensation Program, 100 Justice Building, Salem, OR 97310; (503) 378-5348/6002.

Pennsylvania
Pennsylvania Crime Victim's Compensation Board, 333 Market St., Lobby Level, Harristown Bldg. #2, Harrisburg, PA 17101; (717) 783-5153.

Puerto Rico
No compensation program.

Rhode Island
Victim's Restitution Unit, Room 618, Frank Leicht Bldg., Judicial Complex, 250 Benefit Street, Providence, RI 02903; (401) 277-3263.
South Carolina
South Carolina Crime Victims' Compensation Fund, 1205 Pendleton Street, Room 401,

Columbia, SC 29201; (803) 734-1900, (800) 521-6576.

South Dakota
Victims Compensation Program, 523 E. Capital Ave., Suite 304, Pierre, SD 57501-3182; (605) 773-6317.

Tennessee
Division of Crimes Administration, 11th Floor, Andrew Jackson Bldg., Nashville, TN 37243; (615) 741-2734.

Texas
Office of Attorney General, Crime Victims, P.O. Box 12548 Austin, TX 78711-2548; (512) 448-7956.

Utah
Office of Crime Victim Reparations, 350 E. 500 South, Suite 200, Salt Lake City, UT 84111; (801) 533-4000.

Vermont
Crime Victims Services, P.O. Box 991, Montpelier, UT 05061-0991; (802) 241-1255 or (800) 750-1213.

Virginia
Division of Crime Victims' Compensation, P.O. Box 1794, Richmond, VA 23214; (703) 548-3377.

Virgin Islands
Virgin Islands Criminal Victims Compensation Commission, Department of Human Services,

Crime Victims Programs

Office of the Commissioner, KNUD Hanson Complex, Bldg. A, 1303 Hostitil Ground, Charlotte Amalie, VI 00802; (809) 774-1166.

Washington
Department of Labor and Industries, Crime Victim Compensation Program, P.O. Box 44500, Olympia, WA 98504-4500; (206) 956-4213.

West Virginia
West Virginia Court of Claims, Crime Victims Compensation Fund, 1900 Kanawha Boulevard East, Charleston, WV 25305-0291; (304) 558-3471.

Wisconsin
Crime Victim Compensation, Department of Justice, 222 State Street, P.O. Box 7951, Madison, WI 53707-7951; (608) 266-6470, (800) 446-6564.

Wyoming
Crime Victim Compensation, Office of the Attorney General, 1700 Westland Road, Cheyenne, WY 82002; (307) 635-4050.

U.S. Department Of Education

Besides coordinating the federal education programs, the U.S. Department of Education enforces laws and regulations related to discrimination in federally funded programs, access to school records, and sexual harassment in schools that receive federal funding. For more detailed information, see *School Records* on page 182, *Experimental Testing at School* on page 75, and *Sexual Harassment at School* on page 184.

Region I
Office of Civil Rights, U.S. Department of Education, John W. McCormack Post Office and Court House, Room 222 - Post Office Square, Boston, MA 02109; (617) 223-9317, Fax: (617) 223-9324. Serving: Connecticut, Maine, Massachusetts, New Hampshire, Rhode Island, and Vermont.

Region II
Office for Civil Rights, U.S. Department of Education, 75 Park Place, 12th Floor, New York, NY 10007; (212) 264-7005. Serving: New Jersey, New York, Puerto Rico, and the Virgin Islands.

Region III
Office for Civil Rights, U.S. Department of Education, Gateway Building - 3535 Market Street, Room 6300, Philadelphia, PA 19104-3326; (215) 596-1001, Fax: (215) 596-1094. Serving: Delaware, District of Columbia, Maryland, Pennsylvania, Virginia, and West Virginia.

Region IV
Office for Civil Rights, U.S. Department of Education, 101 Maretta Tower, Room 2702, P.O. Box 2048, Atlanta, GA 30301; (404) 331-2502, Fax: (404) 841-5382. Serving: Alabama, Florida, Georgia, Mississippi, North Carolina, South Carolina, and Tennessee.

Region V
Office for Civil Rights, U.S. Department of Education, 111 N. Canal St., Suite 1094, Chicago, IL 60606-7204; (312) 886-8315, Fax: (312) 353-5147. Serving: Illinois, Indiana, Minnesota, Michigan, Ohio, and Wisconsin.

Region VI
Office for Civil Rights, U.S. Department of Education, 1200 Main Tower, Room 2125, Dallas, TX 75202; (214) 767-3626, Fax: (214) 729-3634. Serving: Arkansas, Louisiana, Mississippi, Oklahoma, and Texas.

Region VII
Office for Civil Rights, U.S. Department of Education, 10220 N. Executive Hill Blvd., 8th Floor, Kansas City, MO 64153-1367; (816) 880-4000, Fax: (816) 891-0578. Serving: Iowa, Kansas,

U.S. Department Of Education

Kentucky, Missouri, and Nebraska.

Region VIII
Office for Civil Rights, U.S. Department of Education, Federal Office Building, 1244 Speer Blvd., Ste. 310, Room 342, Denver, CO 80204; (303) 844-3544, Fax: (303) 564-2524. Serving: Arizona, Colorado, Montana, New Mexico, North Dakota, South Dakota, Utah, and Wyoming.

Region IX
Office for Civil Rights, U.S. Department of Education, 50 United Nations Plaza, Room 205, San Francisco, CA 94102-4987; (415) 437-7520, Fax: (415) 437-7540.

Region X
Office for Civil Rights, U.S. Department of Education, 915 2nd Ave., Room 3310, Seattle, WA 98174-1099; (206) 220-7800, Fax: (206) 220-7806. Serving: Alaska, Guam, Hawaii, Idaho, Nevada, Oregon, Trust Territory of Pacific Island and Washington.

Environmental Protection Agency

The Environmental Protection Agency (EPA) protects the environment by controlling and monitoring air, water, noise, solid waste, radiation, and toxic substance pollution. They investigate reports of pollution and can act to get it stopped. See *Environmental Hazards and Pollution* on page 70 for more detailed information.

Region 1
EPA, John F. Kennedy Federal Building, 1 Congress Street, Boston, MA 02203; (617) 565-3423, or Unleaded Fuel Hotline: (800) 631-2700 in MA or (800) 821-1237 in all other Region 1 states. Serving Connecticut, Massachusetts, Maine, Vermont, New Hampshire, and Rhode Island.

Region 2
EPA, 26 Federal Plaza, New York, NY 10278; (212) 637-3526, or Hazardous Waste Ombudsman: (703) 920-9810, or Headquarters: (800) 424-9348. Serving New Jersey, New York, Puerto Rico, and the Virgin Islands.

Region 3
EPA, 841 Chestnut St., Philadelphia, PA 19107; (215) 566-9800, or the Waste Minimization: (215) 566-0982 and (800) 826-5320 in other Region 3 states; Hazardous Waste Ombudsman: (215) 566-0982. Serving Delaware, Maryland, Pennsylvania, Virginia, West

Virginia, and the District of Columbia.

Region 4
EPA, 345 Courtland Street, NE, Atlanta, GA 30365; (800) 282-0289 in GA, and (800) 241-1754 in other Region 4 states. Hazardous Waste Ombudsman: (404) 347-7603. Serving: Alabama, Florida, Georgia, Kentucky, Mississippi, North Carolina, South Carolina, and Tennessee.

Region 5
EPA, 1701 South 1st Avenue, Maywood, Chicago, IL 60153; (800) 572-2515 in IL, and (800) 621-8431 in other Region 5 states. Hazardous Waste Ombudsman: (312) 353-2000. Serving Illinois, Indiana, Michigan, Minnesota, Ohio, and Wisconsin.

Region 6
EPA, 1445 Ross Ave., 7th Floor, Dallas, TX 75202; (214) 655-2200. Environmental Emergency 24-Hour Hotline: (214) 655-2222; Hazardous Waste Ombudsman

(214) 655-6765. Serving Arkansas, Louisiana, New Mexico, Oklahoma, and Texas.

Region 7
EPA, 726 Minnesota Ave., Kansas City, KS 66101; (913) 551-7003. Action Line for IA, MO, and NE residents: (800) 223-0425; or KS residents: (800) 221-7749. Hazardous Waste Ombudsman: (913) 551-7051. Serving Iowa, Kansas, Missouri, and Nebraska.

Region 8
EPA, 999 18th St., Suite 500, Denver, CO 80202; (303) 293-1603 or (800) 759-4372. Hazardous Waste Ombudsman: (303) 293-1720. Serving Colorado, Montana, North Dakota, South Dakota, Utah, and Wyoming.

Region 9
EPA, 75 Hawthorne St., San Francisco, CA 94105; (415) 744-1500. Hazardous Waste Ombudsman: (415) 744-1730; RCRA Hotline: (415) 540-3780; Superfund Hotline: (800) 231-3075. Serving Arizona, California, Hawaii, and Nevada.

Region 10
EPA, 1200 6th Ave., Seattle, WA 98101; (206) 553-1200. Hazardous Waste Ombudsman: (206) 553-1090. Serving Alaska, Idaho, Oregon, and Washington.

Office Of Federal Contract Compliance Programs

These offices can assist you with discrimination and other kinds of employer problems, if your company is doing business with the government. See *Federal Contractors* on page 82 for more detailed information.

Region I-Boston
Connecticut, Maine, Massachusetts, New Hampshire, Rhode Island, Vermont: Regional Director for OFCCP/ESA, U.S. Department of Labor, One Congress Street, 11th Floor, Boston, MA 02114; (617) 565-2055.

Region II-New York
New Jersey, New York, Puerto Rico, Virgin Islands: Regional Director for OFCCP/ESA, U.S. Department of Labor, 201 Varick St., Room 764, New York, NY 10014; (212) 337-2007.

Region III-Philadelphia
Delaware, District of Columbia, Maryland, Pennsylvania, Virginia, West Virginia: Regional Director for OFCCP/ESA, U.S. Department of Labor, Gateway Bldg., Room 15340, 3535 Market Street, Philadelphia, PA 19104; (215) 596-6168.

Region IV-Atlanta
Alabama, Florida, Georgia, Kentucky, Mississippi, North Carolina, South Carolina, Tennessee: Regional Director for OFCCP/ESA, U.S. Department of Labor, 1375 Peachtree St., NE, Suite 678, Atlanta, GA 30367; (404) 347-4211.

Region V-Chicago
Illinois, Indiana, Michigan, Minnesota, Ohio, Wisconsin: Regional Director for OFCCP/ESA, U.S. Department of Labor, New Federal Building, Room 570, 230 South Dearborn St., Chicago, IL 60604; (312) 353-0335.

Region VI-Dallas
Arkansas, Louisiana, New Mexico, Oklahoma, Texas: Regional Director for OFCCP/ESA, U.S. Department of Labor, 525 South Griffin St., Federal Building, Room 840, Dallas, TX 75202; (214) 767-4771.

Region VII-Kansas City
Regional Director for OFCCP/ESA, U.S. Department of Labor, Federal Office Building, 911 Walnut Street, Room 2011, Kansas City, MO 64106; (816) 426-5384.

Federal Contract Compliance Programs

Region VIII-Denver
Colorado, Montana, North Dakota, South Dakota, Utah, Wyoming: Regional Director for OFCCP/ESA, U.S. Department of Labor, 1801 California, Ste. 935, Denver, CO 80202; (303) 391-6082.

Region IX-San Francisco
Arizona, California, Guam, Hawaii, Nevada: Regional Director for OFCCP/ESA, U.S. Department of Labor, 71 Stevenson St., Suite 1700, San Francisco, CA 94105; (415) 744-6640.

Region X-Seattle
Alaska, Idaho, Oregon, Washington: Regional Director for OFCCP/ESA, U.S. Department of Labor, 1111 Third Avenue, Suite 610, Seattle, WA 98101-3212; (206) 553-4508.

Federal Information Centers

If you can't quite figure out what federal government agency to contact to help you out with a problem, call the Federal Information Center (Internet: http://fic.info.gov/) nearest you listed below. Set up to help you through the often confusing government bureaucracy, these Centers can direct you toward the appropriate agency that can help you solve problems involving anything from Social Security and Medicare benefits to taxes, pensions, immigration laws, and veterans' benefits.

Alabama
Birmingham, Mobile: (800) 366-2998

Alaska
Anchorage: (800) 729-8003

Arizona
Phoenix: (800) 359-3997

Arkansas
Little Rock: (800) 366-2998

California
Los Angeles, San Diego, San Francisco, Santa Ana: (800) 726-4995
Sacramento: (916) 973-1695

Colorado
Colorado Springs, Denver, Pueblo: (800) 359-3997

Connecticut
Hartford, New Haven: (800) 347-1997

Florida
Fort Lauderdale, Jacksonville, Miami, Orlando, St. Petersburg, Tampa, West Palm Beach: (800) 347-1997

Georgia
Atlanta: (800) 347-1997

Hawaii
Honolulu: (800) 733-5996

Illinois
Chicago: (800) 366-2998

Indiana
Gary: (800) 366-2998
Indianapolis: (800) 347-1997

Iowa
All locations: (800) 735-8004

Kansas
All locations: (800) 735-8004

Kentucky
Louisville: (800) 347-1997

Louisiana
New Orleans: (800) 366-2998

Maryland
Baltimore: (800) 347-1997

Federal Information Centers

Massachusetts
Boston: (800) 347-1997

Michigan
Detroit, Grand Rapids:
(800) 347-1997

Minnesota
Minneapolis: (800) 366-2998

Missouri
St. Louis: (800) 366-2998
All other locations:
(800) 735-8004

Nebraska
Omaha: (800) 366-2998
All other locations:
(800) 735-8004

New Jersey
Newark, Trenton:
(800) 347-1997

New Mexico
Albuquerque: (800) 359-3997

New York
Albany, Buffalo, New York,
Rochester, Syracuse:
(800) 347-1997

North Carolina
Charlotte: (800) 347-1997

Ohio
Akron, Cincinnati, Cleveland, Columbus, Dayton,
Toldeo: (800) 347-1997

Oklahoma
Oklahoma City, Tulsa:
(800) 366-2998

Oregon
Portland: (800) 726-4995

Pennsylvania
Philadelphia, Pittsburgh:
(800) 347-1997

Rhode Island
Providence: (800) 347-1997

Tennessee
Chattanooga: (800) 347-1997
Memphis, Nashville:
(800) 366-2998

Texas
Austin, Dallas, Fort Worth,
Houston, San Antonio:
(800) 366-2998

Utah
Salt Lake City: (800) 359-3997

Virginia
Norfolk, Richmond, Roanoke: (800) 347-1997

Washington
Seattle, Tacoma: (800) 726-4995

Wisconsin
Milwaukee: (800) 366-2998

Federal Trade Commission

The Federal Trade Commission (FTC) is the federal agency that investigates cases of consumer fraud on virtually any subject, including advertising, fake art, jewelry, telemarketing, care labels, rare coins, funerals, contests, dancing schools, door-to-door sales, eye care, generic drugs, miracle cures, manufactured homes, health clubs, indoor tanning, employment services, shopping by mail, time shares, warranties, transmission repairs, home mortgages, credit card fraud, bill collectors, real estate agents, and much more. Although they won't investigate just one complaint against a company, if they receive several like yours, they may decide to investigate and seek reimbursement for those who were cheated. If you want more immediate action taken on your complaint, contact your State Consumer Protection Office listed on page 230.

Atlanta
FTC, 60 Forsyth St., Suite 5M35, SW, Atlanta, GA 30303; (404) 656-1399.

Boston
FTC, 101 Merrimac St., Boston, MA 02114-4719; (617) 429-5960, Fax: (617) 424-5998.

Chicago
FTC, 55 East Monroe St., Chicago, IL 60603; (312) 353-4423, Fax: (312) 353-4438.

Cleveland
FTC, 668 Euclid Ave., Cleveland, OH 44114; (216) 522-4207, Fax: (216) 522-7239.

Dallas
FTC, 1999 Bryan St., Suite 2150, Dallas, TX 75201; (214) 979-0213.

Denver
FTC, 1961 Stout St., Suite 1523, Denver, CO 80202; (303) 844-2271, Fax: (303) 844-3599.

Los Angeles
FTC, 11000 Wilshire Blvd., Suite 13209, Los Angeles, CA 90024; (310) 209-7890.

New York
FTC, 150 William St., Suite 1300, New York, NY 10038; (212) 264-1207, Fax: (212) 264-0459.

San Francisco
FTC, 901 Market St., Suite 570, San Francisco, CA 94103; (415) 356-5270, Fax: (415) 356-5284.

Seattle
FTC, 915 Second Ave., Seattle, WA 98174; (206) 220-6363, Fax: (206) 220-6366.

Food And Drug Administration

If you know of any foods, drugs or medicines, cosmetics, medical devices, radiation emitting electronic products, or veterinary products that you think aren't properly labeled or packaged or that are dangerous or unsanitary, you should report them to one of the Food and Drug Administration (FDA) regional offices listed here. For more detailed information, see *Medical Devices* on page 139, *Tanning Devices and Salons* on page 190, *Product Tampering* on page 169, and *Cosmetics* on page 52.

California
FDA (HFR-P145), 50 United Nations Plaza, Room 524, San Francisco, CA 94102; (415) 556-1364.

FDA (HFR-P245), 1521 West Pico Blvd., Los Angeles, CA 90015; (213) 252-7597.

Colorado
FDA (HFR-SW245), P.O. Box 25087, 6th and Kipling, Denver, CO 80225-0087; (303) 236-3000.

Florida
FDA (HFR-SE245), 7200 Lack Ellenor Drive, Suite 120, Orlando, FL 32809; (407) 855-0900.

FDA (HFR-SE2575), 6601 NW 25th Street, P.O. Box 59-2256, Miami, FL 33159-2256; (305) 526-2919.

Georgia
FDA (HFR-SE145), 60 Eighth St., NE, Atlanta, GA 30309; (404) 347-7355.

Illinois
FDA (HFR-MW145), 300 South Riverside Plaza, Suite 550 South, Chicago, IL 60606; (312) 353-7126.

Indiana
FDA, 101 W. Ohio Street, Suite 1310, Indianapolis, IN 46204; (317) 226-6500.

Louisiana
FDA (HFR-SE445), 4298 Elysian Fields Ave., New Orleans, LA 70122; (504) 589-2420.

Maryland
FDA (HFR-MA245), 900 Madison Ave., Baltimore, MD 21201; (301) 962-3731.

Massachusetts
FDA (HFR-NE245), One Montvale Ave., Stoneham, MA 02180; (617) 279-1675.

Michigan
FDA (HFR-MW245), 1560 E. Jefferson Ave., Detroit, MI 48207; (313) 226-6260.

Food And Drug Administration

Minnesota
FDA (HFR-MW345), 240 Hennepin Ave., Minneapolis, MN 55401; (612) 334-4103.

Missouri
FDA (HFR-SW245), Laclede's Landing, 808 N. Collins St., St. Louis, MO 63102; (314) 425-5021.

FDA (HFR-SW345), 1009 Cherry St., Kansas City, MO 64106; (816) 374-6371.

New Jersey
FDA (HFR-MA345), 61 Main St., West Orange, NJ 07052; (201) 645-3265.

New York
FDA, 850 Third Ave., Brooklyn, NY 11232; (718) 965-5725.

FDA (HFR-NE345), 599 Delaware Ave., Buffalo, NY 14202; (716) 846-4483.

Ohio
FDA (HFR-MA445), 1141 Central Parkway, Cincinnati, OH 45202; (513) 684-3501.

FDA (HFR-MA4525), 3820 Central Rd., P.O. Box 838, Brunswick, OH 44212; (216) 273-1038.

Pennsylvania
FDA (HFR-MA145), Room 900

U.S. Customhouse, 2nd and Chestnut Streets, Philadelphia, PA 19106; (215) 597-0837.

Puerto Rico
FDA (HFR-SE545), P.O. Box 5719, Puerto de Tierra Station, San Juan, PR 00906-5719; (809) 729-6948.

Tennessee
FDA (HFR-SE345), 297 Plus Park Boulevard, Nashville, TN 37217; (615) 781-5372.

Texas
FDA (HFR-SW145), 3032 Bryan Street, Dallas, TX 75204; (214) 655-5315.

FDA (HFR-SW1580), 1445 North Loop West, Suite 420, Houston, TX 77008; (713) 220-2322.

FDA, 10127 Morraco, Suite 119, Room B-406, San Antonio, TX 78206; (512) 229-4528.

Virginia
FDA, 1110 North Glebe Road, Suite 250, Arlington, VA 22201; (703) 285-2578.

Washington
FDA (HFR-P345), 22201 23rd Drive, SE, P.O. Box 3012, Bothell, WA 98041-4421; (206) 483-4953.

Funeral Service Examining Boards

Each state has a funeral examining board that licenses funeral homes, morticians, and embalmers. These offices will investigate your complaints and take whatever actions that they decide are necessary, including formal hearings, arbitrated settlements, and revocation or suspension of licenses to resolve them. See *Funeral Homes* on page 89 for more detailed information.

Alabama
Alabama Board of Funeral Service, 7070 Washington Avenue, Suite 226, Montgomery, AL 36130; (334) 242-4049. Written complaints only.

Alaska
Department of Commerce and Economic Development, Investigations Section, Division of Occupational Licensing, P.O. Box 110806, Anchorage, AK 99811; (907) 465-2695.

Arizona
Arizona State Board of Funeral Directors and Embalmers, 1645 W. Jefferson, Room 410, Phoenix, AZ 85007; (602) 542-3095.

Arkansas
Arkansas State Board of Embalmers and Funeral Directors, 400 Harrison, Suite 203, P.O. Box 2673, Batesville, AR 72501; (501) 698-2072.

California
Board of Funeral Directors and Embalmers, 400 R. St., Suite 2060

Sacramento, CA 95814-6200; (916) 263-3180. Written complaints only.

Colorado
Colorado Funeral Directors and Embalmers Association, Inc., Box 1928, Rawlins, WY 82301; (307) 324-5644.

Connecticut
Department of Health, Hearing Division, 150 Washington St., Hartford, CT 06106; (203) 566-1039.

Delaware
Delaware State Board of Funeral Service Practitioners, P.O. Box 1401, Dover, DE 19903; (302) 739-4522.

District of Columbia
Department of Consumer and Regulatory Affairs, Board of Funeral Directors and Embalmers, Room 923, 614 H. St., NW, Washington, DC 20001; (202) 727-7454.

Funeral Service Examining Boards

Florida
Office of Complaints, Department of Professional Regulation, Board of Funeral Directors and Embalmers, 1940 N. Monroe Street, Tallahassee, FL 32399-0750; (904) 488-8690.

Georgia
Georgia State Board of Funeral Service, 166 Pryor Street, SW, Atlanta, GA 30303; (404) 656-3933.

Hawaii
State of Hawaii Department of Health, Sanitation Branch, 591 Alamoane Boulevard, Honolulu, HI 96813; (808) 586-8000.

Idaho
Bureau of Occupational Licensing, Idaho State Board of Morticians, 2 Owahee Plaza, 1109 Main Street, Suite 220, Boise, ID 83705-2598; (208) 334-3233.

Illinois
Illinois Department of Professional Regulation, Funeral Directors and Embalmers Licensing and Disciplinary Boards, 320 W. Washington Street, Springfield, IL 62786; (217) 785-0800.

Indiana
Indiana Professional Licensing Agency, I.G.C. North, Room 1021, 100 N. Senate Avenue, Indianapolis, IN 46204; (317) 232-7215.

Iowa
Board of Mortuary Science Examiners, Iowa Department of Public Health, Lucas State Office Bldg., 321 E. 12th Street, Des Moines, IA 50319-0075; (515) 281-4287.

Kansas
Kansas State Board of Mortuary Arts, 700 S.W. Jackson, Suite 904, Topeka, KS 66603-3758; (913) 296-3980.

Kentucky
State Board of Embalmers and Funeral Directors, 210 E. 4th Street, Cagel Building, P.O. Box 335, Beaver Dam, KY 42320; (502) 274-4515.

Louisiana
State Board of Embalmers and Funeral Directors, 3500 Causeway Boulevard, North Executive Towers, Suite 1232, P.O. Box 8757, Metairie, LA 70011; (504) 838-5109.

Maine
Maine State Board of Funeral Services, Attn: Complaint Officer, State House Station 35, Augusta, ME 04333; (207) 582-8723.

Maryland
State Board of Morticians, 4201 Patterson Ave., Room 315, Baltimore, MD 21215-2299; (410) 764-4792.

Funeral Service Examining Boards

Massachusetts
Board of Registration in Embalming and Funeral Directing, Leverett Saltonstall Building, Room 1512, 100 Cambridge St., Boston, MA 02202; (617) 727-1718.

Michigan
Department of Licensing and Regulation, Board of Examiners in Mortuary Science, Commercial Enforcement Complaints, P.O. Box 30018, Lansing, MI 48909; (517) 355-1688.

Minnesota
Mortuary Science Unit, Minnesota Department of Health, 717 Delaware St., SE, P.O. Box 9441, Minneapolis, MN 55440; (612) 623-5491.

Mississippi
State Board of Funeral Service, 1307 E. Fortification, Jackson, MS 39202; (601) 354-6903.

Missouri
State Board of Embalmers and Funeral Directors, P.O. Box 423, Jefferson City, MO 65102-0423; (314) 751-0813.

Montana
Board of Morticians, P.O. Box 200513, Helena, MT 59620-0407; (406) 444-5433.

Nebraska
Division of Investigation and Enforcement, Bureau of Examining Boards, Department of Health, P.O. Box 95164, Lincoln, NE 68509-5164; (402) 471-2117.

Nevada
Nevada State Board of Funeral Directors and Embalmers, P.O. Box 2462, Reno, NV 89505; (702) 323-3312.

New Hampshire
Board of Registration of Funeral Directors and Embalmers, Health and Welfare Bldg., 6 Hazen Dr., Concord, NH 03301-6527; (603) 271-4651.

New Jersey
State Board of Mortuary Science of New Jersey, P.O. Box 45009, Room 513, Newark, NJ 07101; (201) 504-6425.

New Mexico
New Mexico State Board of Thanatopractice, 725 St. Michaels Dr., P.O. Box 25101, Santa Fe, NM 87504; (505) 827-7177. Complaints must be sworn and notarized.

New York
Bureau of Funeral Directing, New York State Department of Health, Corning Tower, Empire State Plaza, Albany, NY 12237-0681; (518) 402-0785.

Funeral Service Examining Boards

North Carolina
North Carolina State Board of Mortuary Science, 412 N. Wilmington St., Raleigh, NC 27601; (919) 733-9380.

North Dakota
North Dakota Board of Funeral Service, Box 633, Devils Lake, ND 58301; (701) 662-2511

Ohio
Board of Embalmers and Funeral Directors of Ohio, 77 S. High St., 16th Floor, Columbus, OH 43266-0313; (614) 466-4252.

Oklahoma
State Board of Embalmers and Funeral Directors, 4545 N. Lincoln Blvd., Suite 175, Oklahoma City, OK 73105; (405) 525-0158.

Oregon
State Mortuary and Cemetery Board, Portland State Office Bldg., Suite 430, 800 NE Oregon Street #21, Portland, OR 97232; (503) 731-4040.

Pennsylvania
Board of Funeral Directors, P.O. Box 2649, Harrisburg, PA 17105-2649; (717) 783-1253.

Rhode Island
Board of Examiners in Embalming and Funeral Directing, Division of Professional Regulation, Dept. of Health, 3 Capital Hill, Room 104, Cannon Bldg., 75 Davis St., Providence, RI 02908; (401) 277-2827.

South Carolina
South Carolina State Board of Funeral Service, P.O. Box 11329, Columbia, SC 29211; (803) 896-4494.

South Dakota
State Board of Funeral Service, 1111 S. Main St., Aberdeen, SD 57401; (605) 741-2378.

Tennessee
Board of Funeral Directors and Embalmers, 500 James Robertson Parkway, Nashville, TN 37243-1144; (615) 741-2378.

Texas
Texas Funeral Service Commission, 510 S. Congress, Suite 206, Austin, TX 78753; (512) 834-9992.

Utah
Division of Occupational and Professional Licensing, State Funeral Service Examiners Board, 160 E. 300 South, 4th Floor, P.O. Box 146741 Salt Lake City, UT 84145-0805; (801) 530-6396.

Vermont
Secretary of State Office, Board of Funeral Service, 109 State St., Montpelier, VT 05609-1106; (802) 828-2387.

Funeral Service Examining Boards

Virginia
Virginia Board of Funeral Directors and Embalmers, 6606 W. Broad St., Southern State Bldg., 4th Floor, Richmond, VA 23230-1717; (804) 662-9907.

Washington
Washington Funeral and Cemetery Unit, Division of Professional Licensing, P.O. Box 9012, Olympia, WA 98507-9012; (206) 586-4905.

West Virginia
West Virginia Board of Embalmers and Funeral Directors, 812 Quarrier St., 4th Floor, Charleston, WV 25301; (304) 588-0302.

Wisconsin
Funeral Directors Examining Board, Division of Enforcement, 1400 E. Washington Ave., P.O. Box 8935, Madison, WI 53708; (608) 266-1630.

Wyoming
Wyoming State Board of Embalming, P.O. Box 349, Worland, WY 82401; (307) 347-4028.

Health Departments

If you've got a complaint about the sanitation or safety conditions at a particular restaurant, fast food franchise, or meatpacking facility, all state health departments have a division that oversees the inspection and certification of food processing, storing, and serving facilities. They also will investigate reports of unsanitary conditions or they will refer you to the proper local health agency that jurisdiction. For more detailed information, see *Restaurants* on page 181.

Alabama
Department of Public Health, Bureau of Environmental Health, 434 Monroe St., Room 317, Montgomery, AL 63130; (334) 613-5200, Fax: (334) 240-3387.

Alaska
Department of Environmental Conservation, Division of Environmental Health, 410 Willoughby, #105, Juneau, AK 99801; (907) 465-5066, Fax: (907) 465-5070.

Arizona
State Department of Health Services, Sanitation Section, 3815 N. Black Canyon, Phoenix, AZ 85012; (602) 230-5912.

Arkansas
Department of Health, Environmental Health Protection, 4815 West Markham, #46, Little Rock, AR 72205-3867; (501) 661-2111, Fax: (501) 661-1450.

California
State Department of Health Section, Food and Drug Branch, Room 400, 714 P St., P.O. Box 942732, Sacramento, CA 94234-7320; (916) 445-2263, (916) 657-1425, Fax: (916) 657-1156.

Colorado
Colorado Department of Health, Division of Consumer Protection, 4300 Cherry Creek Drive, South, Denver, CO 80222-1530; (303) 692-3627, (303) 692-2012, Fax: (303) 782-0095.

Connecticut
State Department of Consumer Protection, Food Division, State Office Bldg., 165 Capitol Ave., Hartford, CT 06106; (860) 566-3388.

Delaware
Health Systems Protection, Office of Food Protection, P.O. Box 637, Cooper Building, Dover, DE 19903; (302) 739-4731.

District of Columbia
Department of Consumer Regulatory Affairs, Business Regulations Administration, Food Protection Branch, 614 H Street,

Health Departments

NW, Washington, DC 20001; (202) 727-7250/7170, Fax: (202) 727-8073.

Florida
Bureau of Food and Meat Inspection, Division of Food Safety, 3125 Connor Blvd., M-3, Tallahassee, FL 32399-1650; (904) 488-3951.

Georgia
Department of Agriculture, Consumer Protection Field Forces Division, 19 Martin Luther King Jr. Drive, SW, Atlanta, GA 30334; (404) 656-3621.

Hawaii
State Department of Health & Sanitation, 591 Ala Mona Blvd., 1st Floor, Honolulu, HI 96801; (808) 586-8000.

Idaho
State Department of Health and Welfare, Food Quality Control Section, 450 W. State St., Boise, ID 83720; (208) 334-5938.

Illinois
Dept. of Public Health, Division of Food, Drugs and Dairy, 525 W. Jefferson St., Springfield, IL 62761; (217) 785-2439.

Indiana
State Board of Health, Division of Retail and Manufactured Foods, 1330 West Michigan St., P.O. Box 1964, Indianapolis, IN 46206; (317) 633-0618.

Iowa
State Department of Inspections and Appeals, Food Products Control, Lucas Bldg, Des Moines, IA 50319; (515) 281-6538.

Kansas
State Department of Health and Environment, Division of Health, Food Service Division, Drug and Lodging Section, 109 S.W. 9th St., Suite 604, Topeka, KS 66612-1274; (913) 296-5603.

Kentucky
Cabinet for Human Resources, Environmental Sanitation Safety, 275 East Main St., Frankfort, KY 40621; (502) 564-4856.

Louisiana
State Department of Health and Human Resources, Food and Drug Control Unit, P.O. Box 60630, New Orleans, LA 70160; (504) 568-5402.

Maine
Eating and Lodging, Division of Health Engineering, State House Station #10, Augusta, ME 04333; (207) 287-5671.

Maryland
Department of Food Control, 303 E. Fayette Street, 4th Floor, Baltimore, MD 21202; (301) 396-4424.

Massachusetts
Department of Public Health,

Division of Food and Drugs, 305 South St., Jamaica Plain, MA 02130; (617) 522-3700.

Michigan
Department of Public Health, Food Service Sanitation Program, Consultation Section, P.O. Box 30195, Lansing, MI 48909; (517) 335-9178.

Minnesota
Department of Agriculture, Food Inspection Department, 90 W. Plato Blvd., St. Paul, MN 55107; (612) 296-1592.

Mississippi
State Department of Health, Division of Sanitation, P.O. Box 1700, Jackson, MS 39215; (601) 960-7689.

Missouri
State Department of Health, Bureau of Community Sanitation, 1730 East Elm St., Jefferson City, MO 65101; (314) 751-6095.

Montana
State Department of Health and Environmental Sciences, Food and Consumer Safety Bureau, W. F. Cogswell Building, Capitol Station, Helena, MT 59620; (406) 444-2408.

Nebraska
Bureau of Dairies and Foods, P.O. Box 95064, Lincoln, NE 68509; (402) 471-2536. Licenses and inspects food manufacturers, processors, retail stores and warehouses. Files are open to the public but the only way to obtain a listing is to visit the office and copy the information.

Nevada
State Health Division, Bureau of Health Protection Service, Room 103, 505 E. King St., Carson City, NV 89710; (702) 687-4740.

New Hampshire
Department of Health and Human Service, Division of Public Health, Bureau of Food Protection, 6 Hazen Drive, Concord, NH 03301-6527, (603) 271-4589. Complaints in writing only.

New Jersey
State Health Department, Consumer Health Services, Food and Milk Program, CN-369, 3635 Quacker Bridge Road, Trenton, NJ 08625-0369; (609) 984-1370.

New Mexico
New Mexico Environmental Division, P.O. Box 26100, Santa Fe, NM 87505; (505) 827-2850.

New York
State Health Department, Division of Food Inspection Services, Capital Plaza, One Winners Circle, Albany, NY 12235; (518) 457-3880.

North Carolina
State Department of Agriculture, Food and Drug Protection

Division, One Edenton St., P.O. Box 27647, Raleigh, NC 27611; (919) 733-7366.

North Dakota
Department of Health and Consolidated Laboratories, Division of Consumer Protection, 2635 E. Main Street, P.O. Box 937, Bismarck, ND 58502-0937; (701) 221-6147.

Ohio
Department of Agriculture, Division of Foods, Dairies and Drugs, 8995 E. Main St., Reynoldsburg, OH 43068; (614) 866-6361.

Oklahoma
State Department of Health, Food Protection Service, 1000 NE 10th Street, Oklahoma City, OK 73117-1299; (405) 271-5243.

Oregon
State Department Agriculture, Food and Dairy Division, 635 Capitol St., NE, Salem, OR 97310; (503) 378-3790.

Pennsylvania
Community Health, P.O. Box 2357, 2nd and Chestnut, Harrisburg, PA 17105; (717) 783-3795.

Rhode Island
State Dept. of Health, Division of Food Protection and Sanitation, 3 Capitol Hill, Providence, RI 02908; (401) 277-2750.

South Carolina
Department of Health and Environmental Control, Bureau of Environmental Health, 2600 Bull Street, Columbia, SC 29201; (803) 734-4970.

South Dakota
State Department of Health, Division of Public Health, 523 E. Capitol Street, Pierre, SD 57501; (605) 773-3364.

Tennessee
Dept. of Health, Division of Food and General Sanitation, C-1-136, Cordale Hall Building, Nashville, TN 37247-3901; (615) 741-7206.

Texas
Department of Health, Division of Food and Drugs, 1100 W. 49th Street, Austin, TX 78756; (512) 458-7248.

Utah
Department of Agriculture, Bureau of Consumer Services, Division of Food, 350 North Redwood Road, Salt Lake City, UT 84116; (801) 538-7124.

Vermont
Department of Health and Human Services, Environmental Health Division, 60 Main Street, P.O. Box 70, Burlington, VT 05402; (802) 863-7221.

Virginia
Office of Environmental Health Services, 1500 East Main Street,

Health Departments

Suite 117, Richmond, VA 23219; (804) 786-3559.

Washington
Food Protection Service, State Department of Health, 406 General Administration Building, Olympia, WA 98504, (206) 753-2555.

West Virginia
State Health Department, Environmental Health Services, 815 Quarrier Street, Suite 418, Charleston, WV 25301; (304) 558-2981,

Wisconsin
Department of Health and Social Services, Division of Environmental Sanitation, Washington Square Building, #88, 1414 East Washington Avenue, Madison, WI 53703; (608) 266-2835.

Wyoming
Department of Health, Environmental Health Program, Hathaway Building, #487, Cheyenne, WY 82002; (307) 777-6016.

U.S. Department Of Health And Human Services

As the federal agency responsible for protecting the country's health, the U.S. Department of Health and Human Services has programs that respond to and investigate complaints about hospital care and service, health maintenance organizations, discrimination in health facilities, Medicare and Medicaid benefits, and Hill-Burton free hospital care. For more detailed information, see *Health Maintenance Organizations* on page 107, *Free Medical Care* on page 87, and *Hospital Care and Service* on page 111.

Region I
John F. Kennedy Federal Building, Room 2100, Government Center, Boston, MA 02203; (617) 565-1500. Serving: Connecticut, Maine, Massachusetts, New Hampshire, Rhode Island, and Vermont.

Region II
Jacob K. Javits Federal Building, 26 Federal Plaza, New York, NY 10278; (212) 264-4600. Serving: New York, New Jersey, Puerto Rico, and the Virgin Islands.

Region III
P.O. Box 13716, 3535 Market Street, Philadelphia, PA 19101; (215) 596-6492. Serving: Delaware, Maryland, Pennsylvania, Virginia, West Virginia, and District of Columbia.

Region IV
101 Marietta Tower, 15th Floor, Atlanta, GA 30323; (404) 331-2442. Serving: Alabama, Florida, Georgia, Kentucky, Mississippi,

North Carolina, South Carolina, and Tennessee.

Region V
105 W. Adams Street, Chicago, IL 60603; (312) 353-5160. Serving: Illinois, Indiana, Michigan, Minnesota, Ohio, and Wisconsin.

Region VI
1200 Main Tower Building, Room 1100, Dallas, TX 75202; (214) 767-3301. Serving: Arkansas, Louisiana, New Mexico, Oklahoma, and Texas.

Region VII
601 E. 12th Street, Kansas City, MO 64106; (816) 426-2821. Serving: Iowa, Kansas, Missouri, and Nebraska.

Region VIII
1961 Stout Street, Denver, CO 80294; (303) 844-3372. Serving: Colorado, Montana, North Dakota South Dakota, Utah, and Wyoming.

U.S. Health And Human Services

Region IX
Federal Office Building, 50 United
Nations Plaza, San Francisco, CA
94102; (415) 556-6746. Serving:
Arizona, California, Hawaii,
Nevada, Guam, Trust Territory of
Pacific Islands, and American
Samoa.

Region X
2201 6th Ave., Seattle, WA
98121; (206) 553-0420. Serving:
Alaska, Idaho, Oregon, and
Washington.

Interstate Commerce Commission

The Interstate Commerce Commission's (ICC) job is to make sure that interstate bus, train, truck, and moving companies provide consumers with fair rates and services. If you've got a problem with any of these kinds of companies, contact the ICC regional office serving your state. For more detailed information, see *Moving Companies* on page 144 and *Bus Service* on page 39.

Eastern
ICC, 3535 Market St., Room 16400, Philadelphia, PA 19104; (215) 596-4040. Serving: Alabama, Connecticut, Delaware, District of Columbia, Florida, Georgia, Kentucky, Massachusetts, Maryland, Maine, Mississippi, Ohio, Pennsylvania, North Carolina, New Hampshire, New Jersey, New York, Rhode Island, South Carolina, Tennessee, Virginia, Vermont, and West Virginia.

Central
ICC, 55 Monroe St., Suite 550, Chicago, IL 60603; (312) 353-6204. Serving: Arkansas, Iowa, Illinois, Indiana, Kansas, Louisiana, Michigan, Missouri, Minnesota, Nebraska, North Dakota, Oklahoma, South Dakota, Texas, and Wisconsin.

Western
ICC, 211 Maine St., Suite 500, San Francisco, CA 94105; (415) 744-6520. Serving: Alaska, Arizona, California, Colorado, Idaho, Montana, Nevada, New Mexico, Oregon, Utah, Washington, and Wyoming.

Insurance Regulators

These state offices enforce the laws and regulations for all kinds of insurance, including car, homeowner, and health insurance, and they also handle relevant complaints from consumers. If you have a complaint about your insurance company's policies, and the company won't help you, contact the Insurance Commission in your state. For more detailed information, see *Insurance* on page 117.

Alabama
Insurance Commissioner, 135 South Union Street, 2nd Floor, Montgomery, AL 36130; (334) 269-3550.

Alaska
Division of Insurance, Director of Insurance, P.O. Box 110805, Juneau, AK 99811; (907) 465-2515.

Arizona
Director of Insurance, 3030 N. 3rd Street, Suite 1100, Phoenix, AZ 85012; (602) 912-8444.

Arkansas
Insurance Commissioner, 1123 University Tower Building, Suite 400, Little Rock, AR 72204; (501) 371-2600.

California
Commissioner of Insurance, 100 Van Ness Ave., San Francisco, CA 94102; 1(800) 927-4357 (in All California), or (916) 322-3555 (in Sacramento).

Colorado
Division of Insurance, 1560 Broadway, Suite 850, Denver, CO 80202; (303) 894-7499.

Connecticut
Insurance Commissioner, P.O. Box 816, Hartford, CT 06142-0816; (860) 297-3800.

Delaware
Insurance Commissioner, 841 Silver Lake Blvd., Dover, DE 19901; (302) 739-4251.

District of Columbia
Superintendent of Insurance, P.O. Box 37200, 613 G St., N.W., Ste. 516, Washington, DC 20013-7200; (202) 727-8000.

Florida
Insurance Commissioner, Plaza Level Eleven--The Capitol, Tallahassee, FL 32399-0300; (904) 922-3100, or (800) 342-2762 (toll free in FL).

Georgia
Insurance Commissioner, 2 Martin L. King, Jr., Dr., West Tower,

Insurance Regulators

Room 716, Atlanta, GA 30334; (404) 656-2070.

Guam
Insurance Commissioner, P.O. Box 2796, Agana, GU 96910; 011 (671) 445-5000.

Hawaii
Insurance Commissioner, P.O. Box 3614, Honolulu, HI 96811; (808) 586-2790.

Idaho
Director of Insurance, 500 S. 10th St., Boise, ID 83720; (208) 334-4320.

Illinois
Director of Insurance, 320 W. Washington St., 4th Floor, Springfield, IL 62767; (217) 782-4515.

Indiana
Commissioner of Insurance, 311 W. Washington St., Suite 300, Indianapolis, IN 46204; (317) 232-2385, or (800) 622-4461 (toll-free in IN).

Iowa
Insurance Commissioner, Lucas State Office Building, 6th Floor, Des Moines, IA 50319; (515) 281-5705.

Kansas
Commissioner of Insurance, 420 SW 9th St., Topeka, KS 66612; (913) 296-7829, or (800) 432-2484 (toll free in KS).

Kentucky
Insurance Commissioner, 215 W. Main St., Frankfort, KY 40601; (502) 564-6088.

Louisiana
Commissioner of Insurance, P.O. Box 94214, Baton Rouge, LA 70804-9214; (504) 342-1259.

Maine
Superintendent of Insurance, State House Station 34, Augusta, ME 04333; (207) 624-8475 or (800) 300-5000.

Maryland
Insurance Commissioner Office, 501 St. Paul Place, 7th Floor South, Baltimore, MD 21202; (410) 333-1782, or (800) 492-7521 (toll free in MD).

Massachusetts
Division of Insurance, 280 Friend St., Boston, MA 02114; (617) 727-7189, ext. 300.

Michigan
Michigan Insurance Bureau, 611 W. Ottawa St., 2nd Floor North, Lansing, MI 48933; (517) 373-0240.

Minnesota
Department of Commerce, Commissioner of Insurance, 133 E. 7th Street, St. Paul, MN 55101; (612) 296-2594, (800) 652-9747 (in MN).

Insurance Regulators

Mississippi
Commissioner of Insurance, 1804 Walter Sillers Building, Jackson, MS 39201; (601) 359-3569 or 1(800) 562-2957.

Missouri
Director of Insurance, 301 W. High Street, Room 630, P.O. Box 690, Jefferson City, MO 65102-0690; (573) 751-2640, (800) 726-7390 (MO only).

Montana
Commissioner of Insurance, 126 North Sanders, Mitchell Building, Room 270, Helena, MT 59620; (406) 444-2040, or (800) 332-6148 (toll free in MT).

Nebraska
Director of Insurance, 941 "O" Street, Suite 400, Lincoln, NE 68508; (402) 471-2201.

Nevada
Commissioner of Insurance, 1165 Hotspring Road, Capitol Complex 152, Carson City, NV 89710; (702) 687-4270, or (800) 992-0900 (toll free in NV).

New Hampshire
Insurance Commissioner, 169 Manchester St., Concord, NH 03301; (603) 271-2261, or (800) 852-3416 (toll free in NH).

New Jersey
Commissioner, Department of Insurance, CN325-20 West State St., Trenton, NJ 08625; (609) 984-2444.

New Mexico
Superintendent of Insurance, 500 Old Santa Fe Trail, P.O. Drawer 1269, Santa Fe, NM 87501; (505) 827-4698.

New York
Superintendent of Insurance, 160 W. Broadway, Consumer Bureau, 19th Floor, New York, NY 10013; (212) 602-2488, or (800) 342-3736 (toll free in NY).

North Carolina
Commissioner of Insurance, Dobbs Building, P.O. Box 26387, Raleigh, NC 27611; (919) 733-7343, (800) 662-7777 (within NC).

North Dakota
Commissioner of Insurance, State Capitol Bldg, 5th Floor, 600 East Blvd. Ave., Bismarck, ND 58505-0520; (701) 328-2440, or (800) 247-0560 (toll free in ND).

Ohio
Director of Insurance, 2100 Stella Court, Columbus, OH 43266-0566; (614) 644-2651, or (800) 686-1526 and (800) 686-1527 (toll free in OH).

Oklahoma
Insurance Commissioner, P.O. Box 53408, Oklahoma City, OK 73152; (405) 521-2991, or (800) 522-0071 (toll free in OK).

Insurance Regulators

Oregon
Insurance Commissioner, 440 Labor and Industries Building, Salem, OR 97310; (503) 378-4271.

Pennsylvania
Insurance Commissioner, Strawberry Square, 13th Floor, Harrisburg, PA 17120; (717) 787-2317.

Puerto Rico
Commissioner of Insurance, P.O. Box 8330, Fernandez Juncos Station, Santurce, PR 00910; (809) 722-8686.

Rhode Island
Insurance Commissioner, 233 Richmond Street, Providence, RI 02903; (401) 277-2223.

South Carolina
Insurance Commissioner, 1612 Marion Street, or P.O. Box 100105, Columbia, SC 29202-3105; (803) 737-6150 and (800) 737-6180.

South Dakota
Director of Insurance, 500 E. Capital, Pierre, SD 57501-3940; (605) 773-3563.

Tennessee
Commissioner of Insurance, 500 James Robertson Parkway, Volunteer Plaza, Nashville, TN 37243; (615) 741-2218, or (800) 342-4029 (toll free in TN).

Texas
Department of Insurance, Commissioner of Insurance, P.O. Box 149104, Austin, TX 78714-9104; (512) 463-6464, or (800) 252-3439 (toll free in TX).

Utah
Commissioner of Insurance, 3110 State Office Building, Salt Lake City, UT 84114; (801) 538-3805.

Vermont
Commissioner of Insurance, Banking and Securities, 89 Main St., #20, Montpelier, VT 05620-3101; (802) 828-4884.

Virgin Islands
Commissioner of Insurance, 18 Kongens Garde, St. Thomas, VI 00802; (809) 774-7166.

Virginia
Commissioner of Insurance, 700 Jefferson Building, or P.O. Box 1157, Richmond, VA 23219; (804) 371-9694, or (800) 552-7945 (toll free in VA).

Washington
Insurance Commissioner Office, Insurance Building, P.O. Box 40255, Olympia, WA 98504; (360) 753-3613, or (800) 562-6900 (toll free in WA).

Insurance Regulators

West Virginia
Insurance Commissioner, 2019 Washington St., East, P.O. Box 50540, Charleston, WV 25305; (304) 558-3856, or (800) 642-9004 (toll free in WV).

Wisconsin
Commissioner of Insurance, P.O. Box 7873, Madison, WI 53707-7873; (608) 266-0103, or (800) 236-8517 (toll free in WI).

Wyoming
Commissioner of Insurance, 122 W. 25th St., Cheyenne, WY 82002; (307) 777-7401, (800) 442-4333 (within WY).

Internal Revenue Service
Problem Resolution Centers

These special IRS offices are set up to help those who just cannot get their tax-related problems solved through normal IRS channels. Call the office serving your state to see if you qualify. Also see *Taxes* on page 193 for more information on this program.

Alabama
Birmingham: (205) 731-1177

Alaska
Anchorage: (907) 561-7484

Arizona
Phoenix: (800) 829-1040

Arkansas
Little Rock: (501) 378-6260

California
Laguna Niguel: (714) 643-4182
Los Angeles: (213) 894-6953
Sacramento: (916) 978-4079
San Francisco: (415) 556-5046
San Jose: (408) 291-7132

Colorado
Denver: (303) 446-1012

Connecticut
Hartford: (203) 240-4179

Delaware
Wilmington: (302) 791-4502

Florida
Ft. Lauderdale: (305) 424-2385

Jacksonville: (904) 232-3440

Georgia
Atlanta: (404) 522-0050

Hawaii
Honolulu: (808) 541-1040

Idaho
Boise: (208) 334-1324

Illinois
Springfield: (217) 492-4517

Indiana
Indianapolis: (317) 226-5477

Iowa
Des Moines: (515) 284-4780

Kansas
Wichita: (800) 829-1040

Kentucky
Louisville: (502) 582-6030

Louisiana
New Orleans: (504) 589-3001

Maine
Augusta: (207) 780-3309

IRS Ombudsmen

Maryland
Baltimore: (301) 962-3324

Massachusetts
Boston: (617) 565-1857

Michigan
Detroit: (313) 226-4380

Minnesota
St. Paul: (612) 290-3077

Mississippi
Jackson: (800) 829-1040: (toll-free)

Missouri
St. Louis. (314) 539-6770

Montana
Helena: (406) 449-5244

Nebraska
Omaha: (402) 221-4181

Nevada
Las Vegas: (702) 455-1098

New Jersey
Newark: (201) 645-6698

New Mexico
Albuquerque: (505) 766-3760

New York
Albany: (518) 472-4482
Brooklyn: (718) 488-2083
Buffalo: (716) 846-4574
Manhattan: (212) 264-2850

North Carolina
Greensboro: (919) 333-5497

North Dakota
Fargo: (701) 239-5400

Ohio
Cincinnati: (513) 684-3094
Cleveland: (216) 522-7134

Oklahoma
Oklahoma City: (405) 231-4150

Oregon
Portland: (503) 221-3960

Pennsylvania
Philadelphia: (215) 597-3377
Pittsburgh: (412) 644-5987

Rhode Island
Providence: 1(800) 829-1040

South Carolina
Columbia: (803) 765-5939

South Dakota
Aberdeen: (605) 226-7278, ext. 7278

Tennessee
Nashville: (615) 736-5219

Texas
Dallas: (214) 767-1289
Houston: (713) 653-3660

Utah
Salt Lake City: (801) 524-6287

IRS Ombudsmen

Vermont
    Burlington: 1(800) 829-1040

Virginia
    Richmond: (804) 771-2643

Washington
    Seattle: (206) 442-1040

West Virginia
    Parkersburg: (304) 420-6616

Wisconsin
    Milwaukee: (414) 297-3046

Wyoming
    Cheyenne: (307) 772-2489

U.S. Department Of Justice
Antitrust Offices

This office handles complaints about price fixing, bid rigging, collusion, and antitrust violations. For more detailed information, see *Bids on Government Contracts* on page 33.

Atlanta
Richard B. Russell Bldg., Suite 1176, 75 Spring St., SW, Atlanta, GA 30303; (404) 331-7100.

Chicago
John C. Kluczynski Building, Room 3820, 230 S. Dearborn St., Chicago, IL 60604; (312) 353-7530.

Cleveland
55 Erie View Bldg., Ste. 700, Plaza #9, Cleveland, OH 44111-8216; (216) 522-4070.

Dallas
Earle Cabell Federal Building, Room 8C6, 1100 Commerce St., Dallas, TX 75242; (214) 767-8051.

New York
Room 3630, 26 Federal Plaza, New York, NY 10278-0096; (212) 264-0390.

Philadelphia
Suite 650, West Curtis Center, 7th & Walnut, Philadelphia, PA 19106; (215) 597-7405.

San Francisco
450 Golden Gate Ave., Box 36046, San Francisco, CA 94102; (415) 556-6300.

Washington, D.C.
10th St. & Pennsylvania Ave., NW, Washington, D.C. 20530; (202) 514-2421.

U.S. Department Of Labor

The U.S. Department of Labor works to protect workers' pensions, wages, and overtime rights, and to improve their working conditions. For more detailed information see *Wages and Overtime Pay* on page 203, *Garnishment of Wages* on page 91, *Federal Contractors* on page 82, *Migrant and Farm Workers* on page 142, and *Health and Safety Hazards at Work* on page 101.

Atlanta
U.S. Department of Labor, 1371 Peachtree Street, NE, Room 317, Atlanta, GA 30367; (404) 347-4495; OSHA: (404) 347-3573.

Boston
U.S. Dept of Labor, JFK Bldg, 1 Congress Street, 11th Floor, Boston, MA 02114; (617) 565-2072; OSHA (617) 565-7164.

Chicago
U.S. Department of Labor, New Federal Building, 5th Floor, 230 S. Dearborn Street, IL 60604; (312) 353-4807; OSHA: (312) 353-2220.

Dallas
U.S. Department of Labor, 525 Griffin St., Federal Building, Room 734, Dallas, TX 75202; (214) 767-4777; OSHA: (214) 767-4731.

Denver
U.S. Department of Labor, 1468 Federal Office Building, 1961 Stout St., Denver, CO 80294; (303) 844-4235; OSHA: (303) 844-4235.

Kansas City
U.S. Department of Labor, Federal Office Building, Room 2509, 911 Walnut St., Kansas City, MO 64106; (816) 426-5481; OSHA: (816) 426-5861.

New York
U.S. Department of Labor, 201 Varick St., Room 605, New York, NY 10014; (212) 337-2319; OSHA: (212) 337-2319.

Philadelphia
U.S. Department of Labor, Gateway Building, Room 14120, 3535 Market St., Philadelphia, PA 19104; (215) 596-1139; OSHA: (215) 596-1201.

San Francisco
U.S. Department of Labor, 71 Stevenson St., Room 1035, San Francisco, CA 94102; (415) 975-4740; OSHA: (415) 744-6670.

Seattle
U.S. Department of Labor, 1111 3rd Ave., Ste. 805, Seattle, WA 98101; (206) 553-7620; OSHA (206) 553-5930.

National Labor Relations Board

The National Labor Relations Board (NLRB) protects employees' rights to conduct union-type activities, such as discussing their working conditions and salaries with one another and bringing complaints to the attention of management. See *Working Conditions* on page 205 for more detailed information on what the NLRB can do for you.

Alaska
222 West 7th Avenue, #21, Anchorage, AK 99513-3546; (907) 271-5015, Fax: (907) 271-3055.

Arizona
234 N. Central Ave., Suite 440, Phoenix, AZ 85004-2212; (602) 379-3361, Fax: (602) 379-4982.

Arkansas
425 W. Capital St., Room 375, Little Rock, AR 72201-3489; (501) 324-6311, Fax: (501) 324-5009.

California
888 S. Figueroa St., 9th Floor, Los Angeles, CA 90017-5455; (213) 894-5200, Fax: (213) 894-2778.

11000 Wilshire Blvd., Room 12100, Los Angeles, CA 90024-3682; (310) 235-7352, Fax: (310) 235-7420.

1301 Clay St., Room 300N, Oakland, CA 94612-5211; (510) 637-3300, Fax: (510) 637-3315. 555 W. Beech St., Suite 302, San Diego, CA 92101-2939; (619) 557-6184, Fax: (619) 557-6358.

901 Market St., Room 400, San Francisco, CA 94103-1735; (415) 356-5206, Fax: (415) 356-5156.

Colorado
600 17th St., 3rd Floor, South Tower, Denver, CO 80202-5433; (303) 844-3551, Fax: (303) 844-6249.

Connecticut
One Commercial Plaza, 21st Floor, Hartford, CT 06103-3599; (860) 240-3522, Fax: (860) 240-3564.

District of Columbia
Franklin Court Bldg., 1099 14th St., Suite 5530, Washington, DC 20037-1560; (202) 208-3000, Fax: (202) 208-3013.

Florida
400 W. Bay St., Room 214, Box 35091, Jacksonville, FL 32202-4412; (904) 232-3768, Fax: (904) 232-3146.

51 SW First Avenue, Room 1320, Miami, FL 33130-1608; (305) 536-5391, Fax: (305) 536-5320.

Suite 530, Enterprise, 201 E. Kennedy Blvd., Tampa, FL 33602-4081; (813) 228-2641, Fax: (813) 228-2874.

Georgia
101 Marietta St., NW, Suite 2400, Atlanta, GA 30323-3301; (404) 331-2896, Fax: (404) 331-2858.

Hawaii
300 Ala Moana Blvd., Room 7318, Honolulu, HI 96850-4980; (808) 541-2814, Fax: (808) 541-2818.

Illinois
200 W. Adams St., Suite 800, Chicago, IL 60606-5208; (312) 353-7570, Fax: (312) 886-1341.

300 Hamilton Blvd., Suite 200, Peoria, IL 61602-1246; (309) 671-7080, Fax: (309) 671-7095.

Indiana
575 N. Pennsylvania St., Room 238, Indianapolis, IN 46204-1577; (317) 226-7430, Fax: (317) 226-5103.

Iowa
210 Walnut St., Room 909, Des Moines, IA 50309-2116; (515) 284-4391, Fax: (515) 284-4713.

Kansas
8600 Farley St., Suite 100, Mission, KS 66212-4677; (913) 967-3000, Fax: (913) 967-3010.

Louisiana
1515 Poydras St., Room 610, New Orleans, LA 70112-3723; (504) 589-6361, Fax: (504) 589-4069.

Maryland
103 S. Gay St., 8th Floor, Baltimore, MD 21202-4026; (410) 962-2822, Fax: (410) 962-2198.

Massachusetts
10 Causeway St., 6th Floor, Boston, MA 02222-1072; (617) 565-6700, Fax: (617) 565-6725.

Michigan
477 Michigan Ave., Room 300, Detroit, MI 48226-2569; (313) 226-3200, Fax: (313) 226-2090.

82 Ionia NW, Room 330, Grand Rapids, MI 49503-3022; (616) 456-2679, Fax: (616) 456-2596.

Minnesota
110 S. 4th St., Room 316, Minneapolis, MN 55401-2291; (612) 348-1757, Fax: (612) 348-1785.

Missouri
1222 Spruce St., Room 8-302, St. Louis, MO 63101-2829; (314) 539-7770, Fax: (314) 539-7794

New Jersey
970 Broad St., Room 1600, Newark, NJ 07102-2570; (201) 645-2100, Fax: (201) 645-3852.

New Mexico
505 Marquette Ave., NW, Room

National Labor Relations Board

1820, Albuquerque, NM 87102-2181; (505) 248-5125, Fax: (505) 248-5134.

New York
Clinton Avenue & N. Pearl Street, Room 342, Albany, NY 12207-2350; (518) 431-4155, Fax: (518) 431-4157.

Jay Street and Myrtle Avenue, 10th Floor, Brooklyn, NY 11201-4201, (718) 330-7713, Fax: (718) 330-7579.

111 W. Huron St., Room 901, Buffalo, NY 14202-2387; (716) 551-4931, Fax: (716) 551-4972.

26 Federal Plaza, Room 3614, New York, NY 10278-0104; (212) 264-0300, Fax: (212) 264-8427.

Nevada
600 Las Vegas Boulevard, South, Room 400, Las Vegas, NV 89101-6637; (702) 388-6416, Fax: (702) 388-6248.

North Carolina
4035 University Parkway, Suite 200, Winston-Salem, NC 27106-3325; (910) 631-5201, Fax: (910) 631-5210.

Ohio
550 Main St., Room 3003, Cincinnati, OH 45202-3721; (513) 684-3686, Fax: (513) 684-3946.

1240 E. 9th St., Room 1695, Cleveland, OH 44199-2086; (216) 522-3715, Fax: (216) 522-2418.

Oklahoma
111 W. 5th Street, Suite 990, Tulsa, OK 74127-8916; (918) 581-7951, Fax: (918) 581-7970.

Oregon
222 SW Columbia St., Room 401, Portland, OR 97201-5878; (503) 326-3085, Fax: (503) 326-5387.

Pennsylvania
615 Chestnut St., 7th Floor, Philadelphia, PA 19106-4404; (215) 597-7601, Fax: (215) 597-7658.

1000 Liberty Ave, Room 1501, Pittsburgh, PA 15222-4173, (412) 395-6844, Fax: (412) 395-5956.

Puerto Rico
Plaza Las Americas, 525 F.D. Roosevelt Ave., Suite 1002, Hato Rey, PR 00918-1720; (787) 766-5347, Fax: (787) 766-5478.

Tennessee
1407 Union Ave., Suite 800, Memphis, TN 38104-3627; (901) 722-2725.

801 Broadway, Room 716, Nashville, TN 37203-3816; (615) 736-5921.

Texas
P.O. Box 23159, El Paso, TX 79923; (915) 565-2470, Fax: (915) 565-0847.

819 Taylor St., Room 8A24, Fort Worth, TX 76102-6178; (817)

National Labor Relations Board

978-2921, Fax: (817) 978-2928.

40 Louisiana St., Suite 550, Houston, TX 77002-2649; (713) 718-4622, Fax: (713) 718-4640.

615 E. Houston St., Room 565, San Antonio, TX 78205-2040; (210) 229-6140, Fax: (210) 472-6143.

Washington
915 Second Ave., Room 2948, Seattle, WA 98174-1078; (206) 220-6300, Fax: (206) 220-6305.

Wisconsin
310 W. Wisconsin Ave., Suite 700, Milwaukee, WI 53203-2211; (414) 297-3861, Fax: (414) 297-3880.

Lawyer Programs

Often affiliated with the State Bar Associations, these offices can help you resolve ethical, billing, and theft complaints against lawyers in your state. The Attorney Grievance programs deal with ethical complaints, the Fee Arbitration programs will help resolve billing complaints, and the Client Security Trust Funds provides money to clients who have had money stolen from them by their lawyers. See *Lawyers* on page 127 for more detailed information.

Alabama
Attorney Grievances
Alabama State Bar, Center for Professional Responsibility, P.O. 671, Montgomery, AL 36104; (205) 269-1515.

Client Security Trust Fund & Fee Arbitration
Alabama State Bar, P.O. Box 671, Montgomery, AL 36104; (205) 269-1515.

Alaska
Attorney Grievances, Client Security Trust Fund, & Fee Arbitration
Alaska Bar Association, P.O. Box 100279, 510 L. St., Suite 602, Anchorage, AK 99501; (907) 272-7469.

Arizona
Attorney Grievances, Client Security Trust Fund, & Fee Arbitration
Chief Bar Counsel, State Bar of Arizona, 363 N. First Ave., Phoenix, AZ 85003-1580; (602) 252-4804.

Arkansas
Attorney Grievances
Committee on Professional Conduct, 364 Prospect Building, 1501 N. University, Little Rock, AR 72207; (501) 664-8658.

Client Security Trust Fund
Clerk, Clerk Office, 625 Marshall St., Little Rock, AR 72201; (501) 682-6849.

California
Attorney Grievances
Southern California
Chief Trial Counsel, State Bar of California, 333 S. Deaudry Ave., 9th Floor, Los Angeles, CA 90017; (213) 765-1029, or (800) 843-9053 (toll-free in CA).

Northern California
Chief Trial Counsel, State Bar of California, 555 Franklin St., San Francisco, CA 94102; (415) 561-8200, or (800) 843-9053 (toll-free in CA).

Client Security Trust Fund
Southern California Grievance Committee, State Bar of California, 333 S. Deaudry Ave., 9th Floor, Los Angeles, CA 90017; (213) 580-5140.

Fee Arbitration
Chief Trial Counsel, State Bar of California, 555 Franklin St., San Francisco, CA 94102; (415) 561-8200, or (800) 843-9053 (toll-free in CA).

Colorado
Attorney Grievances S.C.D.C
Disciplinary Counsel, Supreme Court of Colorado, Dominion Plaza Bldg., 600 17th St., Suite 510 S., Denver, CO 80202; (303) 893-8121.

Client Security Trust Fund
Colorado Bar Association, 1900 Grant St., Suite 950, Denver, CO 80203-4309; (303) 860-1112, or (800) 332-6736 (toll-free in CO).

Fee Arbitration
Legal Fee Arbitration Committee, Colorado Bar Association, 1900 Grant St., Suite 950, Denver, CO 80203-4309; (303) 860-1112, or (800) 332-6736 (toll-free in CO).

Connecticut
Attorney Grievances
Statewide Grievance Committee, P.O. Box 260888, Hartford, CT 06126-0888; (203) 247-6264.

Client Security Trust Fund
Boyer, Hogan, Evan, State Bar Association, 101 Corporate Place Rocky Hill, CT 06067-1894; (203) 787-1250

Committee on Arbitration of Fee Disputes
State Bar Association, 101 Corporate Place, Rocky Hill, CT 06067-1894; (203) 721-0025.

Delaware
Attorney Grievances
Office of Disciplinary Counsel, 831 Tatnall Street, Wilmington, DE 19801; (302) 571-8703.

Client Security Trust Fund
Kimmel, Wiese, Carter, P.O. Box 272, Wilmington, DE 19899; (302) 571-0800.

Fee Dispute Conciliation and Mediation Committee
Colin Shalk, Attorney, P.O. Box 1276, Wilmington, DE 19899; (302) 594-4500.

District of Columbia
Attorney Grievances
Office of Bar Counsel, 515 5th St., NW, Building A, Room 127, Washington, DC 20001; (202) 638-1501.

Client Security Trust Fund
District of Columbia Bar, 1707 L St., NW, 6th Floor, Washington, DC 20036; (202) 331-3883.

Lawyer Programs

Fee Arbitration
Attorney-Client Arbitration Board, District of Columbia Bar, 1707 L St., NW, 6th Floor, Washington, DC 20036; (202) 331-3883.

Florida
Attorney Grievances, Client Security Trust Fund, & Fee Arbitration
Staff Counsel, Florida Bar, 650 Apalachee Parkway, Tallahassee, FL 32399-2300; (904) 561-5839, or (800) 342-8060 (toll-free in FL), or (800) 874-0005 (toll-free out-of-state).

Georgia
Attorney Grievances, Client Security Trust Fund, & Committee on Arbitration of Fee Disputes
State Bar of Georgia, Office of General Counsel, 800 Hurt Bldg., 50 Hurt Plaza, Atlanta, GA 30303; (404) 527-8720.

Hawaii
Attorney Grievances
Office of Disciplinary Counsel, Supreme Court of the State of Hawaii, 1164 Bishop St., Suite 600, Honolulu, HI 96813; (808) 521-4591.

Client Security Trust Fund
Hawaii Supreme Court Clerk, P.O. Box 2560, Honolulu, HI 96804; (808) 599-8938.

Fee Arbitration
Attorney-Client Coordination Committee, Hawaii State Bar Association, P.O. Box 26, Honolulu, HI 96810; (808) 537-1868.

Idaho
Attorney Grievances, Client Security Trust Fund, & Fee Arbitration
Bar Counsel, Idaho State Bar, P.O. Box 895, Boise, ID 83701; (208) 334-4500.

Illinois
Attorney Grievances
Attorney Registration and Disciplinary Commission of the Supreme Court of Illinois, 203 N. Wabash Ave., Suite 1900, Chicago, IL 60601-2472; (312) 346-0690, or (800) 826-8625 (toll-free in IL).

Attorney Registration and Disciplinary Commission of the Supreme Court of Illinois, One North Old Capitol Plaza, Suite 345, Springfield, IL 62701-1507; (217) 522-6838, or (800) 252-8048 (toll-free in IL).

Client Security Trust Fund & Fee Arbitration
Bar of Illinois, Illinois Bar Center, Springfield, IL 62701; (217) 525-1760.

Lawyer Programs

Indiana
Attorney Grievances
Disciplinary Commission of the Supreme Court of Indiana, 150 W. Market Street, Room 628, Indianapolis, IN 46204; (317) 232-1807.

Clients' Financial Assistance Fund
Attn: Jack Lyle, Indiana State Bar Association, 230 E. Ohio Street, 4th Floor, Indianapolis, IN 46204; (317) 639-5465.

Fee Arbitration
Contact Clients' Financial Assistance Fund for referral to local programs.

Iowa
Attorney Grievances and Fee Arbitration
Iowa State Bar Association, 521 E. Locust, Des Moines, IA 50309; (515) 243-0027, or (800) 532-1100 (in-state).

Client Security Trust Fund
Client Security Trust Fund Commission, Iowa Supreme Court, Iowa State House, State Capitol, Des Moines, IA 50319; (515) 246-8076.

Kansas
Attorney Grievances
Disciplinary Administrator, Supreme Court of Kansas, 3706 S. Topeka Avenue, Suite 100, Topeka, KS 66609; (913) 296-2486.

Client Security Trust Fund & Fee Arbitration
Kansas Bar Association, P.O. Box 1037, Topeka, KS 66601-1037; (913) 234-5696.

Kentucky
Attorney Grievances, Client Security Trust Fund, Fee Arbitration
Kentucky Bar Association, 514 W. Main, Frankfort, KY 40601-1883; (502) 564-3795.

Louisiana
Grievance & Client Security Trust Fund
Executive Counsel, Louisiana State Bar Association, 601 St. Charles Avenue, New Orleans, LA 70130; (504) 293-3900, or (800) 421-5722 (toll-free in LA).

Maine
Attorney Grievances and Fee Arbitration
Maine Board of Overseers of the Bar, P.O. Box 1820, Augusta, ME 04332-1820; (207) 623-1121.

Maryland
Attorney Grievance Commission and the Committee on Resolution of Fee Disputes
100 Community Place, Suite 3301, Crownsville, MD 21032;

(410) 514-7051, or (800) 492-1660 (toll-free in MD).

Client Security Trust Fund
P.O. Box 284, 18222 Flower Hill Way, Gaithersburg, MD 20879-5300; (301) 990-8812.

Massachusetts
Attorney Grievances and Client Security Trust Fund
Massachusetts Board of Bar Overseers, 75 Federal St., Boston, MA 02110; (617) 357-1860.

Fee Arbitration
Massachusetts Bar Association, Fee Arbitration Board, Attn: Stacy Shunk, 20 West St., Boston, MA 02111-1218; (617) 542-3602.

Michigan
Attorney Grievances
Michigan Attorney Grievance Commission, 243 W. Congress, Marquette Bldg., Suite 256, Detroit, MI 48226; (313) 961-6585.

Client Security Trust Fund and Fee Arbitration
State Bar of Michigan, 306 Townsend St., Lansing, MI 48933-2083; (517) 372-9030.

Minnesota
Attorney Grievances and Client Security Trust Fund

Office of Lawyers' Professional Responsibility, 520 Lafayette Rd., First Floor, St. Paul, MN 55155-4196; (612) 296-3952, or (800) 657-3601 (toll-free in MN).

Fee Arbitration
Minnesota Bar Association, 514 Nicollet Mall, Suite 300, Minneapolis, MN 55402; (612) 333-1183, or (800) 882-MSBA (toll-free in MN).

Mississippi
Attorney Grievances, Client Security Trust Fund, & Fee Arbitration
Mississippi State Bar, P.O. Box 2168, Jackson, MS 39225-2168; (601) 948-4471, or (800) 682-6423 (toll-free in MS).

Missouri
Attorney Grievances
Office of Chief Disciplinary Council, 3335 American Avenue, Jefferson City, MO 65119; (816) 826-7890.

Client Security Trust Fund & Fee Arbitration
Missouri Bar Association, P.O. Box 119, Jefferson City, MO 65102; (314) 635-7400.

Montana
Attorney Grievances
Commission on Practice of the Supreme Court of Montana, Justice Building, Room 315, 215

N. Sanders, Helena, MT 59620-3002; (406) 442-7660.

Client Security Trust Fund & Fee Arbitration
State Bar of Montana, P.O. Box 577, Helena, MT 59624; (406) 442-7660.

Nebraska
Attorney Grievances
Counsel for Discipline, Nebraska State Bar Association, 635 S. 14th St., Lincoln, NE 68508; (402) 475-7091.

Client Security Fund
P.O. Box 790, Grand Island, NE 68802; (308) 382-1930.

Nevada
Attorney Grievances, Client Security Trust Fund, & Fee Arbitration
State Bar of Nevada, 201 Las Vegas Blvd., Suite 200, Las Vegas, NV 89101; (702) 382-2200.

New Hampshire
Attorney Grievances
New Hampshire Supreme Court, Professional Conduct Committee, 4 Park Street, Suite 304, Concord, NH 03301; (603) 224-5828.
Clients' Indemnity Fund & Fee Resolution Committee
New Hampshire Bar Association, 112 Pleasant Street, Concord, NH 03301; (603) 224-6942.

New Jersey
Attorney Grievances & Fee Arbitration
Supreme Court of New Jersey, Richard J. Hughes Justice Complex, CN-963, Trenton, NJ 08625; (609) 530-4008.

Client Security Trust Fund
Supreme Court of New Jersey, Richard J. Hughes Justice Complex, CN-961, Trenton, NJ 08625; (609) 984-7179.

New Mexico
Attorney Grievances
Disciplinary Board of the Supreme Court of New Mexico, 400 Gold SW, Suite 1100, Albuquerque, NM 87102; (505) 842-5781.

Fee Arbitration
State Bar of New Mexico, Fee Arbitration Committee, P.O. Box 25883, Albuquerque, NM 87125; (505) 842-6132, or (800) 876-6227 (toll-free in NM).

New York
Attorney Grievances
Departmental Disciplinary Committee for the First Judicial Department, 41 Madison Ave., 39th Floor, New York, NY 10010; (212) 685-1000.
New York State Grievance Committee for the 2nd and 11th Judicial Districts, 210 Joralemon Street, Municipal Bldg., Room 1200, Brooklyn, NY 11201; (718) 624-7851.

Grievance Committee for the 9th Judicial District, Crosswest Office Center, 399 Knollwood Road, Suite 200, White Plains, NY 10603; (914) 949-4540.

New York State Grievance Committee for the 10th Judicial District, 900 Ellison Avenue, Suite 304, Westbury, NY 11590; (516) 364-7344.

3rd Department Committee on Professional Standards, Alfred E. Smith Building, 22nd Floor, P.O. Box 7013, Capitol Station Annex, Albany, NY 12225-0013; (518) 474-8816.

Appellate Division, Supreme Court, 4th Judicial Department, Office of Grievance Committee, 1036 Ellicott Square Building, Buffalo, NY 14203; (716) 858-1190.

Lawyers' Fund for Client Protection
55 Elk Street, Albany, NY 12210; (518) 474-8438, or (800) 442-3863 (toll-free in NY).

North Carolina
Attorney Grievances, Client Security Trust Fund, & Fee Arbitration
North Carolina State Bar, P.O. Box 25908, Raleigh, NC 27611; (919) 828-4620.

North Dakota
Attorney Grievances
Disciplinary Board of the Supreme Court, P.O. Box 2297, Bismarck, ND 58502; (701) 328-3925.

Client Security Trust Fund & Fee Arbitration
State Bar Association of North Dakota, P.O. Box 2136, Bismarck, ND 58502; (701) 255-1404, or (800) 472-2685 (toll-free in ND).

Ohio
Attorney Grievances
Office of Disciplinary Counsel of the Supreme Court of Ohio, 175 South 3rd Street, Suite 280, Columbus, OH 43215; (614) 461-0256.

Clients' Security Fund
175 S. 3rd St., Suite 285, Columbus, OH 43215; (614) 225-6053, or (800) 231-1680 (toll-free in OH).

Fee Arbitration
Ohio State Bar Association, 1700 Lake Shore Dr., P.O. Box 16562, Columbus, OH 43216-6562, (614) 487-2050, or (800) 282-6556 (toll-free in OH).

Oklahoma
Attorney Grievances, Client Security Trust Fund, & Fee Arbitration
General Counsel, Oklahoma Bar Center, 1901 N. Lincoln Blvd., P.O. Box 53036, Oklahoma, OK 73152; (405) 524-2365.

Oregon

Attorney Grievances & Client Security Trust Fund
Oregon State Bar, P.O. Box 1689, Lake Oswego, OR 97035; (503) 620-0222.

Pennsylvania

Attorney Grievances & Fee Arbitration District 1:
Office of the Disciplinary Counsel, 121 S. Broad St., Suite 2100, N. American Building, Philadelphia, PA 19107; (215) 560-6296.

District 2:
Office of the Disciplinary Counsel, One Montgomery Plaza, Suite 708, Norristown, PA 19401; (215) 270-1896.

District 3:
Office of the Disciplinary Counsel, Third Floor, 2 Lemoyne Dr., 2nd Floor, Harrisburg, PA 171043 (717) 731-7073.

District 4:
Office of the Disciplinary Counsel, Suite 400, Union Trust Building, 501 Grant St., Pittsburgh, PA 15219; (412) 565-3173.

Pennsylvania Client Security Fund
1515 Market St., Suite 1420, Philadelphia, PA 19102; (215) 560-6335.

Puerto Rico

Attorney Grievances
Commission of Professional Ethics, Colegio de Abogados de Puerto Rico, Apartado 1900, San Juan, PR 00903; (809) 721-3358.

Rhode Island

Attorney Grievances & Fee Arbitration
Disciplinary Board of the Supreme Court of Rhode Island, D.B. of the S.C., John E. Fogarty, Judicial Annex, 24 Weybuffet St., 2nd Floor, Providence, RI 02903; (401) 277-3270.

Client Security Trust Fund
Rhode Island Bar Association, 115 Cedar St., Providence, RI 02903; (401) 421-5740.

South Carolina

Attorney Grievances
Grievance Commission, South Carolina Supreme Court, P.O. Box 11330, Columbia, SC 29211; (803) 734-2038.

Client Security Trust Fund & Fee Arbitration
South Carolina Bar, P.O. Box 608, Columbia, SC 29202-0608; (803) 799-6653.

South Dakota

Attorney Grievances
State Bar of South Dakota, Attn: Tom Barnett, 222 East Capitol, Pierre, SD 57501; (605) 224-7554.

Lawyer Programs

Client Security Trust Fund
State Bar of South Dakota, 222 E. Capitol, Pierre, SD 57501; (605) 224-7554, or (800) 952-2333 (toll-free in SD).

Tennessee
Attorney Grievances & Fee Arbitration
Board of Professional Responsibility of the Supreme Court of Tennessee, 1101 Kermit Dr., Suite 730, Nashville, TN 37217; (615) 361-7500.

Texas
Attorney Grievances, Client Security Trust Fund, & Fee Arbitration
State Bar of Texas, P.O. Box 12487, Capitol Station, Austin, TX 78711; (512) 463-1463.

Utah
Attorney Grievances & Fee Arbitration
Bar Counsel, Utah State Bar, 645 S. 200 East, Salt Lake City, UT 84111-3834; (801) 531-9112.

Client Security Trust Fund
Bar Counsel, Utah State Bar, 645 S. 200 East, Salt Lake City, UT 84111-3834; (801) 531-9077.

Vermont
Attorney Grievances
Professional Conduct Board, P.O. Box 680, Brattleboro, VT 05301; (802) 295-4106.

Client Security Trust Fund & Fee Arbitration
Vermont Bar Association, P.O. Box 100, Montpelier, VT 05601; (802) 223-2020.

Virginia
Attorney Grievances
Virginia State Bar, 707 E. Main St., Suite 1500, Attn: Patricia Rios, Richmond, VA 23219-2900; (804) 775-0500.

Client Security Trust Fund
Virginia State Bar, 707 E. Main St., Suite 1500-7, Attn: Susan Busch, Richmond, VA 23219-2900; (804) 775-0500.

Washington
Attorney Grievances, Client Security Trust Fund, & Fee Arbitration
Washington State Bar Association, 500 Westin Bldg., 2001 6th Ave., Seattle, WA 98121-2599; (206) 727-8255.

West Virginia
Attorney Grievances and Client Security Trust Fund
Legal Ethics Committee, West Virginia State Bar, State Capitol, 2006 Kanawha Blvd. East, Charleston, WV 25311; (304) 558-2456.

Wisconsin
Attorney Grievances
Board of Attorneys Professional Responsibility, Tenney Bldg., 110 E. Main St., Room 410, Madison, WI 53703; (608) 267-7274.

287

Client Security Trust Fund and Fee Arbitration
State Bar of Wisconsin, P.O. Box 7158, Madison, WI 53707; (608) 257-3838.

Wyoming
Attorney Grievances, Client Security Trust Fund, & Fee Arbitration
Wyoming State Bar, P.O. Box 109, Cheyenne, WY 82003-0109; (307) 632-9061.

Licensing Boards

Besides issuing licenses to professionals so that they can do business, the following offices act as consumer watchdogs to make sure that those with licenses do business fairly and ethically. Not only will these offices investigate complaints against licensed professionals, they also have the ability to revoke or suspend the licenses if the professional repeatedly acts unprofessionally or unethically. Each state listing includes the professionals licensed in that state, including health professionals along with their different licensing offices where noted. See *Licensed Professionals* on page 128 for more detailed information.

Alabama
State Occupational Information Coordinating Community (SO-ICC), P.O. Box 5690, 401 Adams Ave., Montgomery, AL 36104; (205) 242-2990. Licensing boards and professions: accountants, aircraft personnel, architects, auctioneers, audiologists, speech pathologists, bar pilots, water transportation personnel, boxer and wrestler trainers, classroom teachers, coal mine foremen/ mine electricians, cosmetologists, counselors, dentists, dental hygienists, chiropractors, doctors of medicine, physician's assistants, surgeon's assistants, school bus drivers, embalmer/funeral directors, engineer-in-training and professional engineers, land surveyors, fire fighters, foresters, general contractors, hearing aid specialists, heating and air conditioning contractors, insurance agents, interior designers, landscape architects, landscape horticulturist/planters, lawyers, pest control operators and fumigators, tree surgeons, law enforcement personnel, nurses, nursing home administrators, optometrists, pharmacists, physical therapists, physical therapist assistants, plumbers, podiatrists, polygraph examiners, psychologists, real estate brokers, security salespersons, social workers, veterinarians.

Alaska
Division of Occupational Licensing, Department of Commerce and Economic Development, State of Alaska, PO Box 110806, Juneau, AK 99811-0806; (907) 465-2534. Licensing boards and professions: architects, engineers, land surveyors, audiologists, barbers and hairdressers, chiropractors, collection agencies, construction contractors, concert promoters, dental professionals, dispensing opticians, electrical administrators, geologists, guides, hearing aid dealers, marine pilots, physicians, morticians, naturopaths, nursing, nursing home administrators, optometrists, pharmacists, physical therapists, psychologists, public accountants, veterinarians.

Contacts Close To Home

Arizona

Arizona Department of Revenue, 1600 West Monroe, Phoenix, AZ 85007; (602) 542-4576. Licensing boards and professions: pharmacists, physical therapists, podiatrists, psychologists, chiropractors, dentists, teachers, homeopathic specialists, veterinarians, medical examiners, radiologic technicians, naturopathic physicians, nurses, opticians, optometrists, osteopaths, barbers, cosmetologists, real estate brokers, contractors, technical registrators, insurance agents, physician assistants, nursing care administrators.

Arkansas

Governor's Office, State Capitol Building, Little Rock, AR 72201; (501) 682-2345. Licensing boards and professions: architects, abstracters, accountants, barber examiners, funeral directors, contractors, cosmetologists, dental examiners, electricians, speech pathologists, audiologists, nurses, pharmacists, real estate brokers, veterinary engineers, land surveyors, athletic trainers, chiropractors, collection agencies, counselors, embalmers, foresters, landscape architects, manufactured home builders, physicians, opticians, optometrists, podiatrists, psychologists, sanitarians, social workers, soil classifiers, therapy technologists.

California

State of California, Department of Consumer Affairs, Director and Executives Office, 400 R Street, Suite 3000, Sacramento, CA 95814; (916) 323-2191 (Northern CA), or (415) 553-1814 (San Francisco Bay area), or (213) 974-1452 (Southern CA), or (800) 344-9940 (toll-free in CA). Licensing boards professions: professional engineers, cosmetologists, fabric care technicians, physical therapists, medical quality assurance, physician's assistants, chiropractors, acupuncture specialists, accountants, psychologists, registered nurses, pharmacists, architects, funeral directors, embalmers, landscape architects, veterinarians, animal health technicians, home furnishings decorators, collection and investigative agents, dentists, dental auxiliaries, barbers, behavioral scientists, optometrists, shorthand reporters, structural pest control operators, athletic trainers, vocational nurses, psychiatric technicians, osteopaths, electronic repair dealers, personnel services, geologists and geophysicists, dispensing opticians/ contact lens examiners, respiratory care specialists, nursing home administrators, podiatrists, hearing aid dispensers, speech pathologists, audiologists, tax preparers.

Colorado

Department of Regulatory Agencies, State Services Building, 1560 Broadway, Suite 1550, Denver, CO 80202; (303) 894-7855. Licensing Board/Professions:

accountants, architects, barbers, cosmetologists, chiropractors, dentists, electricians, engineers, hearing aid dealers, insurance agents, land surveyors, mobile home dealers, nurses, nursing home administrators, optometrists, outfitters, pharmacists and pharmacies, physical therapists, physicians, plumbers, psychologists, realtors, ski lift operators, social workers, veterinarians.

Connecticut

Occupational Licensing Division, Department of Consumer Products, 165 Capitol Avenue, Hartford, CT 06106; (203) 566-1107, or (800) 842-2649 (toll-free in CT). Licensed Occupations: electricians, plumbers, heating and cooling specialists, well drillers, elevator installers, home improvement contractors, arborists, TV and radio repair specialists. Licensed Health Professions: Department of Health Services, 150 Washington St., Hartford, CT 06106; (203) 566-7398. Physicians, dentists, optometrists, osteopaths, naturopaths, homeopaths, chiropractors, psychologists, registered nurses, licensed practical nurses, dental hygienists, registered physical therapists, hypertrichologists, audiologists, speech pathologists, podiatrists, hairdressers, barbers, embalmers, funeral directors, sewer installers/cleaners, registered sanitarians, nursing home administrators, hearing aid dealers, opticians,

veterinarians, occupational therapists. Other Licensed Professions: Contact Professional Licensing Division, 165 Capitol Avenue, Room G1, Hartford, CT 06106 (203) 566-1814: architects, landscape architects, engineers, engineers-in-training, land surveyors, pharmacists, patent medicine distributors, mobile manufactured home parks.

Delaware

Division of Professional Regulation, P.O. Box 1401, O'Neil Bldg., Dover, DE 19903; (302) 739-4522. Complaints in writing only. Licensed Professionals: architects, accountants, landscape architects, cosmetologists, barbers, podiatrists, chiropractors, dentists, electricians, adult entertainment, physicians, nurses, real estate brokers, land surveyors, private employment agencies, athletic (wrestling and boxing), deadly weapons dealers, nursing home administrators, funeral directors, social workers, speech pathologists, hearing aid dealers, audiologists, psychologists, veterinarians, optometrists, occupational therapists, pharmacists, river boat pilots.

District of Columbia

Department of Consumer and Regulatory Affairs, 614 H Street NW, Room 108, Washington, DC 20001; (202) 727-7000. Licensing Board/Professions: accountants, architects, barbers, cosmetologists, dentists, dieticians, electricians, funeral directors, physicians, nurses, nursing home administrators, occupational therapists, optometrists, pharmacists, physical therapists, plumbers, podiatrists, engineers, psychologists, real estate agents, refrigeration and air conditioning specialists, social workers, steam and other operating engineers, veterinarians.

Florida
Florida Department of Professional Regulation, Consumer Services, 1940 N. Monroe St., Tallahassee, FL 32399-075; (904) 488-6602. Licensing boards and professions: accountants, architects, barbers, chiropractors, cosmetologists, dentists, dispensing opticians, electrical contractors, professional engineers and land surveyors, landscape architects, funeral directors and embalmers, medical examiners, hearing aid dispensers, naturopathics, nursing home administrators, nurses, optometrists, osteopaths, pharmacists, pilot commissioners, podiatrists, psychologists, real estate brokers, veterinarians, acupuncture technicians, radiological health technicians, laboratory services, entomology specialists, emergency medical personnel.

Georgia
Examining Board Division, Secretary of State, 166 Pryor Street, SW, Atlanta, GA 30303; (404) 656-3900. Licensing boards and professions: accountants, architects, athletic trainers, auctioneers, barbers, chiropractors, construction industry, cosmetologists, professional counselors, social workers, marriage and family therapists, dietitians, dentists, engineers, land surveyors, foresters, funeral directors/ embalmers, geologists, hearing aid dealers and dispensers, landscape architects, librarians, physicians, nurses, nursing home administrators, occupational therapists, dispensing opticians, optometrists, pharmacists, physical therapists, podiatrists, polygraph testers, practical nurses, private detectives and security agencies, psychologists, recreation specialists, sanitarians, speech pathologists, audiologists, used car dealers, used motor vehicle dismantlers, rebuilders, and salvage dealers, veterinarians, water/ wastewater treatment plant operators and laboratory analysts.

Hawaii
Office of the Director, Department of Commerce and Consumer Affairs, P.O. Box 3469, Honolulu, HI 96801; (808) 586-2846. Licensing boards and professions: accountants, acupuncture specialists, barbers, boxers, chiropractors, contractors, cosmetologists, dental examiners, detectives and guards, electricians and plumbers, elevator mechanics, engineers, architects,

land surveyors, landscape architects, hearing aid dealers and fitters, massage specialists, physicians, motor vehicle Industry, motor vehicle repair technicians, naturopaths, nurses, nursing home administrators, dispensing opticians, optometrists, osteopaths, pest control operators, pharmacists, physical therapists, psychologists, real estate brokers, speech pathologists, audiologists, veterinarians, embalmers/ funeral directors, collection agencies, commercial employment agencies, mortgage and collection servicing agents, mortgage brokers and solicitors, port pilots, time sharing and travel agents.

Idaho

State of Idaho, Department of Self-Governing Agencies, Bureau of Occupational Licenses, Owyhua Plaza, 1109 Main Street #220, Boise, ID 83702; (208) 334-3233. Licensing boards and professions: accountants, athletic directors, bartenders, engineers, land surveyors, dentists, geologists, physicians, architects, barbers, chiropractors, cosmetologists, counselors, dentists, environmental health specialists, hearing aid dealers and fitters, landscape architects, morticians, nursing home administrators, optometrists, podiatrists, psychologists, social workers, outfitters and guides, pharmacists, public works contractors, real estate brokers.

Illinois

State of Illinois, Department of Professional Regulations, 320 W. Washington, Third Floor, Springfield, IL 62786; (217) 785-0800. Licensed professions: athletic trainers, architects, barbers, cosmetologists, chiropractors, collection agencies, controlled substance specialists, dentists and dental auxiliaries, polygraph testers, detectives, embalmers, funeral directors, land sales, land surveyors, physicians, nurses, nursing home administrators, occupational therapists, optometrists, pharmacists, physical therapists, podiatrists, boxing and wrestling, engineers, psychologists, accountants, real estate brokers and salespersons, roofing contractors, shorthand reporters, social workers, structural engineers, veterinarians.

Indiana

Indiana Professional Licensing Agency, 1021 State Office Bldg., Indianapolis, IN 46204; (317) 232-3997. Licensing boards and professions: accountants, architects, auctioneers, barbers, beauticians, boxers, engineers and land surveyors, funeral directors, plumbers, real estate agents, TV-radio and watch repair technicians. Licensed health professionals: Indiana Health Professional Bureau, 402 W. Washington, Room 041, Indianapolis, IN 46282; (317) 232-2960 for the following medical specialties: chiropractors, dentists, health facility administrators, nurses, optometrists, pharmacists, sanitarians, speech pathologists, audiologists, psychologists, veterinarians, hearing aid dealers, podiatrists, physical therapists.

Iowa
Bureau of Professional Licensing, Iowa Department of Health, Lucas State Office Building, Des Moines, IA 50319; (515) 281-4401. Licensed professionals: dietitians, funeral directors and embalmers, hearing aid dealers, nursing home administrators, optometrists, ophthalmology dispensers, podiatrists, psychologists, physical and occupational therapists, occupational therapist assistants, social workers, speech pathologists and audiologists, respiratory care therapists, barbers, cosmetologists, chiropractors, nurses, physicians, dentists, pharmacists, veterinarians. Other licensed professionals: Professional Licensing Regulation Division, Department of Commerce, 1918 SE Hulsizer, Ankeny, IA 50021; (515) 281-3183: accountants, engineers and land surveyors, landscape architects, architects, real estate agents.

Kansas
Secretary of State, State Capitol, Consumer Affairs, 200 SE 7th Street, #214, Topeka, KS 66611; (913) 291-4340. Licensing boards: abstracters, accountants, adult home administrators, operating engineers, plumbers and pipefitters, carpenters, electrical workers, attorneys, barbers, cos-

metologists, court reporters, dentists and dental auxiliaries, educators, emergency medical services, healing arts specialists, hearing aid dispensers, insurance agents, land surveyors, embalmers/funeral directors, nurses, optometrists, pharmacists, physical therapists, podiatrists, private schools, real estate agents, engineers, architects, landscape architects, veterinarians.

Kentucky
Division of Occupations and Professions, P.O. Box 456, Frankfort, KY 40602; (502) 564-3296. Licensing boards and professions: hearing aid dealers, nurses, private schools, psychologists, social workers, speech and audiologists. Other licensed professionals: Kentucky Occupational Information Coordinating Committee, 275 E. Main St., Two Center, Frankfort, KY 40621; (502) 564-4258: accountants, agriculture specialists, architects, auctioneers, bar examiners, barbers, chiropractors, dentists, hairdressers, cosmetologists, emergency medical technicians Services, radiation and product safety specialists, insurance agents, medical licensure supervisors, natural resources and environmental protection specialists, nursing home administrators, ophthalmic dispensers, optometric examiners, pharmacists, physical therapists, podiatrists, polygraph examiners, professional engineers and land surveyors, real estate agents, veterinarians.

Contacts Close To Home

Louisiana
Department of Economic Development, 101 France Street, Baton Rouge, LA 70802; (504) 342-5361. Licensing boards and professions: acupuncture assistants, adoption agencies, adult day care administrators, agricultural consultants, alcoholic beverages solicitors, ambulatory surgical centers, arborists, archaeological investigators, architects, auctioneers, barbers, beauticians, bedding and furniture upholsterers, beer distributors, blind business enterprise operators, blood alcohol analysts, embalmers/funeral directors, accountants, shorthand reporters, chiropractors, pesticide applicators, driving school Instructors, sewage/construction contractors, cotton buyers, waste-salvage oil operators, cut flower dealers, dairy product retailers, day care centers, fuels dealers, dentists, drug manufacturers, egg marketers, electrolysis technicians, embalmers, emergency medical technicians, employment service agencies, family support counselors, grain dealers, hearing aid dealers, hemodialysis clinics, home health centers, horticulturists, independent laboratories, sewage system installers, insurance, landscape architects, nurses, lime manufacturers, liquefied gas distributors, livestock dealers, maternity homes, mental and substance abuse clinics, midwives, nursing home administrators, nursery stock dealers, occupational therapists, optometrists, pesticide dealers, pharmacists, physical therapists, physicians, physicians, plant breeders, plumbers, podiatrists, solid waste processors, seafood distributors, psychologists, radiation therapists, radio and television repair technicians, radiologic technologists, real estate brokers, sanitarians, social workers, speech pathologists and audiologists, veterinarians, voice stress analysts.

Maine
Department of Professional and Financial Regulation, State House Station 35, Augusta, ME 04333; (207) 624-8500. Licensing boards and professions: veterinarians, itinerant vendors, consumer credit protection services, insurance agents, athletic trainers, real estate agents, geologists and soil scientists, solar energy auditors, hearing aid dealers and fitters, accountants, arborists, barbers, commercial drivers, education instructors, speech pathologists and audiologists, auctioneers, electricians, funeral directors, foresters, dietitians, nursing home administrators, oil and solid fuel installers, substance abuse counselors, mobile home parks, river pilots, physical therapists, plumbers, psychologists, social workers, radiological technicians, occupational therapists, respiratory care therapists, nurses, dentists, chiropractors, osteopaths, podiatrists, physicians, engineers, attorneys.

Contacts Close To Home

Maryland
Division of Maryland Occupational and Professional Licensing, 501 St. Paul Pl., 9th Floor, Baltimore, MD 21202; (301) 333-6209. Licensed professionals: architects, master electricians, engineers, foresters, hearing aid dealers, landscape architects, pilots, plumbers, land surveyors, public accountants, second hand dealers, precious metal and gem dealers, pawnbrokers, real estate agents and brokers, home improvement contractors, barbers and cosmetologists. Referral to the licensing agency for collection agencies, mortgage brokers and insurance agents can be provided by the office listed above. Other licensed professions: Boards and Commissions, Department of Health and Mental Hygiene, 4201 Patterson Ave., Baltimore, MD 21215; (410) 764-4747: audiologists, chiropractors, dentists, dietitians, electrologists, medical examiners, morticians, nurses, nursing home administrators, optometrists, occupational therapists, pharmacists, physical therapists, podiatrists, professional counselors, psychologists, environmental sanitarians, speech pathologists, social workers, well drillers, water work and waste system operators.

Massachusetts
Division of Registration, 100 Cambridge St., Boston, MA 02202; (617) 727-3074. Licensing

boards and professions: electrologists, gas fitters, hairdressers, health officers, landscape architects, licensed practical nurses, nursing home administrators, optometrists, physician's assistants, podiatrists, pharmacists, plumbers, psychologists, real estate brokers, registered nurses, sanitarians, speech pathologists, audiologists, social workers, tv-repair technicians, physical therapists, occupational therapists, athletic trainers, architects, barbers, barber shops, certified public accountants, chiropractors, dental hygienists, dentists, dispensing opticians, pharmacies, electricians, embalmers, engineers, veterinarians.

Michigan
Michigan Department of License and Regulation, P.O. Box 30018, Lansing, MI 48909; (517) 373-1870. Licensing board and professions: accountants, architects, barbers, athletic control (wrestlers and boxers), builders, carnival amusement rides, cosmetologists.

Minnesota
Office of Consumer Services, Office of Attorney General, 1440 N.C.L. Tower, 455 Minnesota St., St. Paul, MN 55101; (612) 296-3353. Licensing boards and professions: abstracters, accountants, adjusters, alarm and communications contractors, architects, assessors, attorneys, auctioneers, bailbondsmen, barbers, beauticians,

boiler operators, boxing related occupations, brokers, building officials, burglar installers, chiropractors, clergy, cosmetologists, dentists, dental assistants, dental hygienists, private detectives, electricians, energy auditors, engineers, financial counselors/ financial planners, funeral directors/ embalmers/ morticians, hearing aid dispensers, insurance agents, investment advisors, landscape architects, land surveyors, midwives, notary publics, nursing home administrators, optometrists, osteopathic physicians, pawnbrokers, peace officers, pharmacists, physical therapists, physicians, surgeons, physician's assistants, high pressure pipefitters, plumbers, podiatrists, practical nurses, precious metal dealers, process servers, psychologists, real estate brokers, registered nurses, rehabilitation consultants, sanitarians, securities brokers, tax preparers, teachers, tow truck operators, transient merchants, veterinarians, water conditioning contractors and installers, water and waste treatment operators, water well contractors/explorers/engineers.

Mississippi

Secretary of State, P.O. Box 136, Jackson, MS 39205; (601) 359-3123. Licensing boards and professions: agricultural aviation pilots, architects, landscape architects, athletic trainers, funeral directors, chiropractors, dentists, physicians, nurses, nursing home administrators, optometrists, pharmacists, physical therapists, psychologists, veterinarians, barbers, cosmetologists, engineers and land surveyors, foresters, polygraph examiners, public accountants, public contractors, real estate agents.

Missouri

Division of Professional Registration, Department of Economic Development, P.O. Box 1335, 3605 Missouri Blvd., Jefferson City, MO 65102; (314) 751-0293. Licensing boards and professions: accountants, architects/engineers/ land surveyors, athletic trainers, barbers, chiropractors, cosmetologists, professional counselors, dentists, embalmers/ funeral directors, healing arts specialists, employment agencies, hearing aid dealers/fitters, nurses, optometrists, podiatrists, pharmacists, real estate agents, veterinarians, insurance agents, nursing home administrators, lawyers, dental hygienists, physicians, physical therapists, speech pathologists and audiologists, psychologists.

Montana

Professional and Occupational Licensing, Business Regulation, Department of Commerce, 111 N. Jackson St., Helena, MT 59620; (406) 444-3737. Licensing boards and professions: accountants, acupuncturists, architects, athletic trainers, barbers, beer distributors, chiropractors, cosmetologists, dental hygienists, dentists, denturists, electricians, electrologists, employment agencies, engineers and land surveyors, hearing aid dispensers, insurance, landscape architects, lawyers, librarians, medical doctors, morticians, nurses, nursing home administrators, occupational therapists, operating engineers (boiler), optometrists, osteopathic physicians, pawnbrokers, physical therapists, plumbers, podiatrists, polygraph examiners, private investigators, psychologists, contractors, radiologic technologists, real estate brokers and salesmen, sanitarians, securities brokers and salesmen, social workers and counselors, speech pathologists and audiologists, taxidermists, tourist campground and trailer courts, veterinarians, water well drillers.

Nebraska
Bureau of Examining Boards, Nebraska Department of Health, P.O. Box 95007, Lincoln, NE 68509; (402) 471-2115. Licensing boards and health professions: athletic trainers, advanced emergency medical technicians, audiologist/ speech pathologists, cosmetologists, chiropractors, dentists/dental hygienists, embalmers/funeral directors, hearing aid dealers and fitters, pharmacists, podiatrists, optometrists, physical therapists, nurses, nursing home administrators, massage specialists, occupational therapists, professional counselors, psychologists, respira-

tory care specialists, social workers, sanitarians, veterinarians. For other licensing boards and professions, contact the NE state operator at (402) 471-2311 to be connected with the board that licenses the following professions: accountants, engineers/ architects, barbers, abstracters, appraisers, land surveyors, landscape architects.

Nevada
Professional and Occupational Licensing, 1 East Liberty, Suite 311, Reno, NV 89501; (702) 786-0231. Licensing boards and professions: accountants, architects, athletic trainers, audiologists and speech pathologists, barbers, chiropractors, contractors, cosmetologists, dentists, engineers and land surveyors, funeral directors and embalmers, hearing aid specialists, homeopaths, landscape architects, liquefied petroleum gas distributors, marriage and family counselors, physicians, naturopathic healing arts specialists, nurses, dispensing opticians, optometrists, oriental medicine, osteopaths, pharmacists, physical therapists, podiatrists, private investigators, psychologists, shorthand reporters, taxicab drivers, veterinarians.

New Hampshire
SOICC of New Hampshire, 64 B Old Sun Cook Rd., Concord, NH 03301; (603) 228-9500. Licensing boards and professions: accountants, emergency medical techni-

cians, engineers/architects/land surveyors, attorneys, auctioneers, insurance (bailbondsmen), barbers, cosmetologists, chiropractors, court reporters, dentists, drivers education Instructors, electricians, funeral directors/embalmers, engineers, physicians, private security guards, lobbyists, nurses, nursing home administrators, occupational therapists, optometrists, psychologists, pesticide control operators, pharmacists, plumbers, podiatrists, real estate agents, teacher agents, veterinarians, water supply and pollution control operators.

New Jersey
Director, Centralized Licensing for the Licensing Boards, Division of Consumer Affairs, 375 West State Street, Trenton, NJ 08625; (609) 292-4670. Licensing boards and professions: accountants, architects, barbers, beauticians, dentists, electrical contractors, marriage counselors, plumbers, morticians, nurses, ophthalmic dispensing technicians, optometrists, pharmacists, physical therapists, professional engineers and landscape surveyors, professional planners, psychological examiners, shorthand reporters, veterinarians, public movers and warehousemen, acupuncture specialists, landscape architects, athletic trainers, hearing aid dispensers, chiropractors, opthomologists.

New Mexico
Regulation and Licensing Department, P.O. Box 25101, Santa Fe, NM 87504-1388; (505) 827-7000. Licensing boards and professions: accountants, architects, athletic promoters, barbers, chiropractors, cosmetologists, dentists, engineers and land surveyors, landscape architects, physicians, nurses, nursing home administrators, occupational therapists, optometrists, osteopaths, pharmacists, physical therapists, podiatrists, polygraphers, private investigators, psychologists, realtors, thanatopractice, veterinarians.

New York
New York State Education Department, Division of Professional Licensing, Cultural Education Center, Empire State Plaza, Albany, NY 12230; (518) 474-3852, or (800) 342-3729 (toll-free in NY). Licensed professionals: acupuncturists, architects, audiologists, certified shorthand reporters, chiropractors, dentists, landscape architects, land surveyors, massage therapists, physicians, osteopaths, nurses, occupational therapists, ophthalmic dispensers, optometrists, pharmacists, physical therapists, podiatrists, engineers, psychologists, public accountants, social workers, speech pathologists, veterinarians.

Contacts Close To Home

North Carolina

North Carolina Center for Public Policy Research, P.O. Box 430, Raleigh, NC 27602; (919) 832-2839. Licensing boards and professions: architects, auctioneers, barbers, boiler operators, accountants, chiropractors, cosmetologists, registered counselors, dental, electrical contractors, foresters, general contractors, hearing aid dealers and fitters, landscape architects, landscape contractors, marital and family therapists, physicians, navigators and pilots, morticians, nurses, nursing home administrators, opticians, optometrists, osteopaths, pesticide operators, pharmacists, physical therapists, plumbers and heating specialists, podiatrists, practicing psychologists, private protective services, professional engineers and land surveyors, public librarians, real estate, refrigeration technicians, sanitarians, social workers, speech and language pathologists, structural pest control operators, veterinarians, waste water treatment operators, water treatment facility operators.

North Dakota

North Dakota Legislative Council Library, 600 East Boulevard Avenue, Bismarck, ND 58505; (701) 224-2916. Licensing boards and professions: abstracters, accountants, architects, athletic trainers, audiologists and speech pathologists, barbers, chiropractors, cosmetologists, dentists, dietitians, electricians, embalmers, emergency medical services, engineers and land surveyors, hearing aid dealers and fitters, massage therapists, physicians, nurses, nursing home administrators, occupational therapists, optometrists, pharmacists, physical therapists, plumbers, podiatrists, private investigators, private police security, psychologists, real estate agents, respiratory care specialists, social workers, soil classifiers, veterinarians, water well contractors.

Ohio

State of Ohio, Department of Administrative Services, Division of Computer Services, 30 East Broad St., 40th Floor, Columbus, OH 43215-0409; (614) 466-8029. Licensed professionals: wholesale distributors of dangerous drugs, terminal distributors of dangerous drugs, pharmacists, accountants, barbers, barber shops, beauty shops, managing cosmetologists, cosmetologists, manicurists, architects, landscape architects, practical nurses, registered nurses, surveyors, engineers, surveyors, dentists, dental hygienists, osteopaths, physicians, podiatrists, chiropractors, midwives, embalmers, funeral directors, hat cleaners, dry cleaners, public employment agencies, auctioneers, private investigators, auctioneers.

Oklahoma

Governor's Office, State Capitol, Oklahoma City, OK 73117-1299;

(405) 521-2342 or State Information Operator (405) 521-1601. Licensing board and professions: accountants, real estate agents, physicians, foresters, medicolegals, nursing homes, nurses, optometrists, osteopaths, physicians, pharmacists, polygraph examiners, psychologists, shorthand reporters, social workers, speech pathologists, veterinarians, landscape architects, architects, chiropractors, cosmetologists, dentists, embalmers and funeral directors. For other licensed professionals, contact Occupational Licensing, OK State Health Department, 1000 North East, 10th Street, Oklahoma City, OK 73152; (405) 271-5217: barbers, hearing aid dealers, electricians, water and waste treatment plant operators.

Oregon

Department of Economic Development, Small Business Advocates, 775 Summer Street NE, Salem, OR 97310; (800) 233-3306 (toll-free in OR). Licensing boards and professions: accountants, architects, barbers and hairdressers, builders, contractors, collection agencies, debt consolidators, geologists, landscape architects, landscape contractors, and TV/-radio service dealers, engineering examiners, fire marshals, insurance agents, maritime pilots, real estate agents, tax practitioners.

Pennsylvania

Bureau of Professional and Occupational Affairs, 618 Transportation and Safety Building, Harrisburg, PA 17120-2644; (717) 787-8503, or (800) 822-2113 (toll-free in PA). Licensing boards and professions: accountants, architects, auctioneers, barbers, cosmetology, funeral directors, landscape architects, professional engineers, real estate agents. For licensed health professions, contact Bureau of Professional and Occupational Affairs, Secretary of State, 618 Transportation and Safety Building, Harrisburg, PA 17120; (717) 783-1400: dentists, physicians, nurses, nursing home administrators, occupational therapists, optometrists, osteopaths, pharmacists, physical therapists, podiatrists, psychologists, speech-language and hearing specialists, veterinarians, navigators.

Rhode Island

State Attorney General, Consumer Protection, 72 Pine Street, Providence, RI 02903; (401) 274-4400. Licensing boards and professions: nurses aides, psychologists, respiratory therapists, sanitarians, speech pathologists, veterinarians, physical therapists, plumbers, podiatrists, prosthetists, nurses, nursing home administrators, occupational therapists, opticians, optometrists, osteopaths, physician assistants, embalmers/funeral directors, hairdressers, cosmetologists, manicurists, massage therapists, physicians, midwives, acupuncturists, athletic trainers, audiologists, barbers, barber shops, chiropractors, dentists, dental hygienists, electrologist, architects, coastal resource management, engineers and land surveyors.

South Carolina
South Carolina State Library, 1500 Senate St., Columbia, SC 29211; (803) 734-8666. Licensing boards and professions: accountants, architects, auctioneers, barbers, morticians, chiropractors, contractors, cosmetologists, dentists, engineers, environmental systems (well diggers), foresters, funeral services, landscape architects, physicians, nurses, nursing home administrators, occupational therapists, opticians, optometrists, pharmacists, physical therapists, professional counselors, marriage and family therapists, psychologists, real estate agents, sanitarians, home builder, social workers, speech pathologist/audiologists, veterinarians, athletic trainers (boxing and wrestling), geologists.

South Dakota
Department of Commerce and Regulation, 910 E. Sioux, Pierre, SD 57105; (605) 773-3178. South Dakota Medical and Osteopath examiners, 1323 A. Minnesota Avenue, Sioux Falls, SD 57104; (605) 336-1965. Licensing boards and professions: physicians, osteopaths, physician's assistants, phys-

ical therapists, medical corporations, emergency technicians, abstracters, accountants, barbers, chiropractors, cosmetologists, electricians, engineers/architects, funeral directors, hearing aid dispensers, medical/osteopaths, nurses, nursing home administrators, optometrists, pharmacists, plumbers, podiatrists, psychologists, real estate agents, social workers, veterinarians.

Tennessee
Division of Regulatory Boards, Department of Commerce and Insurance, 500 James Robertson Parkway, Nashville, TN 37243; (615) 741-3449. Licensing boards and professions: accountants, architects and engineers, auctioneers, barbers, collection services, contractors, cosmetologists, funeral directors and embalmers, land surveyors, motor vehicle salesmen and dealers, personnel recruiters, pharmacists, polygraph examiners, real estate. For other licensed health professionals, contact Division of Health Related Professions, Department of Health and Environment, 283 Plus Park Blvd Complex, Nashville, TN 37247; (615) 367-6220: dentists, dental hygienists, podiatrists, physicians, physician's assistants, osteopaths, optometrists, veterinarians, nursing home administrators, dispensing opticians, chiropractors, social workers, hearing aid dispensers, registered professional environmentalists,

marital and family counselors, speech pathology/audiologists, occupational and physical therapists, x-ray technicians, registered nurses, licensed practical nurses.

Texas

Texas Department of Commerce, Office of Business Permit Assistance, P.O. Box 12728, Capitol Station, Austin, TX 78711; (512) 320-0110, or (800) 888-0511 (toll-free in TX). Licensing boards and professions: accountants, architects, barbers, cosmetologists, morticians, educators, public safety, chiropractors, psychologists, dentists, real estate agents, engineers, veterinarians, insurance agents, land surveyors, landscape architects, fitting and dispensing of hearing aids, private investigators and private security agencies, polygraph, Vocational nurses, nursing home administrators, physicians, optometrists, structural pest control operators, pharmacists, physical therapists, plumbers, podiatrists, professional counselors, dietitians, speech-language pathology and audiology.

Utah

Division of Occupational and Professional Licensing, Department of Business Regulation, Heber M. Wells Building, 160 East 300 South, P.O. Box 45805, Salt Lake City, UT 84145-0805; (801) 530-6628. Licensing boards and professions: accountants, architects, barbers, cosmetologists,

electrologists, chiropractors, podiatrists, dentists, dental hygienists, embalmers, funeral directors, pre-need sellers, engineers, land surveyors, physicians, surgeons, Naturopaths, registered nurses, licensed practical nurses, nurse midwives, nurse anesthetists, nurse specialists, prescriptive practice specialist, IV therapists, optometrists, osteopaths, pharmacists, pharmacies, manufacturing pharmacies, shorthand reporters, veterinarians, health facility administrators, sanitarians, morticians, physical therapists, psychologists, clinical social workers, conduct research on controlled substance, marriage and family therapists, master therapeutic recreational specialists, speech pathologists, audiologists, occupational therapists, hearing aid specialists, massage therapists, massage establishments, acupuncture practitioners, physician assistants, dieticians, contractors.

Vermont

Division of Licensing and Registration, Secretary of State, Pavilion Office Building, 109 State St., Montpelier, VT 05609; (802) 828-2363. Licensing boards and professions: accountants, architects, barbers, boxing control, chiropractors, cosmetologists, dentists, engineers, funeral directors/embalmers, land surveyors, medical board (physicians, podiatrists, real estate brokers, veterinarians, physical therapists,

303

social workers, physician assistants, motor vehicle racing, nurses, nursing home administrators, opticians, optometrists, osteopaths, pharmacies, pharmacist, psychologists, private detectives, security guards, radiological technicians.

Virginia

Virginia Department of Commerce, 3600 W. Broad St., 5th Floor, Richmond, VA 23230; (804) 367-8500. Licensed professions: accountants, architects, auctioneers, audiologists, barbers, boxers, contractors, commercial driver training schools, employment agencies, professional engineers, geologists, hairdressers, harbor pilots, hearing aid dealers and fitters, landscape architects, nursing home administrators, librarians, opticians, polygraph examiners, private security services, real estate brokers, speech pathologists, land surveyors, water and wastewater works operators, wrestlers. For licensed health professions, contact receptionist, Health Professionals: (804) 662-9900. The office listed above can provide you with phone numbers for the following licensing boards: dentists, funeral directors/embalmers, physicians, medical/legal assistants, nurses, optometrists, pharmacists, psychologists, professional counselors, social workers, veterinarians.

Washington

Department of Health, P.O. Box 1099, Olympia, WA 98507; (206) 586-4561. Licensed professions: acupuncturists, auctioneers, architects, barbers, camp club registration/salespersons, chiropractors, cosmetology schools/ instructors, cosmetologists, manicurists, collection agencies, debt adjusters/agencies, dentists, dental hygienists, drugless therapeutic-naturopaths, employment agencies/ managers, professional engineers, engineers-in-training, land surveyors, engineering corporations/ partnerships, escrow officers/ agents, firearms dealers, embalmers, apprentice embalmers, funeral directors, funeral establishments, hearing aid dispensers/trainees, land development registration, landscape architects, massage operators, midwives, notary publics, nursing home administrators, occularists, occupational therapists, dispensing opticians, optometrists, osteopaths, osteopathic physician/ surgeon, osteopathic physician assistants, physicians, surgeons, physician's assistants, limited physician, podiatrists, practical nurses, psychologists, physical therapists, real estate (brokers, salespersons, corporations, partnerships, branch offices), land development representatives, registered nurses, time share registration and salespersons, veterinarians, animal technicians.

West Virginia

Administrative Law Division, Secretary of State, State Capitol, Charleston, WV 25305; (304) 345-4000. Licensing boards and professions: accountants, architects, barbers, beauticians, chiropractors, dentists, and dental hygienists, embalmers and funeral directors, engineers, foresters, hearing-aid dealers, landscape architects, land surveyors, law examiners, physicians, practical nurses, registered nurses, nursing home administrators, occupational therapists, optometrists, osteopaths, pharmacists, physical therapists, psychologists, radiologic technicians, real estate agents, sanitarians, state water resources, veterinarians.

Wisconsin

Department of Regulation and Licensing, P.O. Box 8935, Madison, WI 53708; (608) 266-7482. Licensed professions: accountants, animal technicians, architects, architects, engineers, barbers, bingo organizations, morticians, chiropractors, cosmetologists, distributors of dangerous drugs, dental hygienists, dentists, interior designers, private detectives, drug manufacturers, electrologists, prof.engineers, funeral directors,

hearing aid dealers/ fitters, land surveyors, manicurists, physicians, surgeons, nurse midwives, registered nurses, licensed practical nurses, nursing home administrators, optometrists, pharmacists, physical therapists, physician's assistants, podiatrists, psychologists, raffle organizations, real estate brokers, beauty salons, electrolysis salons, veterinarians.

Wyoming

Governor's Office, State Capitol, Cheyenne, WY 82002; (307) 777-7434. Licensing boards and professions: funeral directors and embalmers, health service administrators, buyers and purchasing agents, shorthand reporters, medical record technicians, accountants and auditors, claims adjusters, appraisers, engineers, architects, surveyors, interior designers and decorators, medical laboratory workers, dental laboratory technicians, opticians, radiological technicians, respiratory technicians, quality control inspectors, security salespeople, insurance agents, real estate agents, physicians, physician's assistants, chiropractors, pharmacists, occupational therapists, activity therapists, physical therapists, speech pathologist and audiologist, veterinarian, optometrist, dietitians, dentists, dental hygienists, registered nurses, licensed practical nurses, emergen-

305

cy medical technicians, nurse's
aides, medical assistants, counselors, lawyers, legal assistants, cosmetologists and barbers.

Medical Boards

Although their powers are different from state to state, most Medical Boards respond to and investigate complaints about the ethical and professional conduct of medical doctors practicing in their states. Most have the ability to revoke or suspend a physician's license or put them on probation. For more detailed information, see *Doctors* on page 61 and *Medical Bills* on page 137.

Alabama
State Board of Medical Examiners, P.O. Box 887, Montgomery, AL 36101; (334) 242-4153.

Alaska
State Medical Board, Frontier State of Alaska Bldg., 3601 C St., Suite 722, Anchorage, AK 99503; (907) 465-2341.

Arizona
State Board of Medical Examiners, 2001 W. Camelback Rd., #300, Phoenix, AZ 85015; (602) 255-3751.

Arkansas
State Medical Board, 2100 River Front Drive, Suite 200, Little Rock, AR 72202; (501) 296-1802.

California
Medical Board of California, 1426 Howe Avenue, Sacramento, CA 98525; (916) 263-2499.

Colorado
Board of Medical Examiners, 1560 Broadway, Suite 1300, Denver, CO 80202-5140; (303) 894-7690.

Connecticut
Division of Medical Quality Assurance, 150 Washington St., Hartford, CT 06106; (203) 566-5296.

Delaware
Board of Medical Practice, Margaret O'Neill Building, 2nd Floor, Federal and Court Sts., Dover, DE 19903; (302) 739-4522.

District of Columbia
Board of Medicine, 614 H Street, NW, Room 108, Washington, DC 20001; (202) 727-5365.

Florida
Board of Medicine, Northwood Centre #60, 1940 N. Monroe St., Tallahassee, FL 32399-0792; (904) 488-8860.

Georgia
Composite State Board of Medical Examiners, 166 Pryor St., SW, Atlanta, GA 30303; (404) 656-3913.

307

Hawaii
Board of Medical Examiners, Department of Commerce and Consumer Affairs, 1010 Richard St., or P.O. Box 3469, Honolulu, HI 96801; (808) 586-2708.

Idaho
State Board of Medicine, 280 N. 8th, Suite 202, Statehouse Mail, Boise, ID 83720-2680; (208) 334-2822.

Illinois
Department of Professional Regulation, 320 W. Washington St., Springfield, IL 62786; (217) 785-0822.

Indiana
Health Professions Service Bureau, 402 W. Washington, Room 041, Indianapolis, IN 46204; (317) 233-4409.

Iowa
State Board of Medical Examiners, State Capitol Complex, 1209 E. Court Ave., Executive Hills West, Des Moines, IA 50319-0180; (515) 281-4258.

Kansas
State Board of Healing Arts, 235 S. Topeka Blvd., Topeka, KS 66603; (913) 296-7413.

Kentucky
Board of Medical Licensure, Hurtuburne Medical Center, 310 Whittington Pkwy, Suite 1B, Louisville, KY 40222; (502) 429-8046.

Louisiana
State Board of Medical Examiners, 630 Camp St., P.O. Box 30250, New Orleans, LA 70190; (504) 524-6763.

Maine
Board of Registration In Medicine, State House Station #137, or Two Bangor St., Augusta, ME 04333; (207) 287-3601.

Maryland
Board of Physician Quality Assurance, 4201 Patterson Ave., 3rd Floor, or P.O. Box 2571, Baltimore, MD 21215; (410) 764-4705.

Massachusetts
Board of Registration In Medicine, Ten West St., 3rd Floor, Boston, MA 02111; (617) 727-3086, ext. 359.

Michigan
Board of Medicine, 611 W. Ottawa St., or P.O. Box 30018, Lansing, MI 48933; (517) 335-0930.

Minnesota
Board of Medical Examiners, 2700 University Ave. SE, Suite 106, St. Paul, MN 55114-1080; (612) 642-0538.

Medical Boards

Mississippi
State Board of Medical Licensure, 2688-D Insurance Center Dr., Jackson, MS 39216; (601) 354-6645.

Missouri
State Board of Registration For The Healing Arts, 3605 Missouri Blvd., or P.O. Box 4, Jefferson City, MO 65102; (314) 751-0098.

Montana
Board of Medical Examiners, P.O. Box 200513, 111 N. Jackson, Helena, MT 59620-0513; (406) 444-4000.

Nebraska
State Board of Examiners in Medicine and Surgery, 301 Centennial Mall South, or P.O. Box 95007, Lincoln, NE 68509-5007; (402) 471-2115.

Nevada
State Board of Medical Examiners, 1105 Terminal Way, Suite 301, or P.O. Box 7238, Reno, NV 89510; (702) 688-2559.

New Hampshire
Board of Registration in Medicine, Health and Welfare Building, Hazen Dr., Concord, NH 03301; (603) 271-1203.

New Jersey
State Board of Medical Examiners, 28 W. State St., Room 602, Trenton, NJ 08625; (609) 826-7100.

New Mexico
State Board of Medical Examiners, 491 Old Santa Fe Trail, Lamy Building, 2nd Floor, or P.O. Box 20001, Santa Fe, NM 87504; (505) 827-5002.

New York
State Board for Medicine, Room 3023, Cultural Education Center, Empire State Plaza, Albany, NY 12230; (518) 474-3830.

New York Board for Professional Medial Conduct, New York State Department of Health, #438, Corning Tower Building, Empire State Plaza, Albany, NY 12237-0614; (518) 474-8357.

North Carolina
Board of Medical Examiners, P.O. Box 20007, or 1203 Front Street, Raleigh, NC 27619; (919) 828-1212.

North Dakota
State Board of Medical Examiners, City Center Plaza, 418 E. Broadway, Suite 12, Bismarck, ND 58501; (701) 223-9485.

Ohio
State Medical Board, 77 S. High Street, 17th Floor, Columbus, OH 43266-0315; (614) 466-3934.

Oklahoma
State Board of Medical Licensure and Supervision, 5104 N. Francis, Suite C, Oklahoma City, OK 73118; (405) 848-2189.

Medical Boards

Oregon
Board of Medical Examiners, 620 Crown Plaza, 1500 SW First Ave., Portland, OR 97201-5826; (503) 229-5770.

Pennsylvania
State Board of Medicine, Transportation and Safety Building, Room 612, Common-wealth Ave. & Forster Street, Harrisburg, PA 17105-2649; (717) 787-2381.

Puerto Rico
Board of Medical Examiners, Kennedy Ave., ILA Building, Hogar del Obrero Portuario, Piso 8, Puerto Nuevo, PR 00920; (809) 782-8989.

Rhode Island
Board of Licensure and Discipline, Department of Health, 3 Capitol Hill, Cannon Building, Room 205, Providence, RI 02908; (401) 277-3855.

South Carolina
State Board of Medical Examiners, P.O. Box 12245, 1220 Pickens St., Columbia, SC 29211; (803) 734-9300.

South Dakota
State Board of Medical and Osteopathic Examiners, 1323 S. Minnesota Ave., Sioux Falls, SD 57105; (605) 334-8343.

Tennessee
State Board of Medical Examiners, 283 Plus Park Blvd., Nashville, TN 37247-1010; (615) 367-6231.

Texas
State Board of Medical Examiners, 12 Center Creek, #300, Austin, TX 78714-9134; (512) 834-7728.

Utah
Physicians Licensing Board, Division of Occupational and Professional Licensing, Heber M Wells Building, 4th Floor, 160 E. 300 South, Salt Lake City, UT 84145; (801) 530-6633.

Vermont
Board of Medical Practice, Licensing and Registration, Pavilion Office Building, 109 State Street, Montpelier, VT 05609; (802) 828-2674, (800) 439-8683 (VT).

Virginia
Board of Medicine, 6606 W. Broad Street, 4th Floor, Richmond, VA 23230-1770; (804) 662-9900.

Virgin Islands
Board of Medical Examiners, Department of Health, 48 Sugar Estate, St. Thomas, VI 00802; (809) 774-0117.

Medical Boards

Washington
Board of Medical Examiners, Department of Health Licensing, 1300 Quince St., EY25, or P.O. Box 7866, Olympia, WA 98504; (360) 586-8934.

West Virginia
Board of Medicine, 101 Dee Dr., Charleston, WV 25311; (304) 558-2921.

Wisconsin
Medical Examining Board, 1400 E. Washington Ave., or P.O. Box 8935, Madison, WI 53708; (608) 266-2112.

Wyoming
Board of Medical Examiners, 211 W. 19th St., 2nd Floor, Cheyenne, WY 82002; (307) 778-7053.

National Marine Fisheries Service

These offices handle complaints about the harassment and illegal hunting of marine mammals. See *Marine Mammal Protection* on page 133 for more detailed information.

Alaska
P.O. Box 021668, Juneau, AK 99802-1668; (907) 586-7225

Northeast
8484 Georgia Ave., Silver Spring, MD 20910; (301) 427-2300.

Northwest
7600 Sandpoint Way, NE

C15700, Seattle, WA 98115; (206) 526-6133

Southeast
9450 Koger Blvd., Suite 106, St. Petersburg, FL 33702.

Southwest
300 S. Ferry, Room 2022, Terminal Island, CA.

Nursing Home Ombudsmen

Often associated with the State Agencies on Aging, these consumer programs specialize in responding to, investigating, and resolving complaints involving nursing homes, such as abusive treatment by the staff, discrimination, billing errors, substandard service, and much more. For more detailed information, see *Nursing Homes* on page 147.

Alabama
Commission on Aging, 7070 Washington Ave., R.F.A. Plaza, #470, Montgomery, AL 36130; (800) 243-5463, (205) 242-5743.

Alaska
Office of the Older Alaskans Ombudsman, P.O. Box 110209, Anchorage, AK 99811; (907) 465-3250, (800) 478-9996 (long term care); also accepts collect calls from older persons.

Arizona
Aging and Adult Administration, 1789 W. Jefferson, Phoenix, AZ 85007; (602) 542-4446.

Arkansas
Division of Aging and Adult Services, 1417 Donaghey Plaza South, P.O. Box 1437, Little Rock, AR 72203-1437; (501) 682-2441, (800) 852-5494.

California
Department of Aging, 1600 K St., Sacramento, CA 95814; (916) 322-3887, or toll free in-state: (800) 231-4024.

Colorado
The Legal Center, 1575 Sherman Street, 4th Floor, Denver, CO 80203; (303) 866-3851, or toll free in-state: (800) 288-1376.

Connecticut
Department on Aging, 175 Main St., Hartford, CT 06106; (203) 566-7772, or toll free in-state: (800) 443-9946.

Delaware
Division on Aging, 1901 N. DuPont Highway, 2nd Floor Annex, New Castle, DE 19720; (302) 577-4791.

District of Columbia
Legal Counsel for the Elderly, 601 E Street, NW, Building A, 4th Floor, Washington, DC 20049; (202) 662-4933.

Florida
Department of Elder Affairs, 1317 Windwood Boulevard, Building 1, Room 317, Tallahassee, FL 32301; (904) 922-5297.

313

Nursing Home Ombudsmen

Georgia
Office of Aging, Dept of Human Resources, 878 Peachtree St., NE, Suite 632, Atlanta, GA 30309; (404) 894-5333.

Hawaii
Executive Office on Aging, 335 Merchant St., Room 241, Honolulu, HI 96813; (808) 586-0100.

Idaho
Office on Aging, State House, Room 108, Boise, ID 83720; (208) 334-3833.

Illinois
Department on Aging, 421 East Capitol Ave., Springfield, IL 62701; (217) 785-3356, or toll free: (800) 252-8966.

Indiana
Aging Division, Department of Human Services, 402 W. Washington St., Indianapolis, IN 46207-7083; (317) 232-7020, or toll free in-state: (800) 622-4484.

Iowa
Department of Elder Affairs, 914 Grand Ave., 200 Jewett Building, Suite 236, Des Moines, IA 50319; (515) 281-5187, or toll free in-state: (800) 532-3213.

Kansas
Department on Aging, State Office Building, 122 South Docking, 915 Southwest Harrison St., Topeka, KS 66612-4986; (913) 296-4986, or toll free in KS: (800) 432-3535.

Kentucky
Division for Aging Services, Department for Social Services, 275 East Main St., Frankfort, KY 40621; (502) 564-6930, or toll free in-state: (800) 372-2991.

Louisiana
Governors Office of Elder Affairs, P.O. Box 80374, 4550 N. Boulevard, Baton Rouge, LA 70898-3074; (504) 925-1700, (800) 259-4990.

Maine
Bureau of Elder and Adult Services, State House, Station 11, August, ME 04333; (207) 624-5335.

Maryland
Office on Aging, 301 West Preston Street, 10th Floor, Baltimore, MD 21201; (410) 225-1100, or toll free in-state: (800) 243-3425.

Massachusetts
Executive Office of Elder Affairs, 1 Ashburton Place, Boston, MA 02101; (617) 727-7750, or toll free in-state: (800) 872-0166.

Michigan
Offices of Services to the Aging, 611 W. Ottawa St., P.O. Box 30026, Lansing, MI 48909; (517) 373-8230.

Minnesota
Board on Aging, Office of Ombudsman for Older Minneso-

Nursing Home Ombudsmen

tans, 444 Lafayette Rd., St. Paul, MN 55155-3843; (612) 296-2770, or (800) 333-2433.

Mississippi
Division of Aging and Adult Services, 455 N. Lamar St., Jackson, MS 39202; (601) 359-6770, or toll free in-state: (800) 345-6347.

Missouri
Division of Aging, P.O. Box 1337, Jefferson City, MO 65102; (314) 751-3082, or toll free in-state: (800) 392-0210.

Montana
Governor's Office on Aging, State Capitol Station, Helena, MT 59620; (406) 444-3111, or toll free in-state: (800) 332-2272.

Nebraska
Department on Aging, State Office Building, 301 Centennial Mall South, Lincoln, NE 68509; (402) 471-2306, or 2307, (800) 942-7830.

Nevada
Division for Aging Services, Department of Human Resources, 340 N. 11th St., Suite 114, Las Vegas, NV 89101; (702) 486-3545.

New Hampshire
Division of Elderly and Adult Services, 6 Hazen Dr., Concord, NH 03301; (603) 271-4375, or toll free in-state: (800) 442-5640.

New Jersey
Department of Community Affairs, Division on Aging, 101 S. Broad and Front Sts., CN 807, Trenton, NJ 08625-0807; (609) 984-3951 or (800) 792-8820.

New Mexico
Agency on Aging, 224 East Palace Ave., Ground Floor, Santa Fe, NM 87501; (505) 827-7640, or toll free in-state: (800) 432-2080.

New York
Office for the Aging, Nelson A. Rockefeller Building, ESP, Albany, NY 12223; (518) 474-5731, or toll free in-state: (800) 342-9871.

North Carolina
Division of Aging, Department of Human Resources, 693 Palmer Drive, Raleigh, NC 27626-0531; (919) 733-3983, or toll free in-state: (800) 662-7030.

North Dakota
Aging Services, Department of Human Services, 600 East Boulevard, Bismarck, ND 58507-7070; (701) 224-2577, or toll free in-state: (800) 472-2622.

Ohio
Department of Aging, 50 West Broad Street, 8th Floor, Columbus, OH 43266-0501; (614) 466-1221, toll free in-state: (800) 282-1206.

Nursing Home Ombudsmen

Oklahoma
Special Unit on Aging, P.O. Box 25352, Oklahoma City, OK 73125; (405) 521-2327.

Oregon
Office of LTC Ombudsman, 2475 Lancaster Drive, Building B, #9, Salem, OR 97310; (503) 378-6533, or toll free in-state: (800) 522-2602.

Pennsylvania
Department of Aging, 231 State St., Barto Building, Harrisburg, PA 17101; (717) 783-1550.

Puerto Rico
Office of Elder Affairs, P.O. Box 11398, Old San Juan Station, San Juan, PR 00910; (809) 722-2429.

Rhode Island
Department of Elderly Affairs, 160 Pine St., Providence, RI 02903; (401) 277-2858, or toll free in-state: (800) 322-2880.

South Carolina
Office of the Governor, Div. of Ombudsman & Citizens' Service, 1205 Pendleton St., Columbia, SC 29201; (803) 735-0210.

South Dakota
Office of Adult Services and Aging, 700 Governors Dr., Pierre, SD 57501; (605) 773-3656.

Tennessee
Commission on Aging, 706 Church St., Suite 201, Nashville, TN 37243; (615) 741-2056.

Texas
Department on Aging, P.O. Box 12786, Capitol Station, Austin, TX 78711; (512) 444-2727, or toll free in-state: (800) 252-9240.

Utah
Division of Aging and Adult Services, P.O. Box 45500, 120 N. 200 West, Rm. 401, Salt Lake City, UT 84103; (801) 538-3910.

Vermont
Department of Rehabilitation and Aging, 103 South Main St., Waterbury, VT 05671-2301; (802) 241-2400.

Virginia
Department for the Aging, 700 East Franklin St., 10th Floor, Richmond, VA 23219; (804) 225-2271, toll free in-state: (800) 552-4464, or (800) 552-3402 (long term care).

Washington
Aging and Adult Services Administration, P.O. Box 40505, Olympia, WA 98504-5050; (206) 586-2768.

West Virginia
Commission on Aging, State Capitol, 1900 Kanola East, Holly Grove, Charleston, WV 25305-0160; (304) 558-3317, or toll free in-state: (800) 642-3671.

Wisconsin
Board on Aging and Long Term Care, One W. Wilson St., P.O.

Nursing Home Ombudsmen

Box 7851, Madison, WI 53707-7851; (608) 266-2536.

Wyoming
Commission on Aging, Hathaway Bldg., 2300 Capitol Ave., Room 139, Cheyenne, WY 82002; (307) 777-7986 or (800) 442-2766.

Pharmacy Boards

The following State Pharmacy Boards will investigate complaints against pharmacies and pharmacists involving the quality and quantity of prescriptions dispensed, the professional conduct of pharmacists, and other related issues. Also see *Pharmacists and Pharmacies* on page 157 for more detailed information.

Alabama
Alabama State Board of Pharmacy, 1 Perimeter Park South, Suite 425 South, Birmingham, AL 35243; (205) 967-0130, Fax: (205) 967-1009.

Alaska
Department of Commerce and Economic Development, Division of Occupational Licensing, P.O. Box 110806, Juneau, AK 99811; (907) 465-2500, Fax: (907) 465-5442.

Arizona
State Board of Pharmacy, 5060 North 19th Avenue, Suite 101, Phoenix, AZ 85015; (602) 255-5125, Fax: (602) 255-5740. Complaints in writing only.

Arkansas
Board of Pharmacy, 101 E. Capitol Ave, #218, Little Rock, AR 72201; (501) 682-0190, Fax: (501) 682-0195.

California
State Board of Pharmacy, 400 R Street, #4070, Sacramento, CA 95814; (916) 445-5014, Fax: (916) 327-6308.

Colorado
Board of Pharmacy, 1560 Broadway, Suite 1310, Denver, CO 80202; (303) 894-7750, Fax: 303) 894-7764.

Connecticut
Drug Control Division, 165 Capital Ave., Room G-37, Hartford, CT 06106, (203) 566-4490, Fax: (203) 566-7630.

Delaware
Board of Pharmacies, Cooper Bldg., Room 205, Federal & Waters St., Dover, DE 19901; (302) 739-4708, Fax: (302) 739-3071.

District of Columbia
Board of Pharmacy, Department of Consumer and Regulatory Affairs, Pharmaceutical and Medical Control Division, 614 H Street, NW, Room 904, Washington, D.C. 20001; (202) 727-7465. Complaints in writing only.

318

Contacts Close To Home

Florida
State Department of Health and Rehabilitative Services, Pharmacy Program Office, 1317 Winewood Blvd. Tallahassee, FL 32399; (904) 487-1257, Fax: (904) 922-5367.

Georgia
Board of Pharmacy, 166 Pryor St. S.W., Atlanta, GA 30303; (404) 656-3912. Complaints in writing only.

Hawaii
R.I.C.O., P.O. Box 3469, Honolulu, HI 96804; (808) 586-2698.

Idaho
Board of Pharmacy, 280 North 8th St., Suite 204, Boise, ID 83720; (208) 334-2356.

Illinois
State Board of Pharmacy, 100 W. Randolph, Chicago, IL 60601; (312) 814-4573.

Indiana
State Board of Pharmacy, 402 W. Washington St., #041, Indianapolis, IN 46024-2739; (317) 232-1140.

Iowa
Board of Pharmacy, Attn: Chief Investigator, 1209 East Court, Des Moines, IA 50319; (515) 281-5944.

Kansas
Board of Pharmacy, Landon State Office Building, 900 Jackson St., Room 513, Topeka, KS 66612; (913) 296-4056.

Kentucky
Board of Pharmacy, 1024 Capital Center Drive, Suite 210, Frankfort, KY 40601; (502) 573-1580.

Louisiana
Board of Pharmacy, 5615 Corporate Blvd. Suite 8E, Baton Rouge, LA 70808-2537; (504) 925-6496.

Maine
Department of Professional Regulations, State House #35, Augusta, ME 04333; (207) 624-8603.

Maryland
Board of Pharmacy, 4201 Patterson Ave., Baltimore, MD 21215; (410) 764-4755.

Massachusetts
State Board of Pharmacy, State Office Building, Government Center, 100 Cambridge St., Room 1514, Boston, MA 02202; (617) 727-9954.

Michigan
Board of Pharmacy, P.O. Box 30018, Lansing, MI 48909; (517) 373-0620.

Pharmacy Boards

Minnesota
Board of Pharmacy, 2700 University Ave., West #107, St. Paul, MN 55114-1079; (612) 642-0541.

Mississippi
State Board of Pharmacy, P.O. Box 24507, Jackson, MS 39204; (601) 354-6750.

Missouri
State Board of Pharmacy, 3605 Missouri Blvd., Jefferson City, MO 65109; (573) 751-0091.

Montana
State Board of Pharmacy, 111 N. Jackson Street, P.O. Box 200513, Helena, MT 59620-0513; (406) 761-5131.

Nebraska
Bureau of Examining Boards, State Department of Health, Attn: Board of Pharmacy, 301 Centennial Mall South, P.O. Box 95007, Lincoln, NE 68509; (402) 471-2115.

Nevada
State Board of Pharmacy, 1201 Terminal Way, Suite 212, Reno, NV 89502; (702) 322-0691.

New Hampshire
State Board of Pharmacy, 57 Regional Drive, Concord, NH 03301; (603) 271-2350.

New Jersey
Board of Pharmacy, P.O. Box 45013, Newark, NJ 07101; (201) 504-6450.

New Mexico
Board of Pharmacy, University Towers, Suite 400B, 1650 University Boulevard, NE, Albuquerque, NM 87102; (505) 841-9102.

New York
Office of Professional Discipline, One Park Ave., New York, NY 10016; (212) 951-6400.

North Carolina
Board of Pharmacy, P.O. Box 459, Carrboro, NC 27510; (919) 942-4454.

North Dakota
State Board of Pharmacy, P.O. Box 1354, Bismarck, ND 58502; (701) 328-9535.

Ohio
State Board of Pharmacy, 77 South High St., 17th Floor, Columbus, OH 43266-0320; (614) 466-4143.

Oklahoma
State Board of Pharmacy, 4545 N. Lincoln, Suite 112, Oklahoma City, OK 73105; (405) 521-3815.

Oregon
Board of Pharmacy, 800 NE Oregon Street #9, Suite 425, Portland, OR 97232; (503) 731-4032.

Pharmacy Boards

Pennsylvania
Board of Pharmacy, P.O. Box 2649, Harrisburg, PA 17105; (717) 783-7157.

Puerto Rico
Board of Pharmacy, Department of Health, Call Box 10,2000, Santruce, PR 00908; (809) 725-8161.

Rhode Island
State Department of Health and Drug Control, 304 Cannon Bldg., 3 Capitol Hill, Providence, RI 02908; (401) 277-2837.

South Carolina
State Board of Pharmacy, 1026 Sumter St., Room 209, P.O. Box 11927, Columbia, SC 29211; (803) 734-1010.

South Dakota
State Board of Pharmacy, P.O. Box 518, 222 E. Capitol Ave., Suite 7, Pierre, SD 57501; (605) 224-2338.

Tennessee
Board of Pharmacy, 500 James Robertson Pkwy., 2nd Floor, Nashville, TN 37243-1143; (615) 741-2718.

Texas
State Board of Pharmacy, 8505 Cross Park Drive, Suite 110, Austin, TX 78754; (512) 305-8000.

Utah
Board of Pharmacy, Heber Wells Building, 160 East 300 South, P.O. Box 45805, Salt Lake City, UT 84145-0805; (801) 530-6767.

Vermont
State Board of Pharmacy, 109 State Street, Montpelier, VT 05609-1106; (802) 828-2875.

Virginia
State Board of Pharmacy, 6606 West Broad, 6th Floor, Richmond, VA 23230-1717; (804) 662-9911.

Washington
Board of Pharmacy, 1300 Quince SE, Mail Stop 7863, Washington Education Association Building, Olympia, WA 98504-7863; (360) 753-6834.

West Virginia
State Board of Pharmacy, 236 Capital St., Charleston, WV 25301; (304) 558-0558.

Wisconsin
State Department of Regulation and Licensing, P.O. Box 8935, Madison, WI 53708; (608) 266-2812.

Wyoming
State Board of Pharmacy, 1720 South Poplar St., Suite 5, Casper, WY 82601; (307) 234-0294.

Radon Offices

The following offices will tell you about radon health risks in your area, how to get your house tested, and where to find a licensed contractor who can correct radon leaks in your house. See *Radon* on page 176 for more detailed information.

Alabama
Division of Radiation Control, Alabama Department of Public Health, 434 Monroe #510, Montgomery, AL 36130; (334) 613-5391, (800) 582-1866.

Alaska
Radiological Health Program, Alaska Department of Health and Social Services, Box 110613, Juneau, AK 99811-0613; (907) 474-7201.

Arizona
Arizona Radiation Regulatory Agency, 4814 S. 40th St., Phoenix, AZ 85040; (602) 255-4845.

Arkansas
Division of Radiation Control and Emergency Management, Arkansas Department of Health, Lot 30, 4815 W. Markham St., Little Rock, AR 72205-3867; (501) 661-2301.

California
California Department of Health Services, Room 334, 2151 Berkeley Way, Berkeley, CA 94704; (510) 540-3014.

Radiation Management, County of Los Angeles, Department of Health Services, 2615 S. Grand Ave., Los Angeles, CA 90007; (213) 744-3244.

Colorado
Radiation Control Division, Colorado Department of Health, 4300 Cherry Creek Dr. South, Denver, CO 80222-1530; (303) 692-3042.

Connecticut
Radon Program, Toxic Hazards Section, Connecticut Department of Health Services, 150 Washington St., Hartford, CT 06106; (203) 240-9041.

Delaware
Division of Public Health, Delaware Bureau of Environmental Health, P.O. Box 637, Dover, DE 19901; (302) 739-4371, or (800) 554-4636 (toll-free in DE).

District of Columbia
D.C. Department of Consumer and Regulatory Affairs, 613 G Street, NW, Room 1014, Washington, DC 20001; (202) 727-7195.

Radon Offices

Florida
Office of Radiation Control, Department of Health and Rehabilitative Services, 1317 Winewood Blvd., Tallahassee, FL 32399-0700; (904) 488-1525, or (800) 543-8279 (toll-free in FL).

Georgia
Environmental Protection Division, Georgia Department of Human Resources, 878 Peachtree St., Room 100, Atlanta, GA 30309; (404) 651-5120, (800) 745-0037.

Hawaii
Environmental Protection and Health Services Division, Hawaii Department of Health, 591 Ala Moana Blvd., Room 136, Honolulu, HI 96813; (808) 586-4700.

Idaho
Office of Environmental Health, Division of Health, Idaho Department of Health and Welfare, 4th Floor, 450 W. State St., Boise, ID 83720; (208) 334-6584 or (800) 445-8647.

Illinois
Illinois Department of Nuclear Safety, Office of Environmental Safety, 1301 Knotts St., Springfield, IL 62703; (217) 786-6384 or (800) 325-1245.

Indiana
Division of Industrial Hygiene & Radiological Health, Indiana State Board of Health, 1330 W. Michigan St., P.O. Box 1964, Indianapolis, IN 46206-1964; (317) 633-0153, or (800) 272-9723 (toll-free in IN).

Iowa
Bureau of Radiological Health, Iowa Department of Public Health, Lucas State Office Bldg., Des Moines, IA 50319-0075; (515) 281-7781, or (800) 383-5992 (toll-free in IA).

Kansas
Bureau of Air Quality and Radiation Control, Kansas Department of Health and Environment, 109 SW 9th Street, Mills Building, #602, Topeka, KS 66612-1274, (913) 296-6183.

Kentucky
Radiation Control Branch, Division of Radiation and Product Safety, Department of Health Services, Cabinet for Human Resources, 275 E. Main St., Frankfort, KY 40621; (502) 564-3700.

Louisiana
Louisiana Nuclear Energy Division, P.O. Box 14690, Baton Rouge, LA 70898-4690; (504) 765-0160.

Louisiana Radiation Protection Service, P.O. Box 82135, 7290 Blue Bonett, 2nd Floor, Baton Rouge, LA 70810.

323

Radon Offices

Maine
Indoor Air Program, Division of Health Engineering, Maine Department of Human Services, 157 Capitol Street, State House Station 10, Augusta, ME 04333; (207) 289-3826 or (800) 232-0842.

Maryland
Center for Radiological Health, Maryland Department of Environment, 2500 Broening Highway, Baltimore, MD 21224; (410) 631-3300, or (800) 872-3666 (toll-free in MD).

Massachusetts
Radiation Control Program, Massachusetts Department of Public Health, 23 Service Center, North Hampton, MA 01060; (413) 586-7525, or (617) 727-6214 in Boston.

Michigan
Division of Radiological Health, Michigan Department of Public Health, 3423 N. Logan, P.O. Box 30195, Martin Luther King Jr. Blvd., Lansing, MI 48909; (517) 335-8037.

Minnesota
Section of Radiation Control, Environmental Health Division, Minnesota Department of Health, 925 Delaware St., SE, P.O. Box 59040, Minneapolis, MN 55459-0040; (612) 627-5033 or (800) 798-9050.

Mississippi
Division of Radiological Health, Mississippi Department of Health, 3150 Lawson St., P.O. Box 1700, Jackson, MS 39215-1700; (601) 354-6657 or (800) 626-7739.

Missouri
Bureau of Radiological Health, Missouri Department of Health, 1730 E. Elm, P.O. Box 570, Jefferson City, MO 65102; (314) 751-6083, or (800) 669-7236 (toll-free in MO).

Montana
Occupational Radiation Health Bureau, Montana Dept of Health and Environmental Sciences, Cogswell Bldg., Helena, MT 59620; (406) 444-3671.

Nebraska
Division of Radiological Health, Nebraska Department of Health, 301 Centennial Mall South, P.O. Box 95007, Lincoln, NE 68509; (402) 471-2168 or (800) 471-0594.

Nevada
Radiological Health Section, Health Division, Nevada Department of Human Resources, 505 East King Street, #101, Carson City, NV 89710; (702) 687-5394.

New Hampshire
Bureau of Radiological Health, Division of Public Health Services, Health and Welfare

Radon Offices

Building, 6 Hazen Drive, Concord, NH 03301-6527; (603) 271-4674 or (800) 852-3345.

New Jersey
Radiation Protection Element, New Jersey Department of Environmental Protection, 729 Alexander Road, Princeton, NJ 08540; (609) 987-6402, or (800) 648-0394 (toll-free in NJ).

New Mexico
Radiation Licensing and Registration Section, New Mexico Environmental Improvement Division, P.O. Box 26110, Market Place, Suite 4, Santa Fe, NM 87502; (505) 827-4301.

New York
Bureau of Environmental Radiation Protection, New York State Health Department, 2 University Plaza, Albany, NY 12237; (518) 458-6450, or (800) 458-1158.

North Carolina
Radiation Protection Section, Division of Facility Services, North Carolina Department of Human Resources, 3825 Barett Dr., Raleigh, NC 27609; (919) 733-4141.

North Dakota
North Dakota Department of Health, Missouri Office Building, 1200 Missouri Avenue, Room 304 P.O. Box 5120, Bismarck, ND 58502-5520; (701) 221-5188.

Ohio
Radiological Health Program, Ohio Department of Health, 35 E. Chestnut Street, P.O. Box 118, Columbus, OH 43266-0118; (614) 644-2727, or (800) 523-4439 (toll-free in OH).

Oklahoma
Radiation and Special Hazards Service, Consumer Protection Service #0202, 1000 NE 10th Street, Oklahoma City, OK 73117-1299; (405) 271-5221.

Oregon
Oregon State Health Department, Radiation Control Section, 800 NE Oregon, #705, Portland, OR 97232; (503) 731-5797 or (800) 422-6012.

Pennsylvania
Pennsylvania Department of Environmental Resources, Bureau of Radiation Protection, P.O. Box 2063, Harrisburg, PA 17105-2063; (717) 787-2480, or (800) 23-RADON (in PA).

Puerto Rico
Puerto Rico Radiological Health Division, G.P.O. Call Box 70184, Rio Piedras, PR 00936; (809) 767-3563.

Rhode Island
Division of Occupational Health and Radiation, Rhode Island Department of Health, 206 Cannon Bldg., 3 Capitol Hill, Providence, RI 02908; (401) 277-2438.

Radon Offices

South Carolina
Bureau of Radiological Health, South Carolina Department of Health and Environmental Control, 2600 Bull St., Columbia, SC 29201; (803) 734-4700/4631 or (800) 768-0362.

South Dakota
Division of Public Health, Licensing & Linesure, Radiation Protection, 445 E. Capitol, Pierre, SD 57501-3181; (605) 773-3364.

Tennessee
Division of Air Pollution Control, Bureau of Environmental Health, Department of Health and Environment, Custom House, 701 Broadway, Nashville, TN 37219-5403; (615) 522-0733 or (800) 232-1139.

Texas
Bureau of Radiation Control, Texas Department of Health, 1100 W. 49th St., Austin, TX 78756-3189; (512) 834-6688 or (800) 241-6688.

Utah
State of Utah, Division of Radiation Control, 168 North, 1950 West, P.O. Box 144850, Salt Lake City, UT 84114-4850; (801) 536-4250 or (800) 458-0145.

Vermont
Division of Occupational and Radiological Health, Vermont Department of Health, 10 Baldwin St., Montpelier, VT 05602; (802) 828-2886 or (800) 640-0601.

Virginia
Bureau of Radiological Health, Department of Health, 1500 E. Main Street, #104A, P.O. Box 2448, Richmond, VA 23218; (804) 786-5932, or (800) 468-0138 (toll-free in VA).

Virgin Islands
Division of Environmental Protection, Department of Planning and Natural Resources, 50 Nisky Center, #231,N, #458 Charlotte Amalie, St. Thomas, VI 00802; (809) 774-3320.

Washington
Environmental Protection Section, Washington Office of Radiation Protection, Thurston AirDustrial Center, Bldg. 5, P.O. Box 47827, Olympia, WA 98504; (206) 586-3303, or (800) 323-9727 (toll-free in WA).

West Virginia
Department of Environmental Health, West Virginia Department of Health, Radiological Division, 815 Quarrier Street, #418, Charleston, WV 25301; (304) 348-3526 or (800) 922-1255.

Wisconsin
Radiation Protection Section, Division of Health, Department of Health & Social Services, P.O. Box 309, Madison, WI 53701-0309; (608) 267-4795.

Wyoming
Environmental Health, Department of Health & Social Service, Hathway Bldg., 4th Floor, Cheyenne, WY 82002-0710; (307) 777-6015.

Real Estate Commissions

The following offices license real estate agents in their states, and they also investigate complaints about agents and brokers involving such issues as misrepresentation, coercion, and theft from escrow accounts. See *Real Estate Agents & Brokers* on page 179 for more detailed information.

Alabama
Real Estate Commission, 1201 Carmichael Way, Montgomery, AL 36102; (205) 242-5544.

Alaska
State of Alaska Division of Occupational Licensing, Real Estate Division, Suite 722, 3601 C St., Anchorage, AK 99503; (907) 563-2169.

Arizona
Real Estate Department, 202 Earll Dr., Suite 400, Phoenix, AZ 85012; (602) 279-2909.

Arkansas
Real Estate Commission, 612 Summit, Little Rock, AR 72201-4770; (501) 682-2732.

California
Department of Real Estate, Attn: Regulatory, P.O. Box 187000, Sacramento, CA 95818-7000; (916) 739-3684.

Colorado
Real Estate Commission, 1776 Logan St., 4th Floor, Denver, CO 80203; (303) 894-2166.

Connecticut
Department of Consumer Protection, Real Estate Division, Attn: Examiner, State Office Building, 165 Capitol Ave., Hartford, CT 06106; (203) 566-5131.

Delaware
Real Estate Commission, Department of Consumer and Regulatory Affairs, 614 H St., NW, Washington, DC 20001; (202) 727-7468.

Florida
Division of Real Estate, Attn: Complaints, P.O. Box 1900, Orlando, FL 32802-1900; (407) 423-6058.

Georgia
Real Estate Commission, Suite 500, 148 International Blvd., NE, Atlanta, GA 30303-1734; (404) 656-3916.

Hawaii
Real Estate Commission, 250 S. King St., Room 702, Honolulu, HI 96813; (808) 586-2643.

Real Estate Commissions

Idaho
Real Estate Commission, Statehouse Mail, Boise, ID 83720; (208) 334-3285.

Illinois
Real Estate Enforcement Division, Department of Professional Regulation, 320 W. Washington St., IL 62786; (217) 785-0800, or (217) 782-0943.

Indiana
Professional Licensing Agency, 1021 State Office Building, Indianapolis, IN 46204; (317) 232-3997.

Iowa
Real Estate Examining Board, 1918 SE Hulsizer Ave., Ankeny, IA 50021; (515) 281-3183.

Kansas
Real Estate Commission, 900 Jackson St., Room 501, Topeka, KS 66612-1220; (913) 296-3411.

Kentucky
Real Estate Commission, 10200 Linn Station Rd., Ste. 201, Louisville, KY 40223; (502) 425-4273.

Louisiana
Real Estate Commission, P.O. Box 14785, Baton Rouge, LA 70898; (504) 925-4800.

Maine
Real Estate Commission, Statehouse Station 35, Augusta, ME 04333; (207) 582-8727.

Maryland
Real Estate Commission, 501 St. Paul Place, 8th Floor, Baltimore, MD 21201; (301) 333-6230.

Massachusetts
Board of Registration, Real Estate, 100 Cambridge St., Boston, MA 02202; (617) 727-3074.

Michigan
Department of Licensing and Registration, P.O. Box 30018, Lansing, MI 48909; (517) 373-1870.

Minnesota
Licensing Unit, Enforcement Division, 133 East 7th Street, St. Paul, MN 55101; (612) 296-2488.

Mississippi
Real Estate Commission, 1920 Dunbarton Dr., Jackson, MS 39216; (601) 987-3969.

Missouri
Real Estate Commission, P.O. Box 1339, Jefferson City, MO 65102; (314) 751-2628.

Montana
Board of Realty, 111 N. Jackson, Helena, MT 59620; (406) 444-2961.

Nebraska
Real Estate Commission, P.O. Box 94667, Lincoln, NE 68509-4667; (402) 471-2004.

329

Real Estate Commissions

Nevada
Real Estate Division, Attn: Complaints Department, 1665 Hotsprings Road, Carson City, NV 89710; (702) 687-4280.

New Hampshire
Real Estate Commission, 95 Pleasant Street, Spaulding Building, Johnson Hall, Concord, NH 03301; (603) 271-2701.

New Jersey
Real Estate Commission, 20 W. State Street, Investigations, 8th Floor, CN 328, Trenton, NJ 08625; (609) 292-8280.

New Mexico
Real Estate Commission, 1650 University Blvd. NE, Suite 490, Albuquerque, NM 87102; (505) 841-9120.

New York
Licensing Services Division, Department of State, 84 Holland Ave., Albany NY 12231; (518) 474-4664.

North Carolina
Real Estate Commission, P.O. Box 17100, Raleigh, NC 27619-7100; (919) 733-9580.

North Dakota
Real Estate Commission, P.O. Box 727, Bismarck, ND 58502; (701) 224-2749.

Ohio
Division of Real Estate, 77 S. High St., Columbus, OH 43266-0547; (614) 466-4100.

Oklahoma
Real Estate Commission, 4040 N. Lincoln Blvd., Suite 100, Oklahoma City, OK 73105; (405) 521-3387.

Oregon
Real Estate Agency, 158 12th St. NE, Salem, OR 97310; (503) 378-4170.

Pennsylvania
Department of General Services, Bureau of Real Estate, 505 North Office Bldg., Harrisburg, PA 17105; (717) 787-4394.

Rhode Island
Licensing and Consumer Protection Division, 233 Richmond St., Suite 230, Providence, RI 02903-4230; (401) 277-2416.

South Carolina
Real Estate Commission, 1201 Main Street, Suite 1500, Columbia, SC 29201; (803) 737-0700.

Tennessee
Real Estate Commission, Div. of Regulatory Boards, 500 James Robertson Parkway, Nashville, TN 37243; (615) 741-2273.

Real Estate Commissions

Texas
Real Estate Commission, P.O. Box 12188, Austin, TX 78711-2188; (512) 459-6544.

Utah
Division of Real Estate, P.O. Box 45802, Salt Lake City, UT 84145; (801) 530-6747.

Vermont
Real Estate Commission, 26 Terrace St., Montpelier, VT 05602; (802) 828-3228.

Virginia
Real Estate Board, Department of Commerce, 3600 W. Broad St., 5th Floor, Richmond, VA 23230; (804) 367-8526.

Washington
Real Estate Disciplinary Section, P.O. Box 9015, Olympia, WA 98504; (206) 586-4602.

West Virginia
Real Estate Commission, 1033 Quarrier St., Suite 400, Charleston, WV 25301; (304) 558-3555.

Wisconsin
Department of Regulation & Licensing, Attn: Marlene Maly, P.O. Box 8935, Madison, WI 53708; (608) 266-0648.

Wyoming
Real Estate Commission, 2nd Floor, Barrett Bldg., Cheyenne, WY 82002; (307) 777-7141.

Securities And Exchange Commission

The Securities and Exchange Commission (SEC) oversees the securities markets in the U.S. to make sure that they operate in a fair and orderly way so that investors are protected from fraudulent practices. Stock brokers and investment advisers who participate in the market are required to be registered with the SEC, and if they violate any of the SEC's rules while doing business, the SEC has the authority to suspend them. If you've got a complaint about a stock broker or investment adviser, contact the SEC regional office nearest you for help in resolving the dispute. See *Stockbrokers* on page 188 for more detailed information.

New York Regional Office
14th Floor, 75 Park Place, New York, NY 10007; (212) 264-1636. Serving: New York and New Jersey.

Boston
J. W. McCormirck, P.O. Court House, Suite 700, 90 Devonshire St., Boston, MA 02109; (617) 223-9900. Serving: Maine, New Hampshire, Vermont, Massachusetts, Rhode Island, and Connecticut.

Philadelphia
The Curtis Center, Suite 1005 E., 601 Walnut St., Philadelphia, PA 19106; (215) 597-3100. Serving: Pennsylvania, Delaware, Maryland, Virginia, West Virginia, and District of Columbia.

Chicago
500 West Madison, Suite 40, Chicago, IL 60601-2511; (312) 353-7390. Serving: Ohio, Kentucky, Wisconsin, Indiana, Iowa, Illinois, Minnesota, and Missouri.

Fort Worth
8th Floor, 411 West 7th Street, Fort Worth, TX 76102; (817) 334-3821. Serving: Oklahoma, Arkansas, Texas, Louisiana west of the Atchafalaya River, and Kansas.

Denver
1801 California, Suite 4800, Denver, CO 80202; (303) 391-6800. Serving: North Dakota, South Dakota, Wyoming, Nebraska, Colorado, New Mexico, and Utah.

Salt Lake City
50 South Main Street, Key Bank Tower, Suite 500, Salt Lake City, UT 84144; (801) 524-5796.

Securities And Exchange Commission

Los Angeles
5670 Wilshire Blvd., 11th Floor, Los Angeles, CA 90036-3648; (213) 965-3998. Serving: Nevada, Arizona, California, Hawaii, and Guam.

San Francisco
Suite 470, 901 Market St., San Francisco, CA 94103; (415) 744-3140.

Seattle
3040 Jackson Federal Building, 915 Second Ave., Seattle, WA 98174; (206) 553-7990. Serving: Montana, Idaho, Washington, Oregon, and Alaska.

Atlanta
Suite 788, 1375 Peachtree St., NE, Atlanta, GA 30367; (404) 842-7600. Serving: Tennessee, Virgin Islands, Puerto Rico, North Carolina, South Carolina, Georgia, Alabama, Mississippi, Florida, and Louisiana east of the Atchafalaya River.

Miami
1401 Brickel Ave., Suite 200, Miami, FL 33131; (305) 536-7459.

Office Of Thrift Supervision

As part of the U.S. Department of the Treasury, the Office of Thrift Supervision oversees federally-insured savings and loan institutions, making sure that they operate fairly and within federal guidelines. They also respond to and investigate individual consumer complaints that involve the services of these savings and loans. See *Banking Services* on page 28 for more detailed information.

Boston
745 Atlantic Ave., Suite 405, Boston, MA 02111; (617) 457-1900

New York
One World Trade Center, FL 103, New York, NY 10048; (212) 912-4600

Pittsburgh
One Riverfront Center, 20 Stanwix St., Pittsburgh, PA 15222-4893; (412) 288-3400

Atlanta
P.O. Box 105217, Atlanta, GA 30348-5217; (404) 888-0771

Cincinnati
525 Vine St., Cincinnati, OH 45202; (513) 762-6100

Indianapolis
8250 Woodfield Crossing Blvd., Suite 305, Indianapolis, IN 46240; (317) 465-1600

Chicago
111 E. Wacker Dr., Suite 800, Chicago, IL 60601-4360; (312) 565-5300

Des Moines
Regency West #2, Ste. 300, 1401 50th St. W., Des Moines, IA 50266-5924; (515) 222-2100

Dallas
P.O. Box 619027, Dallas/Fort Worth, TX 75261-9027; (214) 581-2000

Topeka
8500 W. 110th St., Ste. 400, Overland Park, KS 66210; (913) 339-5000

San Francisco
P.O. Box 7165, San Francisco, CA 94120; (415) 616-1500

Seattle
1501 Fourth Ave., FL 19, Seattle, WA 98101-1693; (206) 727-5200 (For Consumer Complaints go to San Francisco Office)

334

Utility Commissions

These state offices regulate consumer services and rates for gas, electricity, water, telephone, and moving companies. Many of these offices handle consumer complaints, and sometimes, if they receive a number of complaints about the same utility problem, they will conduct formal investigations. For more detailed information, see *Utility Companies* on page 201.

Alabama
Public Service Commission, P.O. Box 991, Montgomery, AL 36101; (205) 242 5211, or (800) 392-8050 (toll free in AL).

Alaska
Public Utilities Commission, 1016 West 6th Avenue, Suite 400, Anchorage, AK 99501; (907) 276-6222, Fax: (907) 276-0160.

Arizona
Corporation Commission, 1200 W. Washington St., Phoenix, AZ 85007; (602) 542-3935, (800) 222-7000.

Arkansas
Public Service Commission, 1000 Center St., P.O. Box 400, Little Rock, AR 72203-0400; (501) 682-1453, or (800) 482-1164 (toll free in AR).

California
Public Utilities Commission, 505 Van Ness Ave., Room 5218, San Francisco, CA 94102; (415) 703-3703 or (800) 649-7570.

Colorado
Public Utilities Commission, 1580 Logan St., Logan Tower, Office Level 2, Denver, CO 80203; (303) 894-2070, or (800) 888-0170 (toll free in CO).

Connecticut
Department of Public Utility Control, One Central Park Plaza, New Britain, CT 06051; (203) 827-1553, or (800) 382-4586 (toll free in CT).

Delaware
Public Service Commission, 1560 South DuPont Highway, P.O. Box 457, Dover, DE 19903; (302) 739-4247, or (800) 282-8574 (toll free in DE).

District of Columbia
Public Service Commission, 450 5th St., N.W., Washington, DC 20001; (202) 626-5110, (800) 737-4772.

Florida
Public Service Commission, 101 E. Gaines St., Tallahassee, FL 32399-0850; (904) 488-7238, or (800) 342-3552 (toll free in FL).

Utility Commissions

Georgia
Public Service Commission, 244 Washington St., S.W., Atlanta, GA 30334; (404) 656-4512, or (800) 282-5813 (toll free in GA).

Hawaii
Public Utilities Commission, 465 S. King St., Room 103, Honolulu, HI 96813; (808) 586-2020.

Idaho
Public Utilities Commission, State House, Boise, ID 83720; (208) 334-3912, (800) 432-0369.

Illinois
Commerce Commission, 527 E. Capitol Ave., P.O. Box 19280, Springfield, IL 62794; (217) 782-7907.

Indiana
Utility Regulatory Commission, Indiana Government Center, 302 W. Washington St., Ste. E306, Indianapolis, IN 46204; (317) 232-2701.

Iowa
State Utilities Board, Lucas State Office Building, 5th Floor, Des Moines, IA 50319; (515) 281-5979.

Kansas
State Corporation Commission, 1500 S.W. Arrowhead Rd., Topeka, KS 66604; (913) 271-3166, or (800) 662-0027 (toll free in KS).

Kentucky
Public Service Commission, 730 Schenkel Lane, P.O. Box 615, Frankfort, KY 40602; (502) 564-3940, (800) 772-4636.

Louisiana
Public Service Commission, One American Place, Suite 1630, P.O. Box 91154, Baton Rouge, LA 70825; (504) 342-6687, or (800) 256-2413 (toll free in LA).

Maine
Public Utilities Commission, State House Station 18, Augusta, ME 04333; (207) 289-3831, or (800) 452-4699 (toll free in ME).

Maryland
Public Service Commission, 231 E. Baltimore St., Baltimore, MD 21202; (410) 333-6000, or (800) 492-0474 (toll free in MD).

Massachusetts
Department of Public Utilities, 100 Cambridge St., 12th Floor, Boston, MA 02202; (617) 727-3500, (800) 392-6066.

Michigan
Public Service Commission, 6545 Mercantile Way, P.O. Box 30221, Lansing, MI 48909; (517) 334-6445, or (800) 292-9555 (toll free in MI).

Minnesota
Public Utilities Commission, 350 Metro Square Bldg., 121 E. 7th Place, St. Paul, MN 55501; (612)

296-7124, or (800) 852-8747 (toll free in MN).

Mississippi
Public Service Commission, P.O. Box 1174, Jackson, MS 39215; (601) 961-5400, (800) 356-6430.

Missouri
Public Service Commission, P.O. Box 360, Jefferson City, MO 65102; (314) 751-3243, or (800) 392-4211 (toll free in MO).

Montana
Public Service Commission, 1701 Prospect Ave., Helena, MT 59620-2601; (406) 444-6199.

Nebraska
Public Service Commission, 300 The Atrium, 1200 N Street, P.O. Box 94927, Lincoln, NE 68509; (402) 471-3101, or (800) 526-0017.

Nevada
Public Service Commission, 727 Fairview Drive, Carson City, NV 89710; (702) 687-6550.

New Hampshire
Public Utilities Commission, 8 Old Suncook Road, Building #1, Concord, NH 03301; (603) 271-2431, or (800) 852-3793 (toll free in NH).

New Jersey
Board of Public Utilities, Two Gateway Center, Newark, NJ 07102; (201) 648-2027, or (800)

624-0241 (toll free in NJ).

New Mexico
Public Service Commission, Marianne Hall, 224 E. Palace Ave., Santa Fe, NM 87501-2013; (505) 827-6940.

New York
Public Service Commission, 3 Empire State Plaza, Albany, NY 12223; (518) 474-5527, or (800) 342-3377 (toll free in NY).

North Carolina
Utilities Commission, P.O. Box 29510-0510, Raleigh, NC 27626; (919) 733-4249.

North Dakota
Public Service Commission, State Capitol Building, 12th Floor, Bismarck, ND 58505; (701) 224-2400, or (800) 932-2400 (toll free in ND).

Ohio
Public Utilities Commission, 180 E. Broad St., Columbus, OH 43266-0573; (614) 466-3292, or (800) 466-8180 (toll free in OH).

Oklahoma
Corporation Commission, Jim Thorpe Office Building, 2101 N. Lincoln, Oklahoma City, OK 73105; (405) 521-2264, or (800) 522-8154 (toll free in OK).

Oregon
Public Utility Commission, 550 Capital Street, N.E., Salem, OR

97310-1380; (503) 378-6611, or
(800) 522-2404 (toll free in OR).

Pennsylvania
Public Utility Commission, P.O.
Box 3265, Harrisburg, PA 17120;
(717) 787-4301, or (800) 782-
1110 (toll free in PA).

Puerto Rico
Public Service Commission, Call
Box 870, Hato Rey, PR 00919-
0870; (809) 758-6264.

Rhode Island
Public Utilities Commission, 100
Orange Street, Providence, RI
02903; (401) 277-3500, or (800)
341-1000 (toll free in RI).

South Carolina
Public Service Commission, P.O.
Drawer 11649, Columbia, SC
29211; (803) 737-5270, or (800)
922-1531 (toll free in SC).

South Dakota
Public Utilities Commission, 500
E. Capitol Avenue, Pierre, SD
57501; (605) 773-3201, (800)
332-1782.

Tennessee
Public Service Commission, 460
James Robertson Parkway,
Nashville, TN 37243; (615) 741-
3125, or (800) 342-8359 (toll free
in TN).

Texas
Public Utility Commission, 7800
Shoal Creek Blvd., Suite 400N,
Austin, TX 78757; (512) 458-
0100.

Utah
Public Service Commission, 160
E. 300 South, P.O. Box 45585,
Salt Lake City, UT 84145; (801)
530-6716.

Vermont
Public Service Board, 89 Main St.,
City Center, 3rd Floor, Drawer 20,
Montpelier, VT 05620-2701;
(802) 828-2358, or (800) 622-
4496 (toll free in VT).

Virgin Islands
Public Services Commission, P.O.
Box 40, Charlotte Amalie, St.
Thomas, VI 00804; (809) 776-
1291, Fax: (809) 774-4971.

Virginia
State Corporation Commission,
P.O. Box 1197, Richmond, VA
23209; (804) 371-9208, or (800)
552-7945 (toll free in VA).

Washington
Utilities and Transportation
Commission, P.O. Box 47250,
Olympia, WA 98504; (206) 753-
6423, or (800) 562-6150 (toll free
in WA).

Utility Commissions

West Virginia
Public Service Commission, P.O. Box 812, Charleston, WV 25323; (304) 340-0300, or (800) 344-5113 (toll free in WV).

Wisconsin
Public Service Commission, 4802 Sheboygan Ave., P.O. Box 7854, WI 53707; (608) 266-2001.

Wyoming
Public Service Commission, 700 W. 21st St., Cheyenne, WY 82002; (307) 777-7427, Fax: (307) 777-5700.

Weights And Measures Offices

These offices enforce laws and regulations about the weights of packaged items such as food and household products. These offices also check the accuracy of weighing and measuring devices, such as supermarket and delicatessen scales, gasoline pumps, taxicab meters, and rental car odometers. See *Delicatessens* on page 60 and *Firewood* on page 84 for more detailed information.

Alabama
Weights and Measures Division, Department of Agriculture, P.O. Box 3336, Montgomery, AL 36193; (334) 240-7133.

Alaska
Weights and Measures, Department of Commerce and Economic Development, 12050 Industry Way, Bldg. O, Anchorage, AK 99515; (907) 345-7750, Internet: 222.state.ak. us/local/aupages/commerce/ms. com.

Arizona
Weights and Measures Division, Department of Administration, 9535 E. Doubletree Ranch Rd., Scottsdale, AZ 85258; (602) 255-1950.

Arkansas
Bureau of Standards, 4608 W. 61st St., Little Rock, AR 72209; (501) 324-9681.

California
Division of Measurement Standards, Department of Food and Agriculture, 8500 Fruitridge Rd., Sacramento, CA 95826; (916)

229-3000, or on the Internet: www.cdfa.ca.gov/measurement.

Colorado
Measurements Standards Section, Department of Agriculture, 3125 Wyandot, Denver, CO 80211; (303) 477-4220.

Connecticut
Department of Consumer Protection, Weights and Measures Division, State Office Building, Room 29-A, 165 Capitol Ave., Hartford, CT 06106; (860) 566-4778.

Delaware
Office of Weights and Measures, Department of Agriculture, 2320 South Dupont Highway, Dover, DE 19901; (302) 739-4811.

District of Columbia
Weights and Measures Branch, Department of Consumer and Regulatory Affairs, 1110 U St., S.E., Washington, DC 20020; (202) 645-6706.

Florida
Department of Agriculture and Consumer Services, Bureau of

340

Weights And Measures Offices

Weights and Measures, 3125 Conner Blvd., Lab #2, Tallahassee, FL 32399-1650; (904) 488-9140.

Georgia
Department of Agriculture, Fuel and Measure Division, 19 Martin Luther King Dr., Room 321, Atlanta, GA 30334; (404) 656-9308.

Hawaii
Department of Agriculture, Measurement Standards, 725 Ilelo St., Honolulu, HI 96813; (808) 586-0870.

Idaho
Department of Agriculture, Bureau of Weights and Measures, 2216 Kellogg Lane, Boise, ID 83712; (208) 334-2170.

Illinois
Department of Agriculture, Weights and Measures Program, 801 E. Sangamon Ave., P.O. Box 19281, Springfield, IL 62794-9281; (217) 782-3817.

Indiana
Weights and Measures Program, State Board of Health, 1330 W. Michigan St., Indianapolis, IN 46206; (317) 383-6350.

Iowa
Iowa Department of Agriculture Attn: Weights and Measures Division, Henry A. Wallace Building, Des Moines, IA 50319; (515) 281-5716.

Kansas
Weights and Measures Division, State Board of Agriculture, 2016 South West 37th Street, Topeka, KS 66611-2570; (913) 267-4641.

Kentucky
Division of Weights and Measures, Department of Agriculture, 106 W. 2nd Street, Frankfort, KY 40601; (502) 564-4870.

Louisiana
Department of Agriculture, Weights and Measures, 5825 Frloida Blvd., Baton Rouge, LA 70821-3098; (504) 925-3780.

Maine
Maine Department of Agriculture, Division of Regulations, State House Station #28, Augusta, ME 04333; (207) 287-2161.

Maryland
Maryland Department of Agriculture, Weights and Measures Section, 50 Harry S. Truman Parkway, Annapolis, MD 21401; (410) 841-5790, Internet: www.mda.state.md.us/ geninfo/ genera5.htm.
Massachusetts
Division of Standards, One Ashburton Place, Room 115, John McCormick Building, Boston, MA 02108; (617) 727-3480.

Weights And Measures Offices

Michigan
Department of Agriculture, Food Division, Ottawa Bldg North, 4th Floor, P.O. Box 30017, Lansing, MI 48909; (517) 373-1060, Internet: www.mda.state.mi.us/hot/lab/inter.html.

Minnesota
Division of Weights and Measures, Department of Public Service, 2277 Highway 36, Suite 150, St. Paul, MN 55113; (612) 639-4010, Internet: www.dpsi.state.mn.us.

Mississippi
Department of Agriculture, Weights and Measures Division, P.O. Box 1609, Jackson, MS 39215; (601) 354-7077.

Missouri
Department of Agriculture, Weights and Measures Division, 1616 Missouri Blvd., Jefferson City, MO 65102; (573) 751-4316.

Montana
Bureau of Weights and Measures, Department of Commerce, 1520 East 5th Avenue, Room 50, Helena, MT 59620; (406) 444-3134.

Nebraska
Department of Agriculture, Division of Weights and Measures, 301 Centennial Mall South, 4th Floor, or P.O. Box 94757, Lincoln, NE 68509; (402) 471-4292.

Nevada
Department of Agriculture, Bureau of Weights and Measures, 2150 Frazier Ave., Sparks, NV 89431; (702) 688-1166.

New Hampshire
Department of Agriculture, Bureau of Weights and Measures, Caller Box 2042, Concord, NH 03302-2042; (603) 271-3551.

New Jersey
State Office of Weights and Measures, 1261 Routes 1 and 9 South, Avenel, NJ 07001; (908) 815-4840.

New Mexico
Department of Agriculture, Division of Standards and Consumer Services, P.O. Box 30005, Department 3170, Las Cruces, NM 88003-0005; (505) 646-1616.

New York
Bureau of Weights and Measures, Dept of Agriculture, One Winner Circle, Albany, NY 12235; (518) 457-3452.

North Carolina
Department of Agriculture, Consumer Standards Division, P.O. Box 27647, Raleigh, NC 27611; (919) 733-3313.

North Dakota
Division of Weights and Measures, State Capitol, 12th Floor, Bismarck, MD 58505;

Weights And Measures Offices

(701) 328-2413, Internet: www. pcg.psc.state.nd.us.

Ohio
Division of Weights and Measures, Department of Agriculture, 8995 E. Main St., Reynoldsburg, OH 43068; (614) 728-6290.

Oklahoma
Agricultural Products Division, Department of Agriculture, 2800 N. Lincoln Blvd., Oklahoma City, OK 73105; (405) 521-3864, ext. 243.

Oregon
Measurement Standards, Department of Agriculture, 635 Capitol St., N.E., Salem, OR 97310-0110; (503) 551-0469.

Pennsylvania
Dept of Agriculture, Bureau of Weights and Measures, 2301 N. Cameron St., Harrisburg, PA 17110; (717) 787-9089.

Puerto Rico
Auxiliary Secretary for Complaints, Department of Consumer Affairs, P.O. Box 41059, Minillas Station, Santurce, PR 00940; (809) 724-5153.

Rhode Island
Department of Labor, Supervising Metrologist, Weights & Measures Division, 610 Manton Ave., Providence, RI 02907; (401) 457-1867.

South Carolina
Consumer Services Division, Department of Agriculture, P.O. Box 11280, Columbia, SC 29211; (803) 737-9690.

South Dakota
Division of Commercial Inspection and Regulation, 118 West Capitol, Pierre, SD 57501; (605) 773-3697.

Tennessee
Department of Agriculture, Standards Administration, Weights and Measures, P.O. Box 40627, Melrose Station, Nashville, TN 37204; (615) 360-0109.

Texas
Enforcement Coordinator, Weights and Measures Section, Department of Agriculture, P.O. Box 12847, Austin, TX 78711; (512) 463-7607, or (800) 835-5832 (toll free in TX), Internet: www.agr.state.tx.us.

Utah
Division of Weights and Measures, State Department of Agriculture, P.O. Box 146500, Salt Lake City, UT 84116; (801) 538-7150, Internet: www.ag.state.ut.us.

Vermont
Department of Agriculture, Division of Weights and Measures and Retail Inspection, 116 State Street, Drawer 20, Montpelier, VT 05620; (802) 828-2436.

Weights And Measures Offices

Virgin Islands
Weights and Measures Division, Golden Rock Shopping Center, Christiansted, St. Croix, VI 00820; (809) 773-2226.

Virginia
Weights and Measures Bureau, Department of Agriculture and Consumer Services, P.O. Box 1163, Room 402, Richmond, VA 23209; (804) 786-2476.

Washington
Weights and Measures, Department of Agriculture, P.O. Box 42560, Olympia, WA 98504-2560; (360) 902-1856.

West Virginia
Department of Labor, Division of Weights and Measures, 570 MacCorkle Ave. West, St. Auben, WV 25177; (304) 722-0602.

Wisconsin
Bureau of Weights and Measures, Department of Agriculture, Trade and Consumer Protection, 2811 Agriculture Drive, or P.O. Box 8911, Madison, WI 53708; (608) 224-4920, or (800) 422-7128 (toll free in WI).

Wyoming
Consumer/Compliance Division, Department of Agriculture, 2219 Carey Avenue, Cheyenne, WY 82002; (307) 777-6590.

Whistleblower Hotlines

Many federal departments and agencies have hotlines, many toll-free, into the offices of the Inspector Generals, the in-house auditors that investigate government fraud, waste, and mismanagement. These whistleblower hotlines are set up to encourage federal employees, state employees, contractors, and private citizens to report any such complaints. See *Government Waste & Mismanagement* on page 97 for more information about these hotlines.

U.S. Department of Agriculture
Office of Inspector General, USDA, P.O. Box 23399, Washington, DC 20026; (202) 690-1622, or (800) 424-9121 (toll-free).

U.S. Department of Commerce
Department of Commerce, OIG, P.O. Box 612, Ben Franklin Station, Washington, DC 20044; (202) 482-2495, or (800) 424-5197 (toll-free).

U.S. Department of Defense
Defense Hotline, The Pentagon, Washington, DC 20301-1900; (703) 693-5080, or (800) 424-9098 (toll-free).

U.S. Department of Education
OIG Hotline, 600 Independence Ave., Washington, DC 20202-1510; (202) 205-5770, or (800) 647-8733.

U.S. Department of Energy
OIG Hotline, 1000 Independence Ave., SW, Washington, DC 20585; (202) 205-5770, or (800) 541-1625.

U.S. Department of Health and Human Services
OIG Hotline, P.O. Box 17303, Baltimore, MD 21203-7303; (800) 368-5779 (toll-free).

U.S. Department of Housing and Urban Development
OIG, 451 7th St., SW, Washington, DC 20410; (202) 708-4200, (800) 347-3735 (toll-free).

U.S. Department of the Interior
1550 Wilson Blvd. #402, Arlington, VA 22209; (703) 235-9399, (800) 424-5081 (toll-free).

U.S. Department of Justice
Office of the Inspector General Hotline, P.O. Box 27606, Washington, DC 20038; (800) 869-4499 (toll-free).

U.S. Department of Labor
200 Constitution Ave., NW, Room S5514, Washington, DC 20210; (202) 219-5227, or (800) 347-3756.

Whistleblower Hotlines

U.S. Department of State
OIG, 2201 C St., NW, New State Building, Room 6821, Washington, DC 20520; (202) 647-3320.

U.S. Department of Transportation
U.S. DOT, OIG, Attn: Hotline Center, P.O. Box 23178, Washington, DC 20026-0178; (202) 366-1461, or (800) 424-9071 (toll-free).

U.S. Department of the Treasury
OIG, 1500 Pennsylvania Ave., NW, Room 2412, Washington, DC 20220; (202) 622-1090, or (800) 359-3898 (toll-free).

U.S. Department of Veterans Affairs
941 N. Capital, Washington, DC 20421; (202) 233-5394, or (800) 488-8244 (toll-free).

Environmental Protection Agency
EPA, OIG Hotline, 401 M St., SW, Room 307C NE Mall, Washington, DC 20460; (202) 260-4977, or (800) 424-4000 (toll-free).

General Accounting Office
GAO, 600 E. St. NW, Ste. 1000, Washington, DC 20548; (202) 272-5557, or (800) 424-5454.

General Services Administration
Hotline Officer, GSA/OIG (JI), Washington, DC 20405; (202) 501-1780, or (800) 424-5210 (toll-free).

National Aeronautics and Space Administration
NASA Inspector General, P.O. Box 23089, L'Enfant Station, Washington, DC 20026; (202) 755-3402, or (800) 424-9183 (toll-free).

Nuclear Regulatory Commission
NRC, OIG, MS/EWW542, Washington, DC 20555; (202) 492-7301, or (800) 233-3497 (toll-free).

Office of Personnel Management
OPM, 1900 E St., NW, Room 6831, Washington, DC 20415; (202) 606-2423.

Railroad Retirement Board
Office of Inspector General, Office of Investigation, 844 N. Rush St., Room 450, Chicago, IL 60611; (312) 751-4336, or (800) 772-4258.

Small Business Administration
SBA, 409 3rd St. SW, Washington, DC 20416; (202) 205-7151, (800) 767-0385.

Tennessee Valley Authority
TVA, 400 West Summit Hill Drive, Knoxville, TN 37902; (615) 632-3550, or (800) 323-3835 (toll-free).

Whistleblower Hotlines

U.S. Agency for International Development
OIG Hotline, P.O. Box 12894 Rosslyn Station, Arlington, VA 22209; (703) 875-4999, (800) 230-6539.

U.S. Information Agency
USIA, Donohoe Building, Room 1100, 400 6th St., SW, Washington, DC 20547; (202) 401-7931, (202) 401-7206 Investigations).

Index

Index

Index

Index

Index

Index

Index

Index

Index

Index

Index

Index

Index

Index

Index

Index

Index

Index